Cake &Loaf

Cake & Loaf

Satisfy Your Cravings with Over 85 Recipes
for Everyday Baking and Sweet Treats

NICKEY MILLER

JOSIE RUDDERHAM

PENGUIN

an imprint of Penguin Canada, a division of Penguin Random House Canada Limited

Canada • USA • UK • Ireland • Australia • New Zealand • India • South Africa • China

First published 2022

www.penguinrandomhouse.ca

LIBRARY AND ARCHIVES CANADA CATALOGUING IN PUBLICATION

Title: Cake & Loaf : satisfy your cravings with over 85 recipes for everyday baking and special
    treats / Josie Rudderham and Nickey Miller.
Other titles: Cake and Loaf
Names: Rudderham, Josie, author. | Miller, Nickey, author.
Identifiers: Canadiana (print) 20210210524 | Canadiana (ebook) 20210210540 |
    ISBN 9780735239838 (softcover) | ISBN 9780735239845 (EPUB)
Subjects: LCSH: Baking. | LCSH: Desserts. | LCSH: Confectionery. | LCGFT: Cookbooks.
Classification: LCC TX765 .R83 2022 | DDC 641.7/1—dc23

Cover and interior design by Kate Sinclair
Food and Prop Styling by Nickey Miller and Josie Rudderham
Food Photography and Illustrations by Nickey Miller
Portrait Photography by Tamara Campbell

Printed in China

10 9 8 7 6 5 4 3 2 1

For Luke: My rock, my nest, my soulmate. —Josie

For Alex: I love and appreciate you, and most of all thank you for understanding the drive and determination it takes and allowing me to disappear and reappear, always supporting and never questioning. —Nickey

For our employees past and present: Without you, none of this would be possible. Thank you for being the best co-workers we could have asked for.

Contents

CAKES

TARTS AND PIES

ICINGS, BUTTERCREAMS, AND FILLINGS

local • responsible • healthy • delicious
Cake & Loaf
BAKERY
www.cakeandloaf.com
Baked
IN HAMILTON

Our Story

WELCOME TO CAKE & LOAF BAKERY. We are Josie Rudderham and Nickey Miller, co-owners and founders of the bakery, and we are honoured that you have chosen to pick up our book and let us enter your kitchen. It is such a privilege and beyond any expectations we had for our little neighbourhood bakery to be sharing these recipes far and wide. We hope you enjoy the recipes, learn more about baking, and maybe have a giggle at our stories. As business owners, we have experienced more than a decade of personal and professional growth that has challenged us to confront many uncomfortable truths and has allowed us to transform in ways we had never dreamed. For better and for worse, here is our story.

We sat down for our first coffee date in late 2007. It had been four years since we had first met during our pastry apprenticeship at Niagara College and had connected over our shared hometown of Hamilton, Ontario. We were both a little nervous and excited to learn more about each other; we were, after all, pretty much strangers. We traded stories about the struggles we had each faced in the culinary industry. We connected over our shared desire to open our own businesses. Bakeries with a difference that were environmentally sustainable. Bakeries that put strong values over profit in every decision made. An accepting and open environment that would foster creativity and trust, free of the sexual harassment and toxic environment that can be common in some kitchens. Quickly, it became obvious that we shared the same dream, a passion for food, and a desire to give more than we take from our community. Nickey already had an experienced bakery manager's drive, paired with natural creative talent. She was creating gorgeous cakes in her spare time and brought the refined pastry skills that Josie lacked. Josie had an entrepreneurial spirit and leadership skills. She had grown up steeped in cooking seasonal, from-scratch

food every day in her home. That coffee date was only the second time we had hung out socially, but by the end of that day we were committed to opening a bakery together. Some called it entrepreneurial love at first sight, and many called it incredibly foolish, but we had a dream and we were ready to chase it.

We quickly started scouring the city for real estate, and by early 2008 we had secured the perfect home for our one-day bakery. The two-and-a-half-storey red brick home was classic Hamilton turn-of-the-century architecture and had housed a well-loved barbershop for decades. With the help of our wonderful families and friends, we gutted the house, removing all the old plumbing, electrical, plaster and lathe, and flooring. We did our best to salvage what we could—from the original hardwood floors on the main floor to the chunky doors and window trim—to try to maintain a homey feel in the bakery. Everything else we rebuilt. At twenty-five and twenty-six years old, we did not have much renovation experience, but with our fathers' guidance, we taught ourselves to lay hardwood floors, install drywall and tile, and do simple plumbing and electrical. We were excited to start building our bakery, but the world had other plans. The economic downturn of 2008 left us doubting whether our business was still a good idea. Who would buy premium pastries and breads in such an uncertain financial climate? As a result, Nickey continued to build her skills as a bakery manager with a side hustle of custom cakes in her mother's kitchen and Josie began building her family. Months of municipal red tape meant that there was no way we could start baking out of our new shop. Instead, we did what entrepreneurs do: you fake it until you make it. We had Josie's home kitchen licensed and launched a Community Supported Bakery (CSB) program. Working from the model of successful Community Supported Agriculture (CSA) programs, we figured that if it worked for small-scale farming, maybe it could work well for baked goods too. The program was unique in Canada at the time, but our bet paid off and after a few months of promoting the venture we had fifty families picking up weekly baskets full of breads, pastries, and preserves. In 2010, Cake & Loaf Bakery Ltd. was officially incorporated. "Cake" for Nickey and her gorgeous cake creations, generous nature, and more refined aesthetic, and "Loaf" for Josie and her rustic breads, pastries, and stubborn politics.

We finally opened our brick-and-mortar bakery on Dundurn Street in August 2011. Our business was based on four core principles: Local, Healthy, Responsible, and Delicious. Our commitment to these foundations has carried through everything we do, from recipe development to the social activism that has defined Cake & Loaf ever since. Local means supporting local farmers and makers, sourcing ingredients as

locally as possible, and not sacrificing to find a lower price. It means seeking out opportunities to give back wherever we can and a continued involvement in our small and greater community. Healthy means embracing and supporting the mental and physical health of both our employees and our customers. It means being a safe space, advocating for a living wage for all, and providing a work-life balance that recognizes the unique needs of each individual we employ. Responsible means planning for the future through environmental initiatives, extensive student training programs, and ingredient and packaging selections. It means we always make our business decisions based on principles over profit. One of our earliest and easiest wins for environmental responsibility was our recycling and composting program. To this day, we never create more than one bag of garbage a week and usually fill ten to twelve green bins of compost. Finally and most importantly, delicious means that we test a recipe until we can hear the groans of pleasure throughout the bakery. If we are not falling over ourselves for another bite, it is not good enough yet.

Entrepreneurship is a daily leap of faith and a roller coaster of emotions. We have had days when we are literally holding each other up and in tears over a sense of powerlessness or a decision gone wrong. We have had perfect moments when all the planning aligned and we could not believe this is our life. Cake & Loaf has been not only a business, but also the centre of our hopes and dreams. It's our small corner of the world to make a better place. We are so grateful to have had the privilege of working with dozens of talented bakers, enthusiastic students, inspiring collaborators, supportive customers, and devoted employees. It is definitely not all sunny memories, but we are here to share the joy, and the best way we can do that is by bringing some Cake & Loaf deliciousness into your home. While you are baking your way through this book, we do hope that you will take a moment to think of bakers all over the country who are not yet making a living wage or who are facing unfair working conditions. What can you do to support makers in your community? Ask your favourite small business directly: Do you pay a living wage? Tell them you are willing to pay an extra couple of dollars to support a living wage business. Put your money where your ethics are. If we want to live in communities with thriving small businesses that add character and variety to our neighbourhoods, we need to pay for those goods. If we wish to reduce our environmental footprint and contribute to solving the climate crisis, we must consider alternatives to our current defaults. Prioritize human interactions and products that last, and invest in supporting local over convenience and cheap solutions. We build the world we want to live in with our daily actions. Small, thoughtful steps may seem insignificant, but they do lead to long-term change.

Why are we so political? Because it has never really been about the dough. Cake & Loaf, at its core, has never really been about food. Do not get us wrong, we really love food; eating is probably the best thing we get to do every day. However, when we sat down in that coffee shop and laid out our bakery dreams to each other, they were really about creating a space we wanted to go to every day. To build something that would address as many of the systemic issues we had seen in our own bakery jobs as possible. A place to foster creativity and feminist ideals. A business that would give more than it would take from the community and that centred sustainability in all its decisions. The results have not always been what we intended, and we are still learning how the systems in which we operate affect our biases and how we can continue to be better. It has been a financial challenge. Trying to operate in an effectively non-profit way in a capitalist system is fraught with compromises and disappointments. Luckily, we are resourceful folks and have had the honour of working with many amazing people over the years, so we feel like we have won the life lottery.

Writing this book was a completely unexpected adventure and a humbling experience for us. We have never had formal written recipes at the bakery. Our recipes were literally an ingredient list with two or three sentences, and we trained our bakers in all the secret techniques and skills they would need to complete them. We guess you could say we practise an oral history and passing of knowledge at the bakery, a very collaborative approach. It was definitely a challenge to distill all the years of contributions and small improvements we have made to our recipes. We are grateful to have the chance to share a decade's worth of recipe development with you. We tested the recipes at home ourselves, and we enlisted friends and family and even Josie's children, Finn and Lily, to test many of the recipes. Thank you to Josie's husband, Luke, for supervising recipe testing and always being willing to serve as a quality control taster. During the photo sessions for this book, Nickey set up her spare room as a photography studio and took each shot in her home. Nickey's husband, Alex, can attest to the delicious nature of every product that came through the door.

This book captures the best of our everyday baking and basic cake offerings from the bakery's menu. This is Baking 101; you will find all the pastry fundamentals like pastry cream, butter pastry, and caramel in these pages, as well as more advanced recipes like layered cakes to take you to the next level of culinary achievement. The Morning Baking chapter includes all our daily customer favourites and the recipes we make most frequently at home for our families. Our scone recipes are our most requested, most accessible, and most often made by family and friends. The Cookies chapter is the fastest way to get from snackless to happily eating warm baked goods in a hurry. These are the simplest recipes and a great place to start if you are new to baking. Be sure to keep your cupboards and fridge stocked with pantry basics like flour, cocoa powder, sugar, eggs, butter, vanilla, and your favourite chocolate and you will be able to whip up most cookie recipes in less than thirty minutes. If you are looking to serve a crowd or make something beautiful to flex your baking muscles, turn to our Bars chapter. The bars range from simple Classic Fudge Brownies (page 97) to advanced layered bars like our Snazzy Bars (page 105). They were all designed to be photo-friendly (as well as delicious), so show off your skills!

For parties or to give as gifts, we love sandwich cookies. Basically, they are tiny, layered cakes, but more portable and individual. Our sandwich cookie recipes include buttercreams, compotes, and ganaches, and are a natural next step to cakes.

Both cheesecakes and layered cakes require some planning, so make sure you read the recipe through a few days in advance to ensure you have all the ingredients and the time needed to prepare all the components. We like to divide our cake making into at least two days. The day before you intend to serve the cake or cheesecake, make all the components, including the base cake, for your recipe. This is the longer bake day, as you may need four to six hours to make all the subrecipes for the more complex cakes. Think of it as the "dirty day," since you might end up using every dish in your kitchen or have the whole counter strewn with recipe ingredients and cooling fillings. If you don't have a whole day for baking, divide the recipes out over a week. Most cake subrecipes (though not the cakes themselves) last for weeks, so you have time to plan. The day you want to serve the cake is your "clean day." All the pieces are ready to slot into place, and you will just need an hour or two to assemble the cake. Keep your assembling area sparkling clean and take your time to build your perfect cake. Once you have made one cake, you can make them all.

Pies are always a crowd-pleaser and usually quite nostalgic for folks. Many people have special memories of a lemon meringue pie or fruit crumble pie from their childhood; if you don't have a family recipe to turn to, we hope you'll make our recipes your own. We have included an extensive chapter full of icings, fillings, and other component recipes. Please take these and adapt our recipes to your tastes by swapping out fillings or icings. Fundamentally, we believe that baking should be a little messy and tactile. A sensual sensory experience. Taste as you go, engage in the feeling of flour and sugar on your fingers as you rub a crumble together, embrace the aroma of juicy cooking fruit or caramelizing sugar. Give yourself a cheer when you master a smooth icing finish, relish in the sense of accomplishment that pulling a perfectly baked pie from the oven creates, and take a moment to be present in your kitchen.

Advice for Bakers

1. READ THE WHOLE RECIPE TWICE BEFORE YOU START (THEN MAKE THEM YOUR OWN)

Scanning a recipe will not give you the nitty-gritty details that can make or break the recipe. Nothing is worse than being halfway through a recipe and realizing you were supposed to toast the nuts or make pastry ahead of time. Because our recipes were designed to fit into the ecosystem of a from-scratch seasonal bakery, we have simplified some of them but some still have multiple subrecipes that must be made in advance. Do not worry; no one is judging if you choose to purchase marshmallows instead of making your own. However, we hope you will try it at least once; we promise it will be worth it. Take these recipes and make them your own over time; make them as written the first and maybe a second time and then think about how to make them uniquely yours. If possible, taste as you go. You should always taste every component before assembling a cake or sandwich cookie. Evaluate the taste for your personal palette. Could it use a little salt? More chocolate? A touch more vanilla? Maybe you like a sprinkle of cayenne in your chocolate icing or a little cardamom in your cookie. Just keep in mind swapping liquids for liquids and solids for solids. Anything that is a solid dry good like nuts or chocolate chips can be switched out for dried fruit or seeds. If you are worried about waste, try smaller batches. Do your research on ingredients that differ dramatically from the original ingredient—for example, applesauce for eggs or coconut oil for canola. You may learn something new, and that switch-up may lead to your favourite version of the recipe.

2. WRITE YOURSELF NOTES

We love writing directly in our favourite cookbooks. It is a historical record of your relationship with a cookbook. We also understand that not everyone is okay with

marking up books, but we strongly encourage keeping a recipe diary or logbook for those epiphany moments when you strike recipe gold. Feel free to staple or tuck recipe snippets in there too, or notes on specific websites or a certain cookbook's recipe page and title. Maybe even leave yourself or loved ones love letters in the pages. The beautiful thing is that this is a part of you, and you can pass down your knowledge by gifting this book to the next generation of bakers. There is an equally important but very different note you should always be leaving for yourself. If you have ever worked in food service, you will be very familiar with the term FIFO: first in, first out. This cycling of ingredients is standard in commercial kitchens and should be adopted in all home kitchens as well. Make sure to use older ingredients first before opening a new package and rearrange your cupboards to make sure you are using the oldest ingredients first. It is also a great idea to date everything in your fridge. It is easy to forget how long that extra ganache or fruit compote has been hanging out in the fridge. Make your life easier by dating everything with a permanent marker when you open it or by applying some masking tape to containers to write on.

3. CLEAN AS YOU GO AND WASH YOUR HANDS

If Josie's dad taught her one thing in life, it was to clean as you go. Start any recipe with two clean kitchen cloths: a clean wet cloth for keeping your surface clean or quickly wiping down tools you are still using, and a dry cloth to dry your hands and use as a stabilizer for the bottom of bowls or to handle warm items. After every recipe transition, give your work surface a wipe and ask yourself: Am I going to use this tool again today? If so, wipe it down and set it neatly to the side of your work surface. If you are not going to use that tool again, put it in the sink to soak in soapy water to make dishes easier later. Keep your work surface clean and tidy the entire time you are working, wiping up spills as they occur to avoid any accidental cross-contamination. It is understood that you wash your hands before starting any baking project. In culinary school, you are trained to wash your hands every time you enter the kitchen, even if you are returning from washing your hands in another room. It is a good habit to adopt.

4. WASTE NOT, WANT NOT

For environmental reasons, it's best to invest in reusable piping bags, silicone or wax replacements for plastic wrap, cloths over paper towels, silicone baking sheet liners, and good-quality airtight containers for keeping your baked goods. We hope you also have a favourite apron to throw on to protect your clothes and to hang that dry cloth from. Teach yourself to make paper cones with parchment paper to avoid using single-use plastic bags; the parchment paper is compostable and can be tossed right into most municipal compost bins with any little bits of compote or ganache still inside it. Parchment paper is wonderful to have around to line loaf or bar pans for easier product removal and can often be reused a few times. Just wipe it down with a clean cloth and dry it before using it again. There are good green reasons to do these things, but it is also thrifty and will save you money over the long run. We feel that this policy also extends to how you source your ingredients. The priority should always be to support local farmers and producers in your area. We strongly believe that supporting small businesses and family farms has a quantifiable positive ripple effect on your community. It enriches your community with strong farmers markets, increases access to fresh food for everyone, and maintains a common interest in keeping your food systems safe, accessible, and sustainable. If you are lucky enough to live in an agricultural area, you can probably access some "pick your own" farms. Picking your own fruits or veggies will help you appreciate just how much work goes into harvesting and is a rewarding experience. You can preserve or freeze the excess produce you pick for use all through the year. Many farmers rely on this secondary income to keep their farms in the black, so it is a win-win for everyone. If you have space, growing your own food is even more rewarding, and baking is the perfect way to use any less-than-perfect-looking produce your efforts generate. At the bakery, we grow rhubarb, currants, gooseberries, tomatoes, kale, beets, spinach, herbs, and carrots to use in our recipes. Even with just a window or a small balcony, you can usually grow herbs that will add a fresh twist to your scones or lemon loaf.

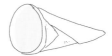

5. TEMPERATURE MAKES A DIFFERENCE

To get the volume and texture you want in your baked goods, you need to make sure your ingredients start at the right temperature, especially for products like cakes. Do not be afraid to microwave butter for a few seconds if it is not soft. Just watch it carefully to avoid any melting. If your eggs are not at room temperature yet and you just cannot wait to get started, place them in a bowl submerged in warm water to come to temperature. In a pinch, we have been known to even quickly microwave dairy to get it to temperature. The ambient temperature of your kitchen can also have an effect, so if it is a particularly chilly or warm day you may have to adjust mixing times. We keep a small kitchen torch on hand to release cheesecakes from their pan or to warm buttercream carefully in the mixing bowl while whipping when the room is just too cold.

6. MISE EN PLACE (EVERYTHING IN ITS PLACE)

There is nothing like having all your ingredients perfectly lined up on the counter, turning on your favourite tunes, having your mug of choice within arm's reach, and relaxing into a day of baking. Taking the time to prepare your mise en place, which is simply having all your ingredients measured and prepped at the beginning of the recipe, allows you the space to relax and just love what you are doing. Prep your fruits and vegetables, dig out those sprinkles from the back of your cupboard, and check out your pantry before assuming you have something. Inherit or thrift an assortment of itty-bitty bowls to use when prepping small amounts—they're not only cute but also useful when building your mise en place. One of the best parts of baking at home for us is the meditative nature of escaping and just immersing ourselves in the moment. Take the time to enjoy the process of mise en place, the love you put into gathering ingredients for your baking, and the tactile experience of a hands-on approach.

7. KNOW YOUR OVEN

Always help your oven perform at its best by baking products on the middle rack and centring your bakeware on that rack to allow for a lot of air circulation around your baking vessel. If you are baking with more than one tray at a time, place one rack in the top third and one rack in the bottom third of your oven. Is your oven hotter than most? Does it run a little cool? Yes, you can invest in an oven thermometer, but you certainly do not have to—just use your senses. Do recipe times usually work for you, or do you have to adjust them? Take notes as you create different dishes to see where your oven falls and then adapt. Newer convection ovens should bake relatively evenly, and you should not have to rotate pans halfway through baking. If you find your oven does not bake evenly, then watch for its hot spots and rotate to accommodate them but always move very quickly when the oven door is open. The worst thing you can do is open an oven repeatedly to rotate pans or check doneness, as this can easily lead to burning the bottom of your product. Each of our ovens has a personality and quirks. Learn to listen to them. For example, when Josie bakes at home she always sets her oven twenty-five degrees higher than the recipe calls for and then turns it down as soon as the product is in the oven. She found that her oven would sometimes overcook the bottoms of items while it struggled to get back up to temperature after she opened the door to insert the product. By increasing the initial temperature and then turning it down, her oven does not blast the products while trying to maintain temperature early in the baking process.

8. FOOD COLOURING AND EXTRACTS

Josie really hates food colouring and never uses it at home. In contrast, Nickey never shies away from using vibrant tones and enjoys using all the colours of the rainbow to express her creativity. A note on gel food colouring and flavour oils and extracts: One drop goes a long way. Start with one or two drops and work your way up from there. Just know that it is harder to step backwards when it comes to food colours that are highly saturated. If you want to remove a yellow undertone and end up with a vibrant cool tone, use a white gel food colouring to mute the yellow and work from there. If you are investing in a few gel colourings, start with white, red, blue, yellow, and green. When making cakes, you'll tend to introduce more colours into your art. However, err on the side of caution when it comes to amounts, as adding too much colour to buttercream and icings may change the flavour and impart a bitter taste, depending on the tone. Do not forget that people will be eating this; they may not want stained teeth or clothing at Grandma's ninetieth birthday celebration! At Cake & Loaf, we tend to avoid dark red or black tones in buttercreams and fondant and opt for a different direction in design. When you are colour matching, physical swatches are always best. Taking a colour from a device screen or printed on paper does not work to your advantage and may skew the tone. Use a swatch or get a colour wheel to add to your collection of tools. This can be useful when needing a reference or choosing the perfect agreed-upon colour when you are creating for friends and family. We resort to extracts, colouring, and oils only when there are no alternatives. Enhance natural flavours by toasting nuts in advance, using fresh substitutes over extracts or oils, using natural colouring like beets or deep yellow farm eggs, and baking seasonally. Vanilla is an omnipresent ingredient in recipes at the bakery, and we strongly advise against using artificial vanilla, which is not the same. Always try to use real flavours, directly from the source, in your baking. Fewer preservatives will yield a better product, and you will feel better about your baking.

Essential Tools and Equipment

1. TOOLS FOR MEASURING

You will need a set of dry cup measures, which usually come in a set of 1, ½, ⅓, and ¼ cups. Look for a simple design made from durable materials that nest into each other for easy storage, and do not be tempted by adorable but impractically shaped measuring cups. We prefer stainless steel with securely riveted handles; they are easy to keep clean and will last for decades. Double-check the volume of the cup measure; cups in this book are based on a 250 mL cup measure. You will also need a set of liquid cup measures for liquids and semi-solids. We suggest Pyrex glass liquid measuring cups that usually come in a set of 1, 2, and 4 cups. We also love an 8-cup glass measuring cup (these often come with silicone lids and are called batter bowls) as the vessel we most frequently use to microwave large quantities. Any liquid measuring cup should be shatter proof and heat resistant and have clearly marked cup increments and ounce or millilitre markings on the side for easy reading. When you are filling the cup, always place it on a level surface and get at eye level to the cup to look at it straight on. If you read it from above, your perspective will skew the reading and you will end up with the wrong volume.

Measuring spoons are needed for measuring small quantities of both liquids and solids. A set should include 1 and ½ tablespoon and 1, ½, ¼, and ⅛ teaspoon measures. We prefer stainless steel in classic round spoon shapes for durability and washability. Ideally look for measuring spoons that are narrow enough to fit into your spice jars and baking powder and baking soda containers.

A digital kitchen scale that measures up to 11 pounds (5 kg) in both half-ounce and one-gram increments is needed to weigh chocolate in many of our recipes, but in a pinch just look online for common conversions to cups for any weight.

2. BOWLS

Most sets of mixing bowls include 6 cups/1.5 quarts (small), 12 cups/3 quarts (medium), and 20 cups/5 quarts (large). This is a good start for any bowl collection, but we would add a 28-cup/7-quart bowl to that list for some of the larger recipes so that you have room to work in the bowl without it overflowing. We prefer stainless steel since it is unbreakable, relatively light to lift, holds heat well as a double boiler, and is non-reactive. There is something quite romantic about using hand-me-down bakeware, and we love heavy old ceramic bowls for their stability while mixing and their vintage charm, but they do not have the same range of practical uses. Tempered glass bowls are also excellent as double boilers and for when you want to microwave anything in a bowl, but they can get heavy and can chip or break over time. If you are building your bowl collection, we suggest getting an extra-large 40-cup/10-quart bowl for doubling recipes and several small bowls, less than 1 cup in volume, for measuring out ingredients for your mise en place. When melting or heating anything in the microwave, we always prefer to use tempered glass measuring cups instead of bowls. They make it easier to pour the liquid out once melted and have a handle that is easy to grab when the glass gets warm.

3. POTS

If you are cooking custards or melting chocolate, you will want good-quality pots with thick bottoms that conduct heat evenly. If you are using the pots as a base for a double boiler or making mostly water-based items like caramel or candied lemon peel, you can get away with a lower quality pot. We suggest having these pot sizes handy: 8-cup/2-quart (small), 16-cup/4-quart (medium), and 24-cup/6-quart (large) saucepans with lids, a large cast-iron skillet, and a wide 4- to 6-quart saucepan. A quality collection of pots and pans can take a lifetime to build as you find what works best for you, your stovetop, and your cooking preferences. It is a good idea to invest in the best cookware you can afford, as these really are items that can last for decades.

4. TOOLS FOR MIXING AND SPREADING

To whisk ingredients together, you will need a sturdy metal whisk. Look for stainless steel construction and thick, well-balanced handles that are comfortable to grip, which will reduce hand and wrist strain. You want sturdy, well-spaced wires that spring back to their original shape if you bend them and that are sealed within the handle so there are no nooks and crannies to trap food or moisture. We generally use balloon whisks, the classic shape you probably think of, with a bulbous end, and we like a 12-inch whisk for most tasks. To stir and mix, you will need a silicone spatula and a wooden spoon. Silicone spatulas generally have an outer layer made of flexible silicone that is great for scraping the contours of pots and bowls and a rigid core of fibreglass, plastic, or wood. Look for spatulas that are completely coated in silicone (including the handle) and avoid ones where the head may become detached or has gaps that may allow moisture to be trapped over time. They are dishwasher safe, should be able to withstand temperatures to 550°F, will not scratch non-stick pans, and will not absorb any smells or colours as they age. They are essential for scraping down bowls while mixing and stirring custards while cooking and are our go-to mixing tool at the bakery. Wooden spoons are not as common in the bakery, as they are harder to sanitize and do not have the flexibility of a silicone spatula, but at home we all have a favourite wooden spoon. They are best for stirring stiff doughs and are also useful when cooking custards, but they can be used for most of the same purposes as silicone spatulas. As wooden spoons age, they naturally take on oils, colours, and smells and even change shape depending on how you hold and use them. They truly become an extension of your body and carry your culinary history within them.

A universal tool at the bakery is the palette knife. Pastry chefs, bread bakers, and cake decorators alike use this tool daily. An extension of your hand, they are used for an endless list of tasks, including spreading fillings, smoothing batters, finishing icing on cakes, mixing small amounts of ingredients, and lifting and placing pieces delicately. There are many different styles and sizes of palette knives, and they go by various names from spreaders to offset spatulas. The great debate is what palette knife is better for which task? The step palette or offset knife has a bend in the flat blade near the handle, which gives you room for your fingers, allows you to place items with a more balanced hand, and avoids overextending your wrist while icing a cake. The straight palette has a flat blade that comes straight out of the handle, and some bakers prefer it for icing cakes. We know many bakers who have more than a dozen different sizes and variations of palette knives in their collections, so the truth is that you should go with what feels right and what gets the job done most effectively. The two most frequently used in the bakery are a small offset palette knife, which has a narrow, flexible 4-inch-long blade with a bend near the wooden handle, and a large step palette knife, which has a stiff, inflexible 8-inch-long blade with a bend near the black hard plastic handle. The smaller one is used for everything, and the larger one is used primarily for icing cakes.

5. TOOLS FOR PORTIONING

We use seven different sizes of spring-loaded scoops at the bakery, but we have simplified the recipes in this book to use just two sizes: a 1½-tablespoon (¾-ounce) scoop for small cookies and a 3-tablespoon (1⅝-ounce) scoop for large cookies and sandwich cookies. The larger scoop also works well for muffins if you scoop rounded or heaped scoops. Check your local professional kitchen supply store for the best quality scoops that will last (we use Vollrath brand). They should be mostly or completely made of stainless steel and have hard plastic, textured handles to provide an excellent grip, even with buttery fingers. The trigger should fit your thumb comfortably and the handle should be ergonomically designed to make it easy to scoop repeatedly without repositioning your hand.

Another crucial portioning tool is a stainless steel ruler at least 18 inches long for measuring while cutting bars and rolling out pastry. You also may want to invest in a 5-inch round cookie cutter for cutting out pastry circles for tarts, although you can certainly cut them out with a paring knife instead.

You will need at least three knives: a small paring knife for preparing fruit, a 10- to 12-inch chef's knife for cutting bars, and a bread knife for slicing cakes. A baker's knives are a very personal preference; just like chefs, we are usually pretty specific about what we like in our knives and this varies a lot from baker to baker. It is a good idea to visit your local kitchen or knife store, speak to an expert, and hold some knives in your hand to decide which is best for you. The good news is you can get away with an entry-level, commercial-grade Henckels knife, which usually has a bright yellow plastic handle and is very affordable, for most tasks. If you are spending a lot of time in the kitchen, it's best to invest in two or three quality knives and build your collection as your culinary tastes grow.

6. BAKING VESSELS

The preferred material for all baking vessels is aluminum or stainless steel—light, shiny metal, not dark-coloured metals. Professional bakers stay away from non-stick coatings. They do not last forever and eventually there is some flaking or scratching of the coating. For the recipes in this book, you will need the following:

- four 13- × 18-inch baking sheets
- one 9- × 13-inch cake pan
- one 8-inch square cake pan

- one 9-inch square cake pan
- one 12-cup muffin tin
- one 24-well mini-muffin pan
- two 6-well or one 12-well doughnut pans
- one 9- × 5-inch loaf pan
- four 6-inch-round, 3-inch-deep cake pans
- one 6-inch springform pan
- one 9-inch springform pan

We have suggested greasing and lining pans with parchment paper in most recipes. Avoid using soap on your pans; just wash them with very hot water and a soft cloth to avoid microabrasions from scrub brushes. Your pans will acquire a beautiful patina and a natural non-stick surface over time. Greasing them is certainly easiest with canola oil cooking spray, but you can get away with many alternatives. Josie's mum and grandmother always saved old butter wrappers in the fridge and used them to wipe down baking pans as a way to grease them with a coating of butter. You can also use a paper towel to apply canola oil or other neutral-tasting oils with low smoke points, such as sunflower oil, in lieu of cooking spray. Just avoid oils, like olive oil, that add their own distinct flavour or have low smoke points.

7. TOOLS FOR DECORATING

You will find that having too many pastry bags is never a bad thing! In your baking toolbox, you should have at least three different sizes of bags for a variety of uses. We prefer to use reusable, washable, featherweight polyester piping bags. These are coated to keep grease from coming through and can be washed easily with hot soapy water, reused, and fitted with a variety of tips and piping bag couplers. We recommend investing in three 16-inch bags, two 14-inch bags, and four 12-inch bags. Disposable plastic piping bags also have their place, for sticky caramels that may need to go in the microwave quickly or royal icings where it is useful to see the colours through the bags. Couplers for piping bags are a great investment. To use a coupler, you simply place the cone piece inside the bag, place the desired tip inside the plastic ring, and screw it onto the cone from the outside of the bag. This is a time saver and makes it simple to switch between different tips and piping techniques. Having sets of both round and star tips will come in handy; you can purchase 10-piece packs that range in size for both round and star tips. A few smaller round tips are always a great option for detail work. We use both Wilton brand, which is for home

baking, and Ateco brand, which caters to more industrial kitchens. Tips are sold in standard numbered sizes. For cakes and decorative details in this cookbook, you'll need No. 804 and 806 round tips, a No. 825 star tip, and No. 1 to 4 round tips for smaller details.

A cake turntable is essential for decorating cakes. It allows you to manipulate the icing evenly while you spin the cake. Add a small slip-free mat between the turntable and your cake board or plate and you are golden. We suggest investing in a sturdy metal turntable for durability and fluid movement, but there are some great low-end plastic turntables out there. Just be sure to purchase a hard plastic turntable that can hold at least 25 pounds (11 kg) without any bend or give in the top surface. A great brand that has held strong at almost all bakeries we have worked at is Ateco brand metal cake turntables.

8. TOOLS FOR SIFTING AND STRAINING

You will need at least one large metal fine-mesh strainer (aka sieve), more than 7 inches wide, for sifting ingredients into a bowl in most of our recipes. You also may want a small 3-inch sieve for sifting small amounts of spices or leaveners. A durable stainless steel mesh sieve will not rust or warp as it ages and should be easy to clean with hot soapy water. Look for handles that will sit securely on top of your large bowl so that you do not have to hold the sieve while you scoop ingredients into it. You want the mesh to be firmly attached to its frame so that you can push on it with a wooden spoon or silicone spatula to force through purées or thick liquids when needed. It is also useful to have a selection of durable, stackable plastic strainers or colanders with varying hole sizes for everything from draining pasta to mascarpone.

9. STAND MIXER

We highly recommend investing in a 6-quart or larger stand mixer. If that is not accessible to you, a handheld mixer will work most of the time, although you may end up with sore hands from all the vibration. It is not impossible to make these recipes by hand, but you will certainly develop some impressive arm muscles. When using any mixer, start at low every time and then work up to the speed requested. Before turning on your mixer, always, always, always check where the speed is set. If you are adding a large portion of dry ingredients to a wet mixture, grab a large clean kitchen towel and cover the head of the mixer, draping it over the top to cover the gap between the bowl and the mixer head. This will act as a barrier shielding you from

that explosive dry ingredient cloud! This also works well to prevent splatter if you are whipping a large amount of cream.

10. OTHER USEFUL TOOLS

A mini kitchen torch or small blowtorch is useful for toasting meringues and caramelizing sugars for crunchy finishes. We love our torch head that attaches directly to the small green propane cylinders you use for camping. It has an adjustable flame and a trigger start that is easy to use and control.

Invest in a candy thermometer that reads up to at least 400°F. The only way to get the chemistry right in baking is to know your temperatures. Candy thermometers that have hangers to keep them securely attached to your pots are great and usually relatively cheap, but for convenience we absolutely adore our digital laser thermometer that can read a temperature without ever touching your product. It is easy to use and does not get all sticky from your bubbling syrups.

Look for sales and purchase a quality immersion blender and a blender or food processor. These are tools you might not use often but that will last for a long time if you care for them properly. You want solid construction from dependable brands like Cuisinart, from whom you will be able to order replacement parts if needed.

Morning Baking

Farmers' Fruit Muffins

Makes 12 muffins

Many of our bakery regulars drop by first thing in the morning to grab a coffee and a muffin. It is the perfect portable morning pick-me-up, and we love showing off whatever local fruit happens to be in season. At home, this is our favourite "clean out the fridge" muffin recipe. We often bake these muffins to use up any fruit that has somehow been forgotten and is about to be past its prime. Everyone loves these muffins because they are a delicious treat for adults and kids alike (great for lunch boxes!) and the recipe is simple enough to make with any little helper. If you are lucky, your helper will get a taste for baking, and it will not be long before you get to sit back and enjoy the spoils. We have used raspberries as shown in the photo, but really any fruit will work. Leave berries whole or cut them in half if they are very large; cut larger fruits into half-inch cubes. Peeling the fruit is optional.

1. Preheat the oven to 350°F. Line a muffin tin with 12 paper liners or generously grease with canola oil cooking spray.

2. Sift the flour, baking powder, cinnamon, and salt into a large bowl and stir together.

3. In a medium bowl, combine the buttermilk, brown sugar, canola oil, eggs, and vanilla. Vigorously whisk together until the sugar is dissolved and the mixture is smooth.

4. Add the wet ingredients to the dry ingredients and stir until almost fully combined. Gently fold in the fruit and stir just until the ingredients are fully incorporated and no dry flour remains. Be careful not to overmix.

5. Fill the muffin cups to the rim with batter. Sprinkle about ½ teaspoon of the turbinado sugar over each muffin before baking. Bake for 25 to 35 minutes, or until a toothpick inserted into the centre of a muffin comes out clean. Cool the muffins in the pan or wait 5 to 10 minutes, then turn them out onto a wire rack. Store in an airtight container at room temperature for up to 3 days.

2½ cups all-purpose flour

1 tablespoon baking powder

½ teaspoon cinnamon

½ teaspoon salt

1 cup buttermilk or plain full-fat yogurt, room temperature

⅔ cup packed dark brown sugar

½ cup canola oil

2 large eggs, room temperature

1 teaspoon pure vanilla extract

1½ cups fresh or frozen fruit (berries whole or cut in half; larger fruit chopped into ½-inch cubes)

2 tablespoons turbinado sugar, for topping

Morning Glory Muffins

Crumble Topping (optional)

1 cup lightly packed dark brown
   sugar

¾ cup all-purpose flour

¾ cup oat flakes

½ cup unsalted butter cut into
   ½-inch cubes, room temperature

½ teaspoon cinnamon

¼ teaspoon salt

Muffins

2½ cups all-purpose flour

1½ teaspoons baking powder

1 teaspoon baking soda

1½ teaspoons cinnamon

½ teaspoon salt

¾ cup packed dark brown sugar

½ cup plain full-fat yogurt or sour
   cream, room temperature

⅓ cup canola oil

2 large eggs, room temperature

1 teaspoon pure vanilla extract

2 cups grated peeled carrots

¾ cup grated peeled apples (Mutsu
   or Jonagold)

½ cup dried cranberries

½ cup unsweetened shredded or
   flaked coconut

½ cup raw pumpkin seeds

¼ cup raw sunflower seeds

Secretly, muffins are everyone's favourite excuse to have cake for breakfast. That is just fine with us! The morning glory is a classic muffin available in coffee shops and bakeries all over the world. For us, the key is to load it with as many delicious and healthy ingredients as we can. Grated apple, carrots, and coconut add a tender texture and sweet flavour, while the seeds add crunch and protein. Peeling the carrots and apples is optional, but giving them a good wash and including the skin will give the muffins a little more texture and nutrition. On rare mornings when Josie is alone in the kitchen, this is her favourite recipe to bake. The ingredients in the bowl form a rainbow as the almost metallic sunflower seeds are piled next to bright orange carrots, shiny red cranberries, green apple skins and pumpkin seeds, and bright white coconut. Embrace this muffin's inner cupcake by topping it with a sweet cinnamon oat crumble for a special breakfast, or just sprinkle it with extra seeds and coconut for a simpler finish.

1. Preheat the oven to 350°F. Line a muffin tin with 12 paper liners or generously grease with canola oil cooking spray.

2. Make the crumble topping, if using: In a medium bowl, combine the brown sugar, flour, oat flakes, butter, cinnamon, and salt. Using your fingers, rub together until the mixture resembles coarse crumbs. Set aside.

3. Make the muffins: Sift the flour, baking powder, baking soda, cinnamon, and salt into a large bowl and stir together.

4. In a medium bowl, whisk together the brown sugar, yogurt, canola oil, eggs, and vanilla until the sugar is dissolved and the mixture is smooth. Add the carrots, apples, cranberries, coconut, pumpkin seeds, and sunflower seeds and stir until evenly distributed.

5. Add the wet ingredients to the dry ingredients, and stir just until the ingredients are fully incorporated and no dry flour remains. Be careful not to overmix.

6. Fill the muffin cups to the rim with batter. Sprinkle the crumble (if using) over the muffins before baking. If you want to skip the crumble topping, these will still be beautiful and delicious. Bake for 25 to 35 minutes, or until a toothpick inserted into the centre of a muffin comes out clean. Cool the muffins in the pan or wait 5 to 10 minutes, then turn them out onto a wire rack. These muffins are best enjoyed on the day of baking, served warm with butter or plain. Store in an airtight container at room temperature for up to 3 days.

Mocha Walnut Crunch Muffins

Throwing away all pretense of practicality and heading firmly into indulgence territory, this beauty is loaded with caffeine, chocolate, and just the right crunchy finish. This muffin does mornings right! We based this recipe on one of our favourite old-school doughnuts: the Walnut Crunch. If you have not had one before, it is a lightly cocoa-flavoured cake doughnut with chopped walnuts and a simple vanilla glaze. This muffin is very reminiscent of that classic doughnut, and the aroma of the ground coffee while baking really rounds out those retro doughnut shop vibes.

1. Preheat the oven to 350°F. Line a muffin tin with 12 paper liners or generously grease with canola oil cooking spray.

2. Make the muffins: Sift the flour, cocoa powder, baking soda, cinnamon, and salt into a large bowl and stir together.

3. In a medium bowl, combine the applesauce and ground coffee and mash together with a fork or wooden spoon until well blended. Add the brown sugar, coffee, granulated sugar, canola oil, eggs, and vanilla and whisk together until the sugar is dissolved. Stir in the chocolate chunks and walnuts.

4. Add the wet ingredients to the dry ingredients, and stir just until the ingredients are fully incorporated and no dry flour remains. Be careful not to overmix.

5. Fill the muffin cups to the rim with batter.

6. Make the topping: In a small bowl, mix together the sugar and ground coffee. Sprinkle the mixture over the muffins, 1 to 2 teaspoons per muffin. This seems like a lot of topping, but it will form a crust that cracks as the muffins bake. Bake for 25 to 35 minutes, or until a toothpick inserted into the centre of a muffin comes out clean. Cool the muffins in the pan or wait 5 to 10 minutes, then turn them out onto a wire rack. Store in an airtight container at room temperature for up to 3 days.

Muffins

2¼ cups all-purpose flour

3 tablespoons cocoa powder

1½ teaspoons baking soda

1 teaspoon cinnamon

½ teaspoon salt

⅓ cup unsweetened applesauce

1½ tablespoons finely ground coffee (use the espresso grind setting)

¾ cup packed dark brown sugar

¾ cup cold coffee

⅓ cup granulated sugar

⅓ cup canola oil

2 large eggs, room temperature

1½ teaspoons pure vanilla extract

¾ cup semi-sweet chocolate chunks

½ cup toasted walnuts, finely chopped

Topping

¼ cup granulated sugar

2 teaspoons finely ground coffee

Fruit Crumble Muffins

Crumble Topping

1 cup all-purpose flour

½ cup granulated sugar

⅓ cup soft vegan margarine, cold
   (we use Crystal)

½ teaspoon cinnamon (optional)

Muffins

1½ cups soy milk or other
   unsweetened non-dairy milk,
   room temperature

1½ tablespoons apple cider
   vinegar or white vinegar

3¾ cups all-purpose flour

2¼ teaspoons baking soda

1 teaspoon cinnamon

¾ teaspoon salt

1½ cups packed dark brown sugar

½ cup canola oil

1½ teaspoons pure vanilla extract

1½ cups fresh or frozen fruit,
   chopped into 1-inch cubes

Variation

Piña Colada Muffin:

Replace ½ cup of the soy milk with
½ cup full-fat canned coconut
milk. Replace the fruit with 1 cup
strained pineapple chunks, 1 cup
unsweetened shredded coconut,
and 2 tablespoons rum. Top with
sweetened flaked coconut before
baking.

This versatile vegan muffin base has been used for dozens of amazing muffin variations at the bakery. It has enough structure to support heavy additions like chocolate chunks but a soft and airy texture that is still appropriate for flavours as subtle as lemon poppy seed. We encourage you to play around with different combinations to find your own signature family recipe. We have gone with a simple blueberry version as shown in the photo, but you can use any fruit from pineapple to blackberries. If your fruit is frozen, do not defrost it before adding it to the batter; simply add four to five minutes to your baking time. We have added a vegan shortbread crumble for the top so that vegans too can rejoice in the joy of cake for breakfast. If you prefer a simpler finish, just sprinkle the muffins with granulated sugar before baking.

1. Preheat the oven to 350°F. Line a muffin tin with 12 paper liners or generously grease with canola oil cooking spray.

2. Make the crumble topping: In a medium bowl, combine the flour, sugar, vegan margarine, and cinnamon, if using. Using your fingers, rub together until the mixture resembles coarse crumbs. Set aside.

3. Make the muffins: In a medium bowl, whisk together the soy milk and apple cider vinegar. Set aside at room temperature and let the soy milk curdle and thicken a little, 10 to 15 minutes. It will look like buttermilk when ready.

4. Sift the flour, baking soda, cinnamon, and salt into a large bowl and stir together.

5. Add the brown sugar, canola oil, and vanilla to the soy milk and vinegar mixture. Whisk until the sugar is dissolved and there is no oily film left around the edges.

6. Add the wet ingredients to the dry ingredients and stir until almost fully combined. Gently fold in the fruit and stir just until the ingredients are fully incorporated and no dry flour remains. Be careful not to overmix.

7. Fill the muffin cups to the rim with batter. Sprinkle the crumble topping over the muffins. Bake for 25 to 35 minutes, or until a toothpick inserted into the centre of a muffin comes out clean. Cool the muffins in the pan or wait 5 to 10 minutes, then turn them out onto a wire rack. These muffins are best enjoyed on the day of baking. Store in an airtight container at room temperature for up to 3 days.

Pumpkin Coconut Muffins

We are not entirely sure of the original source of this recipe. In the early days of the bakery, it came to us via a truly exceptional intern on a typewritten page that was lost to time long ago. We had not been open long, and we were desperately looking for quality vegan recipes. It was a frenzy of recipe testing in the early days of the bakery, and every day the kitchen was full of baked goods waiting to be evaluated. After testing this recipe, everyone adored it immediately. It has become a staple recipe over the last decade and a favourite of young visitors to the bakery. This muffin has the perfect balance of sweet and pumpkin spice with a tender crumb and moisture that keeps this muffin fresh for days.

1. Preheat the oven to 350°F. Line a muffin tin with 12 paper liners or generously grease with canola oil cooking spray.

2. Sift the flour, pumpkin spice, baking powder, baking soda, and salt into a large bowl and stir together.

3. In a medium bowl, combine the brown sugar, pumpkin purée, canola oil, granulated sugar, coconut milk, shredded coconut, and vanilla, and whisk together until the sugars are dissolved and there is no oily film left around the edges.

4. Add the wet ingredients to the dry ingredients, and stir just until the ingredients are fully incorporated and no dry flour remains. Be careful not to overmix.

5. Fill the muffin cups to the rim with batter. Sprinkle the large flake coconut over the muffins before baking, about 1 tablespoon per muffin. Bake for 25 to 35 minutes, or until a toothpick inserted into the centre of a muffin comes out clean. Cool the muffins in the pan or wait 5 to 10 minutes, then turn them out onto a wire rack. Store in an airtight container at room temperature for up to 5 days.

2¼ cups all-purpose flour

1½ teaspoons Pumpkin Spice (page 267)

1 teaspoon baking powder

1 teaspoon baking soda

½ teaspoon salt

1 cup lightly packed dark brown sugar

1 cup pure pumpkin purée

½ cup canola oil

⅓ cup granulated sugar

⅓ cup full-fat canned coconut milk, room temperature

⅓ cup unsweetened shredded coconut

1½ teaspoons pure vanilla extract

¾ cup sweetened large flake coconut, for topping

Vanilla Bean Scones

Scones

½ cup cold unsalted butter

2½ cups all-purpose flour, more
for dusting

⅓ cup granulated sugar, more for
sprinkling (optional)

2 teaspoons baking powder

1 teaspoon baking soda

¾ teaspoon salt

1 cup cold buttermilk

1 large egg

2 teaspoons pure vanilla extract

Egg Wash

1 large egg

1 tablespoon water, room
temperature

Variations

Almond Currant Scones: Add
½ teaspoon almond extract at the
same time as the vanilla extract.
Add ¾ cup roasted sliced almonds
and 1 cup dried currants (soaked
in warm water for 10 minutes and
drained) to the dry ingredients
before mixing in the wet
ingredients in step 5. Egg wash as
instructed and top the scones
with ¼ cup raw sliced almonds
and ¼ cup turbinado sugar before
baking.

Cheese Scones: Add 2 cups grated
old cheddar cheese or your
favourite hard cheese to the dry
ingredients before mixing in the
wet ingredients in step 5. One of
our favourite combinations is a
good aged, salty Beemster and
old cheddar cheese. We often
make a cheddar, mozzarella, and
Asiago combination that is very
popular.

The beauty of this recipe is its ability to take anything, from the best quality freshly picked berries to last night's leftovers, and transform it into baking magic. These fluffy golden gems have a buttery, tender crumb that supports any flavour combination you can dream up. Growing up, Josie was ingrained with a "waste not, want not" approach to cooking, and this recipe was developed specially to make sure that no quality ingredient ever goes to waste at the bakery. Our bakers are trained to check the fridges and gardens each morning and to get creative with their scones. We have made hundreds of variations over the years. These scones stand up equally well as the centrepiece of a hearty breakfast, as a delicate addition to a fancy tea party, or as a robust side to your favourite stew. We have created them as full-size scones, but if you want a more elegant petite version, try them at half the size, reduce the baking time to fifteen to seventeen minutes, and make sixteen scones.

1. Preheat the oven to 400°F. Line a large baking sheet with parchment paper or a silicone baking mat.

2. Make the scones: Using a box grater, grate the cold butter into a small bowl. Store in the refrigerator until needed in step 5.

3. Sift the flour, sugar, baking powder, baking soda, and salt into a large bowl and stir together.

4. In a small bowl, whisk together the buttermilk, egg, and vanilla.

5. Toss the cold grated butter into the dry ingredients until evenly distributed. Create a well in the centre of the dry ingredients, add the wet ingredients, and using a large fork, fold the dry and wet ingredients together. Mix just until all the flour is moist and the dough is still a little shaggy. The dough should be fairly dry but workable.

6. Using as little pressure as possible, form a ball with the dough in the bowl. Lightly dust a work surface with flour. Turn the dough out onto the work surface. Working quickly and with as little kneading as possible, shape the dough into a 6- to 7-inch disc, 1½ to 2 inches thick.

7. Using a large sharp knife or bench scraper, cut the dough into 8 equal wedges and place on the prepared baking sheet 2 to 3 inches apart.

8. Make the egg wash: In a small bowl, whisk together the egg and water. Using a pastry brush, brush the tops of the scones evenly with egg wash. If you would like to add some sparkle, sprinkle some sugar on top before baking. Bake for 18 to 20 minutes or until the scones are evenly browned and the edges look crispy. These scones are best enjoyed warm or at room temperature on the day of baking. Store in an airtight container at room temperature for up to 3 days. The scones can be reheated in the oven at 350°F for 5 minutes.

Pumpkin Spice Scones

Once you master these tender and sweet scones, you will be able to make them in less time than it takes your oven to warm up. They are the perfect breakfast to impress last-minute overnight guests or to please an afternoon snack-craving crowd. If serving them with something savoury, we suggest skipping the glaze and just topping the scones with pumpkin seeds. They can even be baked half-size for sixteen scones; just reduce the baking time to fifteen to seventeen minutes. Mini scones make the most heavenly partner to fall vegetable soups.

1. Preheat the oven to 400°F. Line a large baking sheet with parchment paper or a silicone baking mat.

2. Make the scones: Using a box grater, grate the cold butter into a small bowl. Store in the refrigerator until needed in step 5.

3. Sift the flour, sugar, pumpkin spice, baking powder, baking soda, and salt into a large bowl and stir together.

4. In a small bowl, whisk together the buttermilk, pumpkin purée, egg, and vanilla.

5. Toss the cold grated butter into the dry ingredients until evenly distributed. Create a well in the centre of the dry ingredients, add the wet ingredients, and using a large fork, fold the dry and wet ingredients together. Mix just until all the flour is moist and the dough is still a little shaggy. The dough should be fairly dry but workable.

6. Using as little pressure as possible, form a ball with the dough in the bowl. Lightly dust a work surface with flour. Turn the dough out onto the work surface. Working quickly and with as little kneading as possible, shape the dough into a 6- to 7-inch disc, 1½ to 2 inches thick.

7. Using a large sharp knife or bench scraper, cut the dough into 8 equal wedges and place on the prepared baking sheet 2 to 3 inches apart.

8. Make the egg wash: In a small bowl, whisk together the egg and water. Using a pastry brush, brush the tops of the scones evenly with egg wash. Sprinkle the raw pumpkin seeds (if using) on top of the egg wash. Bake for 18 to 20 minutes or until the scones are evenly browned and the edges look crispy.

9. While the scones are baking, make the glaze: In a small bowl, whisk together the icing sugar and warm water. Glaze the scones as soon as they come out of the oven by spooning the glaze over the scones. These scones are best enjoyed warm or at room temperature on the day of baking. Store in an airtight container at room temperature for up to 3 days. The scones can be reheated in the oven at 350°F for 5 minutes.

Scones

½ cup cold unsalted butter

2¾ cups all-purpose flour, more for dusting

⅓ cup granulated sugar, more for topping

1 tablespoon Pumpkin Spice (page 267)

2 teaspoons baking powder

1 teaspoon baking soda

¾ teaspoon salt

⅔ cup cold buttermilk

½ cup pumpkin purée

1 large egg

1 teaspoon pure vanilla extract

½ cup raw shelled pumpkin seeds, for garnish (optional)

Egg Wash

1 large egg

1 tablespoon water, room temperature

Glaze

½ cup icing sugar

1 to 1½ tablespoons warm water

Bacon and Cheddar Scones

Scones

½ cup cold unsalted butter

2½ cups all-purpose flour, more
   for dusting

¼ cup granulated sugar

2 teaspoons baking powder

1 teaspoon baking soda

¾ teaspoon salt

1 cup cold buttermilk

1 large egg

1½ cups grated old cheddar cheese

¾ cup cooked bacon chopped into
   1-inch pieces, room temperature

Egg Wash

1 large egg

1 tablespoon water, room
   temperature

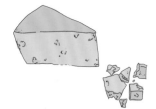

The smell of these scones baking is absolutely intoxicating but biting into them is even better. Make sure to eat them while they are still warm, the cheese is melty, and the smoky bacon chunks are crispy. If you do not catch the magic moment they emerge from the oven, they can be reheated at 350°F for 5 minutes.

We call these "Marley scones." Josie's best friends, Amy and Michael, had an amazing black lab mix named Marley. He was the first dog to play with Josie's babies and the best-trained dog you'd ever meet. He was not just a family pet—he was Michael's best friend. They went everywhere together. Too early in his life, he was diagnosed with cancer, and Amy and Michael were inconsolable. After months of illness they began to see him fade. He had not eaten in seven days and they were facing a difficult decision at the vet's later that day. They happened to have made this recipe that Josie had previously shared with them. They offered Marley a bite and he actually ate some. Then he ate more. He rallied that day and lived for five more loving months. Whenever we make these scones, we always take a moment to remember Marley.

1. Preheat the oven to 400°F. Line a large baking sheet with parchment paper or a silicone baking mat.

2. Make the scones: Using a box grater, grate the cold butter into a small bowl. Store in the refrigerator until needed in step 5.

3. Sift the flour, sugar, baking powder, baking soda, and salt into a large bowl and stir together.

4. In a medium bowl, whisk together the buttermilk and egg.

5. Toss the cold grated butter, grated cheese, and bacon pieces into the dry ingredients until evenly distributed. Create a well in the centre of the dry ingredients, add the wet ingredients, and using a large fork, fold the dry and wet ingredients together. Mix just until all the flour is moist and the dough is still a little shaggy. The dough should be fairly dry but workable.

6. Using as little pressure as possible, form a ball with the dough in the bowl. Lightly dust a work surface with flour. Turn the dough out onto the work surface. Working quickly and with as little kneading as possible, shape the dough into a 6- to 7-inch disc, 1½ to 2 inches thick.

7. Using a large sharp knife or bench scraper, cut the dough into 8 equal wedges and place on the prepared baking sheet 2 to 3 inches apart.

8. Make the egg wash: In a small bowl, whisk together the egg and water. Using a pastry brush, brush the tops of the scones evenly with egg wash. Bake for 18 to 20 minutes or until the scones are evenly browned and the edges look crispy. These scones are best enjoyed warm or at room temperature on the day of baking. Store in an airtight container at room temperature for up to 3 days. The scones can be reheated in the oven at 350°F for 5 minutes.

Lemon Poppy Seed Loaf

Makes one 9- × 5-inch loaf

This classic pound cake base is buttery and dense and oh so perfectly sweet. Sometimes simple is best, and you really cannot go wrong with basic quality flour, butter, eggs, and sugar. The inclusion of tart lemon and nutty poppy seed adds a depth of flavour, as well as a nice visual appeal with the bright yellow and black contrasting the creamy white base. Make sure you invest in local free-range eggs and quality butter and flour for this recipe—it will make a huge difference to the final taste. We love switching this loaf up seasonally by swapping the poppy seeds for one cup of fresh blueberries or raspberries. Just add ten to fifteen minutes to the baking time to make up for the extra moisture of the fruit.

1. Preheat the oven to 350°F. Lightly grease a 9- × 5-inch loaf pan with canola oil cooking spray. Line the pan with parchment paper, allowing excess paper to hang over each side for easy removal.

2. Make the loaf: Sift the flour, baking powder, and salt into a small bowl and stir together.

3. In the bowl of a stand mixer fitted with the paddle attachment, cream the sugar, butter, and lemon zest on medium-high speed until pale and fluffy. Scrape down the sides and bottom of the bowl.

4. Add the eggs, one at a time, and beat well on medium-high speed. Scrape down the sides and bottom of the bowl after each addition.

5. Add the flour mixture, buttermilk, and poppy seeds and mix on low speed until combined, 2 to 3 minutes. The mixture should be smooth and lump-free. Scrape down the sides and bottom of the bowl and mix for 30 more seconds on medium-high speed to make sure everything is well incorporated.

6. Scoop the batter into the prepared loaf pan. Level the top of the batter with a small offset palette knife or spoon. Bake for 80 to 95 minutes, or until a toothpick inserted into the centre of the loaf comes out clean.

7. Meanwhile, make the glaze: In a small bowl, stir together the lemon juice and sugar. The sugar will not totally dissolve in the lemon juice.

8. Remove the loaf from the oven and leave it in the pan. Give the lemon and sugar mixture a quick stir then immediately slowly pour over the loaf, allowing the loaf to absorb the delicious glaze. Let sit for 15 to 20 minutes. Lift the loaf from the pan using the parchment paper handles, remove the paper, and continue to cool on a wire rack for at least 1 hour before slicing. Store in an airtight container at room temperature for up to 5 days.

Loaf

3 cups all-purpose flour

2 teaspoons baking powder

½ teaspoon salt

2 cups granulated sugar

1 cup unsalted butter, room temperature

Zest of 3 lemons

4 large eggs, room temperature

1 cup buttermilk, room temperature

1 tablespoon poppy seeds

Glaze

Juice from 3 lemons

⅔ cup granulated sugar

Carrot Loaf with Dreamy Cream Cheese Icing

Makes one 9- × 5-inch loaf
or one 9-inch square cake

There has always been a lot of debate about the perfect carrot cake at the bakery. The two camps are clear: dense and intensely spicy with no additions or packed with pecans, pineapple, raisins, and coconut. Either way, there is no disagreement about the icing. It must be cream cheese icing, not too sweet and with a touch of vanilla. We have covered our bases in this book with this basic beauty and a loaded version in the cake chapter. This loaf is not only a delicious addition to any tea party or breakfast table but also a lifesaver for new parents. When Josie's daughter was born, her grandmother gifted her a groaning cake. Traditionally, a groaning cake is baked either by the labouring mother to distract her from the pain of early labour or by loved ones in the home. The scrumptious smell of baking cake is meant to carry the mother through the birth and give her a restorative snack once she has delivered. For Josie, that loaded carrot cake imbued with love and support was not just fortifying, it got her through the hardest parts of the first couple of days of new motherhood. Because when you go through such a life-changing shift, there should always be cake (and family) to keep you grounded.

Loaf

2 cups all-purpose flour

1 tablespoon cinnamon

2 teaspoons Pumpkin Spice (page 267)

1 teaspoon freshly grated or ground nutmeg

2 teaspoons baking soda

½ teaspoon baking powder

¾ teaspoon salt

3 cups grated peeled carrots

2 cups packed dark brown sugar

4 large eggs, room temperature

⅓ cup canola oil

1 teaspoon pure vanilla extract

Dreamy Cream Cheese Icing

⅓ batch Dreamy Cream Cheese Icing (page 244)

1. Preheat the oven to 350°F. Lightly grease a 9- × 5-inch loaf pan or 9-inch square cake pan with canola oil cooking spray. Line the pan with parchment paper, allowing excess paper to hang over each side for easy removal.

2. Make the loaf: Sift the flour, cinnamon, pumpkin spice, nutmeg, baking soda, baking powder, and salt into a large bowl and stir together.

3. In a medium bowl, whisk together the grated carrots, brown sugar, eggs, canola oil, and vanilla until the mixture is smooth, the sugar is dissolved, and the eggs are well mixed in.

4. Add the wet ingredients to the dry ingredients, and stir just until the ingredients are fully incorporated and no dry flour remains. Be careful not to overmix.

5. Scoop the batter into the prepared pan. Level the top of the batter with a small offset palette knife or spoon. Bake for 60 to 80 minutes, or until a toothpick inserted into the centre of the loaf comes out clean. Remove from the oven and let cool in the pan to room temperature for at least 2 hours before icing.

6. Ice the loaf: If the dreamy cream cheese icing is freshly made, spread it evenly over the loaf. If the icing has been stored, whip it in the bowl of a stand mixer fitted with the paddle attachment on high speed for 3 to 4 minutes until fluffy again and then ice the loaf. Store covered at room temperature for up to 2 days or in the refrigerator for up to 5 days.

Banana Chocolate Chunk Loaf

Loaf

2 cups all-purpose flour

1 tablespoon baking powder

½ teaspoon salt

1 cup granulated sugar

½ cup unsalted butter, room
    temperature

2 large eggs, room temperature

1½ cups very ripe mashed banana
    (3 to 4 bananas)

1 teaspoon lemon juice

1 cup chocolate chunks

**Dark Chocolate Ganache
(optional)**

2 batches Dark Chocolate
    Ganache (page 254)

A school lunch staple and perfect snack anytime, this loaf is a crowd-pleaser. We went through at least a dozen banana loaf recipe trials in our first couple of months at the bakery before settling on this one, and we hope you will love it as much as we do. If you are feeling indulgent, try it with our chocolate ganache, which should be prepared just as the loaf emerges from the oven. Alternatively, you can add ¼ cup of chocolate chunks to the top of the loaf before baking in lieu of ganache. Heavy on banana flavour but with a light crumb, this loaf keeps well for days. Don't skimp on the chocolate here; you'll want a good-quality dark chocolate to support this timeless classic. This recipe converts well to muffins and will make about sixteen. If making muffins, reduce the baking time to thirty to thirty-five minutes.

1. Preheat the oven to 350°F. Lightly grease a 9- × 5-inch loaf pan with canola oil cooking spray. Line the pan with parchment paper, allowing excess paper to hang over each side for easy removal.

2. Make the loaf: Sift the flour, baking powder, and salt into a small bowl and stir together.

3. In the bowl of a stand mixer fitted with the paddle attachment, cream the sugar and butter on medium-high speed until pale and fluffy. Scrape down the sides and bottom of the bowl.

4. Add the eggs, one at a time, and beat well on medium-high speed. Scrape down the sides and bottom of the bowl after each addition. Add the mashed banana and lemon juice. Mix on medium speed for 1 to 2 minutes until combined.

5. Add the flour mixture and chocolate chunks and mix on low speed until combined.

6. Scoop the batter into the prepared pan. Level the top of the batter with a small offset palette knife or spoon. Bake for 70 to 85 minutes, or until a toothpick inserted into the centre of the loaf comes out clean. Remove from the oven and let sit for at least 30 minutes before removing from the pan and icing.

7. If topping with dark chocolate ganache: Pour the ganache over the loaf while the loaf is still a little warm and the glaze is fresh. Store in an airtight container at room temperature for up to 5 days.

Pumpkin Spice Baked Doughnuts

If you love autumn as much as we do, you know it is all about pairing a piping hot coffee in your favourite cozy mug with a pumpkin spice doughnut on a cool morning when the leaves are just starting to change colour. Fall combines all our favourite things: oversized sweaters and cozy scarves, chilly mornings that lead to sunny afternoons, harvest fruits and vegetables, and a great excuse for pumpkin spice everything. The perfect balance of spices, crunchy sugar exterior, and creamy pumpkin in this doughnut will give you that "fall hug" feeling no matter what season it is. These were introduced to us as doughnut hole-size treats and when we make them at home, we still love that format. Bake them in a mini muffin pan for eight to ten minutes.

1. Preheat the oven to 350°F. Lightly grease two 6-cavity doughnut pans with canola oil cooking spray.

2. Make the doughnuts: Sift the flour, baking powder, salt, cinnamon, nutmeg, allspice, and cloves into a large bowl and stir together.

3. In a medium bowl, whisk together the pumpkin purée, brown sugar, milk, canola oil, egg, and vanilla until the mixture is smooth, the sugar is dissolved, and there is no oily film left around the edges.

4. Add the wet ingredients to the dry ingredients, and stir just until the ingredients are fully incorporated and no dry flour remains. Be careful not to overmix.

5. Using a large spoon or a piping bag fitted with a No. 806 round tip, fill the wells of the pans about three-quarters full. Bake for 12 to 15 minutes, or until a toothpick inserted into the centre of a doughnut comes out clean. Immediately turn the doughnuts out onto a wire rack to cool.

6. Make the topping: Pour the melted butter into a small bowl big enough to submerge a doughnut. In a medium bowl, stir together the sugar and cinnamon.

7. Working quickly, one doughnut at a time, keep one "wet" hand for the butter and one "dry" hand for the cinnamon sugar. Dip each baked doughnut in the melted butter with one hand, then toss it in the cinnamon sugar with the other hand. The key is to dip the doughnuts in the butter quickly so that they are fully coated but do not absorb much butter. Place the coated doughnuts on a wire rack for 10 to 15 minutes before serving. Store in an airtight container at room temperature for up to 3 days. Leftover cinnamon sugar can be stored in an airtight container in the refrigerator for up to 1 month.

Doughnuts

1¾ cups all-purpose flour
2 teaspoons baking powder
½ teaspoon salt
½ teaspoon cinnamon
½ teaspoon freshly grated or ground nutmeg
½ teaspoon ground allspice
⅛ teaspoon ground cloves
¾ cup pure pumpkin purée
½ cup packed dark brown sugar
½ cup whole milk, room temperature
⅓ cup canola oil
1 large egg, room temperature
1 teaspoon pure vanilla extract

Topping

1 cup unsalted butter, melted and warm
2 cups granulated sugar
3 tablespoons cinnamon

Double-Double Baked Doughnuts

Makes 12 doughnuts
and 18 to 24 doughnut holes

Growing up in the 1980s and '90s, a popular coffee chain permeated our childhood memories with the smell of freshly baked doughnuts, coffee, and cigarette smoke. The classic double-double coffee and doughnut has found new life, minus the cigarette smoke! Our doughnut has everything you want: deep coffee flavour, crunchy sugar, and creamy icing. There are a few components to assemble, but we promise it is worth it. Originally developed for Father's Day, the double-double doughnut was such a staff favourite that we have brought it back on multiple occasions. Do not go cheap on the coffee, as it is the star. Find yourself some nice local dark roast, ethically sourced coffee. We recommend baking the doughnuts and doughnut holes separately for even baking.

1. Preheat the oven to 350°F. Lightly grease two 6-cavity doughnut pans and a 24-well mini-muffin pan (for the doughnut holes) with canola oil cooking spray.

2. Make the doughnuts (and doughnut holes): Sift the flour, baking powder, baking soda, and salt into a large bowl. Stir in the espresso powder and nutmeg.

3. In a medium bowl, whisk together the buttermilk, granulated sugar, brown sugar, eggs, melted butter, canola oil, and vanilla until the mixture is smooth and the sugars are dissolved.

4. Add the wet ingredients to the dry ingredients, and stir just until the ingredients are fully incorporated and no dry flour remains. Be careful not to overmix.

5. Using a large spoon or a piping bag fitted with a No. 806 round tip, fill the wells of the doughnut pans about three-quarters full. Fill the cups of the mini-muffin pan halfway full with the remaining batter.

6. Bake the doughnut holes for 8 to 10 minutes, or until a toothpick inserted into the centre of a hole comes out clean. Turn the doughnut holes out onto a baking sheet to cool.

7. Bake the doughnuts for 12 to 15 minutes, or until a toothpick inserted into the centre of a doughnut comes out clean. Turn the doughnuts out onto a wire rack to cool.

8. Make the coffee sugar topping: Pour the melted butter into a small bowl big enough to submerge a doughnut hole. In a medium bowl, stir together the coffee and sugar.

9. Working quickly, one at a time, dip each baked doughnut hole in the melted butter and then toss it in the coffee sugar. The key is to dip the doughnut holes in the butter quickly so that they are fully coated but do not absorb much butter. Place the coated doughnut holes on a wire rack to dry.

Doughnuts (and doughnut holes)

2⅔ cups all-purpose flour

1½ teaspoons baking powder

¼ teaspoon baking soda

¾ teaspoon salt

1 tablespoon espresso powder or finely ground dark roast coffee

½ teaspoon freshly grated or ground nutmeg

1 cup buttermilk, room temperature

½ cup granulated sugar

⅓ cup packed dark brown sugar

2 large eggs, room temperature

¼ cup unsalted butter, melted

¼ cup canola oil

1 teaspoon pure vanilla extract

Coffee Sugar Topping (for the doughnut holes)

1 cup unsalted butter, melted and warm

3 tablespoons finely ground coffee

1 cup granulated sugar

Coffee Icing (for the doughnuts)

2 cups icing sugar

¼ cup hot dark coffee

Continued on next page

10. Make the coffee icing and finish the doughnuts: In a small bowl, whisk together the icing sugar and hot coffee until smooth. You want the icing to be quite thick. If needed, add up to 1 tablespoon coffee to the icing, but you are looking for a fairly stiff mixture, not a glaze.

11. Dip the top of each cooled doughnut halfway into the coffee icing, twisting the doughnut as you lift it to capture as much icing as possible. If the icing does not stick, give the doughnut a bit more wiggle and twist. Place a coffee sugar-coated doughnut hole on top of each iced doughnut while still wet to attach them. Store in an airtight container at room temperature for up to 3 days.

Lemon Meringue Pie Baked Doughnuts

Makes 12 doughnuts

We have always wanted to make fried doughnuts but do not have the space and proper venting for deep fryers. We very ambitiously held a couple of doughnut pop-ups early in the life of the bakery, staying up all night and frying six doughnuts at a time to make more than a thousand to sell to people lined up around the block. It was incredibly fun, we invented some killer doughnuts, and our audacity even earned us a spot on season two of Food Network's *Donut Showdown*. One of the doughnuts we created for our pop-ups was too good to let go of, so we turned it into a baked version. This doughnut is not easy or quick to make but it is worth it—we promise. Once you master the lemon curd, you will find all sorts of reasons to make it. We use the meringue in our pies, and we have simplified the process to make it as easy as possible. The bonus with meringue is you get to play with fire. Who does not love that?

1. Preheat the oven to 350°F. Lightly grease two 6-cavity doughnut pans with canola oil cooking spray.

2. Make the doughnuts: Sift the flour, baking powder, baking soda, and salt into a large bowl and stir together.

3. In a medium bowl, whisk together the buttermilk, granulated sugar, brown sugar, eggs, melted butter, canola oil, lemon zest, and vanilla until the mixture is smooth, the sugars are dissolved, and there is no oily film left around the edges.

4. Add the wet ingredients to the dry ingredients, and stir just until the ingredients are fully incorporated and no dry flour remains. Be careful not to overmix.

5. Using a large spoon or a piping bag fitted with a No. 806 round tip, fill the wells of the doughnut pans about three-quarters full. Bake for 12 to 15 minutes, or until a toothpick inserted into the centre of a doughnut comes out clean.

6. Meanwhile, make the icing sugar glaze: In a small bowl, whisk together the icing sugar and hot water until smooth.

7. Spread the graham cracker crumbs about ½-inch thick on a baking sheet big enough to fit all the doughnuts.

8. Remove the doughnuts from the oven and immediately turn out onto a wire rack. Completely submerge the warm doughnuts, one at a time, in the icing sugar glaze, then lift out and allow the excess icing to drip back into the bowl. Place the wet doughnuts bottom side down on the graham cracker crumbs to dry. As the icing dries, the combination of glaze and graham crumbs will create a "pie crust" on the bottom of the doughnut.

Doughnuts
2⅔ cups all-purpose flour
1½ teaspoons baking powder
¼ teaspoon baking soda
¾ teaspoon salt
1 cup buttermilk, room temperature
½ cup granulated sugar
⅓ cup packed dark brown sugar
2 large eggs, room temperature
¼ cup unsalted butter, melted
¼ cup canola oil
Zest of 1 lemon
1 teaspoon pure vanilla extract
2 cups graham cracker crumbs, for coating

Icing Sugar Glaze
1½ cup icing sugar
1 cups hot water

Lemon Curd
½ batch Lemon Curd (page 270)

Meringue
1 batch Meringue (page 265)

Continued on next page

9. When the doughnuts are cool, using a spoon or a piping bag, fill the hole of each doughnut with the lemon curd. (If, like us, you really love lemon curd and want more of it in your doughnut, use a small spoon to scoop out a larger hole in the top of each doughnut before filling it with curd.)

10. Scoop or pipe the fresh meringue overtop the doughnuts.

11. Using a handheld kitchen torch, toast the meringue. The doughnuts should resemble individual lemon meringue pies. If they do not, they will still be a delicious mess. Store in an airtight container in the refrigerator for up to 3 days. Bring to room temperature before eating.

Old-Fashioned Chocolate Baked Doughnuts

Makes 12 doughnuts

Deep chocolate flavour meets classic doughnut shop mood. This easy doughnut is as quick to make as it is elegant in its simplicity. We love making a batch and then mixing things up with a bunch of different toppings: coconut, chopped peanuts, sprinkles, chocolate chips, candied pecans, or even chopped-up candy bars. Sometimes you just want something that speaks to that inner child, and for us this is it!

1. Preheat the oven to 350°F. Lightly grease two 6-cavity doughnut pans with canola oil cooking spray.

2. Make the doughnuts: Sift the flour, cocoa powder, baking powder, salt, and nutmeg into a large bowl and stir together.

3. In a medium bowl, whisk together the buttermilk, sugar, eggs, canola oil, and vanilla until the mixture is smooth, the sugar is dissolved, and there is no oily film left around the edges.

4. Add the wet ingredients to the dry ingredients. Add the chocolate chips and stir just until the ingredients are fully incorporated and no dry flour remains.

5. Using a large spoon or a piping bag fitted with a No. 806 round tip, fill the wells of the doughnut pans about three-quarters full with the batter. Bake for 12 to 15 minutes, or until a toothpick inserted into the centre of a doughnut comes out clean. Immediately turn the doughnuts out onto a wire rack to cool.

6. Make the chocolate icing: In a medium heat-resistant bowl, melt the chocolate and cream in the microwave in 30-second intervals, stirring after each interval, until smooth, 1 to 2 minutes total.

7. Finish the doughnuts: Place your selected toppings in individual bowls. Dip the top of each cooled doughnut halfway into the chocolate icing, twisting the doughnut as you lift it to capture as much icing as possible. If the icing does not stick, give the doughnut a bit more wiggle and twist. Immediately dip the wet doughnuts, one at a time, in one of your topping choices to encrust the icing in that topping. Place on a wire rack bottom side down and allow the doughnuts to set for 30 minutes, or speed up the process by placing them in the fridge for 10 to 15 minutes. Store in an airtight container at room temperature for up to 3 days.

Doughnuts
1½ cups all-purpose flour
½ cup cocoa powder
2 teaspoons baking powder
1 teaspoon salt
½ teaspoon freshly grated or ground nutmeg
1 cup buttermilk, room temperature
1 cup granulated sugar
2 large eggs, room temperature
¼ cup canola oil
2 teaspoons pure vanilla extract
½ cup mini semi-sweet chocolate chips

Chocolate Icing
7 ounces (200 g/1 cup) semi-sweet chocolate callets or semi-sweet chocolate, chopped
¼ cup whipping (35%) cream

Topping (choose one or a selection)
½ cup chopped roasted peanuts
½ cup sweetened flaked coconut
½ cup colourful sprinkles

Classic Granola

Smells hold magic that can transport you through time and dig up emotions you have long forgotten. For Josie, one of those special smells is granola toasting in the oven. Her mum always seemed to make granola while the family was sleeping. As the granola was baking, the smell would fill the house and sneak into everyone's dreams. Josie still cannot smell granola cooking without being transported back to that feeling of cozy beds, oversized duvets, and waking up to the safety of her family's love. In the following pages, you will find our favourite granola variations, but show your loved ones some foodie affection and make this basic recipe your own with whatever ingredients you like. Our recipes make a lot of granola, but it keeps very well. We love the idea of giving it away as gifts, too.

1 cup grade A dark maple syrup or honey
½ cup coconut oil or unsalted butter, melted
1 tablespoon pure vanilla extract
½ teaspoon cinnamon
½ teaspoon salt
5 cups oat flakes (not quick oats)
3 cups chopped nuts, dried fruit, seeds, chocolate chips, or desired add-ins (optional)

1. Position the oven racks in the upper and lower thirds of the oven. Preheat the oven to 300°F. Line 2 baking sheets with parchment paper or silicone baking mats.

2. In a large bowl, mix together the maple syrup or honey, melted coconut oil or butter, vanilla, cinnamon, and salt until smooth.

3. Add the oats and fold into the liquid until fully coated. If you are adding nuts or seeds to your granola, add them now to give them a flavourful glaze. Do not add the dried fruit or chocolate chips until the granola is baked and cooled.

4. Evenly spread the granola onto the prepared baking sheets and bake for 25 to 30 minutes. Halfway through the baking time, rotate the baking sheets front to back and top to bottom and toss the granola using a large spatula. The granola should feel dry and be uniformly brown when done. It will crisp up as it cools. If you like your granola chunky, allow it to cool on the baking sheets and break it up once it is cool. If you prefer your granola with more individual oat flakes, give it a good stir as soon as it comes out of the oven and let cool on the baking sheets.

5. The granola is delicious plain, but feel free to add up to 3 cups (adjust amount if you added nuts and seeds in step 3; total amount used in the recipe should be 3 cups) of chopped nuts, dried fruit, seeds, chocolate chips, or your favourite add-ins once the granola is completely cooled. Store in airtight containers at room temperature for up to 2 months.

   Tip: To make the granola vegan, use coconut oil and maple syrup instead of butter and honey. The coconut oil will also keep the granola shelf stable for longer. Store in airtight containers at room temperature for up to 3 months.

Double Chocolate Granola

½ cup coconut oil, melted

6 tablespoons packed brown
    sugar

¼ cup cocoa powder

¼ cup grade A dark maple syrup

1 teaspoon pure vanilla extract

½ teaspoon salt

4 cups oat flakes (not quick oats)

⅔ pound (300 g/1½ cups)
    semi-sweet chocolate chips or
    callets

We do not want to get too healthy here. After all, you only live once. If dessert for breakfast is your thing, then this indulgent granola is for you. Use the best chocolate you can find here because it is the star! Kids and kids at heart will love the way it turns your milk chocolatey.

1. Position the oven racks in the upper and lower thirds of the oven. Preheat the oven to 300°F. Line 2 baking sheets with parchment paper or silicone baking mats.

2. In a large bowl, mix together the melted coconut oil, brown sugar, cocoa powder, maple syrup, vanilla, and salt until smooth and homogeneous. Add the oats and fold into the liquid until fully coated.

3. Evenly spread the granola onto the prepared baking sheets and bake for 20 to 25 minutes. Halfway through the baking time, rotate the baking sheets front to back and top to bottom and toss the granola using a large spatula. The granola should feel dry when done. It will crisp up as it cools. If you like your granola chunky, allow it to cool on the baking sheets and break it up once it is cool. If you prefer your granola with more individual oat flakes, give it a good stir as soon as it comes out of the oven and let cool on the baking sheets.

4. When the granola is fully cooled, stir in the chocolate chips. Store in an airtight container at room temperature for up to 3 months.

Peanut Butter Chocolate Chunk Granola

Mix up your granola with this nutty version. We love this granola served with fresh berries for a PB&J experience. It is also delicious over vanilla ice cream or yogurt as a dessert. Different in appearance to the other granolas, this version has a dry, matte finish as opposed to the glossy finish of the classic granola.

1. Position the oven racks in the upper and lower thirds of the oven. Preheat the oven to 300°F. Line 2 baking sheets with parchment paper or silicone baking mats.

2. In a small heat-resistant bowl, heat the maple syrup and peanut butter in the microwave for 1 minute, or until the peanut butter is melted and smooth. Transfer the peanut butter mixture to a large bowl. Add the vanilla and salt and stir until the mixture is smooth. Add the oats and chopped peanuts and fold into the liquid until fully coated.

3. Evenly spread the granola onto the prepared baking sheets and bake for 20 to 25 minutes. Halfway through the baking time, rotate the baking sheets front to back and top to bottom and toss the granola using a large spatula. The granola should feel dry and be uniformly light brown when done. It will crisp up as it cools. Let cool on the baking sheets.

4. When the granola is fully cooled, stir in the chocolate chunks. Store in airtight containers at room temperature for up to 2 months.

½ cup grade A dark maple syrup

½ cup smooth peanut butter (use sweetened, not natural)

1 teaspoon pure vanilla extract

½ teaspoon salt

5 cups oat flakes (not quick oats)

1 cup unsalted peanuts, chopped

2 cups semi-sweet chocolate chunks

Sleepy G Protein Bars

1 cup unsweetened shredded
coconut
½ cup raw pumpkin seeds
½ cup raw sunflower seeds
½ cup sesame seeds
½ cup unsalted butter
¼ cup packed dark brown sugar
1 cup smooth peanut butter (use
sweetened, not natural)
¾ cup natural smooth almond
butter
½ cup honey
1 tablespoon pure vanilla extract
1½ cups oat flakes
1½ cups quick oats
1 cup semi-sweet chocolate chips
½ cup raisins
½ cup dried apricots, chopped
¼ cup flax seeds

Almost a decade ago, Nickey and some friends embarked on an exhausting fifty-plus-kilometre hike in Sleeping Giant Provincial Park that was quite the adventure. When the energy levels were getting low, Nickey's friend offered homemade protein bars to the group. They were jam-packed with everything you would want in an energy bar, not to mention providing a much-needed protein boost to take them all the way home. That evening, Nickey's boyfriend got down on one knee and proposed. Thank goodness for that protein bar! It gave them enough energy to keep their eyes open long enough to celebrate the wonderful surprise ending. The Sleepy G Protein Bar was born and has been a bakery staple ever since. Thank you for sharing your recipe, Catherine, xo.

1. Preheat the oven to 350°F. Line a baking sheet with parchment paper or a silicone baking mat. Grease a 9- × 13-inch cake pan with canola oil cooking spray, then line it with parchment paper, allowing excess paper to hang over each side for easy removal.

2. Place the coconut, pumpkin seeds, sunflower seeds, and sesame seeds on the prepared baking sheet and toast for 10 to 15 minutes, or until they are golden brown and you can smell the toasted seeds. Set aside to cool.

3. Reduce the oven temperature to 300°F.

4. In the bowl of a stand mixer fitted with the paddle attachment, cream the butter and brown sugar on medium-high speed until pale and fluffy, 3 to 5 minutes. Scrape down the sides and bottom of the bowl. Add the peanut and almond butters and mix on high speed for 1 minute. Scrape down the sides and bottom of the bowl once more.

5. Add the honey and vanilla and mix on medium speed just until homogeneous. Scrape down the sides and bottom of the bowl. Add the cooled toasted coconut and seeds, oat flakes, quick oats, chocolate chips, raisins, apricots, and flax seeds and mix on low speed just until combined.

6. Scoop the mixture into the prepared cake pan and, using wet hands, press the mixture firmly and evenly into the pan. Bake for 22 to 26 minutes, or until the surface is golden and almost dry. It will still have a bit of a sheen to it. The outside edges will be a little darker than the centre. Do not be tempted to overbake or the bars will crumble. Underbaked is better than overbaked for this recipe. Allow to cool for at least 2 hours or overnight in the refrigerator. Remove from the pan and cut into 16 bars. Store in an airtight container at room temperature for up to 2 weeks.

Cookies

Chocolate Chunk Cookies

There are few things more comforting in life than a warm chocolate chunk cookie straight from the oven. Paired with a tall cold glass of milk or almond milk, these cookies have gotten us through more than one difficult day. The simplest of recipes, cookies really capture the alchemy of baking. You take everyday staples like flour and butter and with a little love (and chocolate) they're transformed into caramelized, chewy, gooey heaven in your mouth. The secret to these particular cookies is to vigorously whisk the wet ingredients together into a custard-like texture before adding the dry ingredients.

1½ cups all-purpose flour
½ teaspoon baking soda
½ cup unsalted butter, melted and warm
½ cup granulated sugar
½ cup packed dark brown sugar
½ teaspoon salt
1 large egg, room temperature
1 teaspoon pure vanilla extract
7 ounces (200 g/1 cup) good-quality semi-sweet chocolate chunks or semi-sweet chocolate, chopped

1. Preheat the oven to 350°F. Line 2 baking sheets with parchment paper or silicone baking mats.

2. Sift the flour and baking soda into a small bowl and stir together.

3. In a large bowl, whisk together the melted butter, granulated sugar, brown sugar, and salt until the mixture is smooth and there is no oily film left around the edges. Whisk in the egg and vanilla until the mixture is smooth and light in colour.

4. Stir in the flour mixture and chocolate chunks until no dry flour remains. The dough may look a little wet, but it will firm up as the butter cools.

5. Scoop thirteen 1½-tablespoon portions of cookie dough onto each prepared baking sheet, leaving ample space between them. Bake, one sheet at a time, for 12 to 15 minutes, or until the cookies are puffy and lightly browned around the edges. For chewier, gooey cookies, bake until the centre is risen but a little shiny and wet looking. Allow the cookies to cool on the baking sheets. Store in an airtight container at room temperature for up to 5 days.

Double Peanut Butterscotch Cookies

Makes thirty-six 3-inch cookies

2 cups smooth peanut butter (use sweetened, preferably Kraft; not natural)

1 cup granulated sugar

2 large eggs, room temperature

1 teaspoon pure vanilla extract

½ teaspoon salt

½ cup roasted unsalted peanuts, chopped

1 cup butterscotch chips

This flourless cookie is our go-to for gluten-free cookies because it is such an easy base recipe and does not require you to buy any special gluten-free ingredients. Very peanut butter forward with a delicate melt-in-the-mouth texture, this base works with so many different additions. Try candied nuts, any variety of chocolate, or even raisins for a trail mix version. This recipe comes together very quickly in one bowl, so it is also a great recipe to throw together at the last minute. You can use all sorts of kitchen tools to make designs on the tops of your cookies before baking. In the photo, we used a metal meat tenderizer to press the pattern into the dough before baking.

1. Preheat the oven to 350°F. Line 2 baking sheets with parchment paper or silicone baking mats.

2. In a large bowl, mix together the peanut butter, sugar, eggs, vanilla, salt, peanuts, and butterscotch chips until the sugar is fully dissolved and the batter is uniformly mixed.

3. Scoop eighteen 1½-tablespoon portions of cookie dough onto each prepared baking sheet, leaving ample space between them.

4. Using wet hands to prevent the batter from sticking, flatten the cookies with the palm of your hand. Make a pattern on top of the cookies by dipping a potato masher or other metal kitchen utensil (like a fork or tenderizer) in room-temperature water, then lightly pushing it into the dough. Rotate the utensil 90 degrees and lightly push it into the dough again to form a crossed pattern. Bake, one sheet at a time, for 12 to 15 minutes, or until the cookies are puffy and dry on top. Allow the cookies to cool on the baking sheets. Store in an airtight container at room temperature for up to 5 days.

Ginger Crinkle Cookies

Josie's first real baking job was at a little shop called The Elegant Pantry in Hamilton, Ontario. The owner, Ruth, was very generous with her time and patient enough to let an untrained baker get her feet wet in the culinary industry. Sadly, the shop is no longer in business, but this version of a traditional soft molasses cookie evolved from Ruth's recipe. Over the past decade, these unassuming little gems have become a daily staple at the bakery—a favourite of many customers and surprisingly irresistible to kids. They are perfectly balanced with their bitter molasses notes, intense spiciness, tender and sweet interior, and crunchy sugar crust. These are a holiday favourite, but we love them at any time of year.

2 cups all-purpose flour

1 teaspoon baking soda

1 teaspoon baking powder

1½ teaspoons ground ginger

1½ teaspoons cinnamon

⅛ teaspoon ground cloves

3 cups granulated sugar, divided

⅔ cup canola oil

¼ cup refiners molasses

½ teaspoon salt

1 teaspoon pure vanilla extract

1 to 2 teaspoons grated fresh ginger (optional for extra kick)

1 large egg, room temperature

1. Preheat the oven to 350°F. Line 2 baking sheets with parchment paper or silicone baking mats.

2. Sift the flour, baking soda, baking powder, ground ginger, cinnamon, and cloves into a small bowl and stir together.

3. In the bowl of a stand mixer fitted with the paddle attachment, add 1 cup of the sugar and the canola oil, molasses, salt, vanilla, and grated fresh ginger (if using) and beat on low speed just until combined.

4. Add the egg, increase the speed to medium-high, and beat for 2 to 3 minutes until the mixture is smooth and light in colour. Scrape down the sides and bottom of the bowl.

5. Stir in the flour mixture and mix on medium-low speed for 2 to 3 minutes, or until no dry flour remains. The dough may look a little wet, but it will firm up.

6. Using a spatula, scrape the dough into another medium bowl, making sure it is evenly mixed throughout. Cover with plastic wrap or a wax wrap and let sit at room temperature for at least an hour or up to 4 hours.

7. Place the remaining 2 cups sugar in a medium bowl. Scoop three 1½-tablespoon portions of cookie dough at a time and roll in the sugar to coat. Place 13 cookies on each baking sheet, leaving ample space between them. Bake, one sheet at a time, for 12 to 15 minutes, or until the cookies are cracked and puffy. Allow the cookies to cool on the baking sheets. These cookies are best enjoyed on the day of baking. Store in an airtight container at room temperature for up to 5 days.

Funfetti Sugar Cookies

Cookies

2 cups all-purpose flour

1 teaspoon baking powder

1 teaspoon baking soda

½ teaspoon salt

1 cup granulated sugar

½ cup soft vegan margarine, melted and warm (we use Crystal)

3 tablespoons water, room temperature

1 teaspoon pure vanilla extract

1 teaspoon apple cider vinegar

3 tablespoons rainbow nonpareil sprinkles, more for garnish

Icing (optional)

2 cups icing sugar

¼ cup hot water

3 to 4 drops gel food colouring

Variation

Lemon Poppy Seed: Swap out the sprinkles for the zest of 2 lemons and 2 tablespoons of poppy seeds. Add at the same time as the vanilla in step 3.

We are constantly striving to make sure we have delicious vegan offerings for our loyal customers. Until recently, we were still searching and testing for a truly great, everyday vegan cookie, but this recipe has made all our dreams come true. It is a simple but classic buttery sugar cookie base that carries all flavours very well. Feel free to swap a cup of your favourite chocolate, nuts, or dried fruit for the sprinkles if that's more your style. We find people generally love or hate sprinkles, so if you are not a fan, you have options and there's no need to skip making these delicious cookies. To dress up this cookie, we love a simple icing in jewel tones to complement the sprinkles—easy to match to the theme of any event.

1. Preheat the oven to 350°F. Line 2 baking sheets with parchment paper or silicone baking mats.

2. Make the cookies: Sift the flour, baking powder, baking soda, and salt into a small bowl and stir together.

3. In a large bowl, vigorously whisk together the sugar and vegan margarine for 1 to 2 minutes until the mixture is smooth and the sugar has dissolved. Whisk in the water, vanilla, and apple cider vinegar until the mixture is smooth. This may take a few minutes of whisking, depending on your speed.

4. Using a spatula, stir in the flour mixture and mix just until the ingredients are combined and no dry flour remains. The dough may look a little wet, but it will firm up as the margarine cools. Fold in the sprinkles until they are evenly distributed but mixing as little as possible to prevent the sprinkles from leaking colour into the batter.

5. Scoop thirteen 1½-tablespoon portions of cookie dough onto each prepared baking sheet, leaving ample space between them. Gently press down on the cookies to flatten them to about ½-inch thickness. Bake, one sheet at a time, for 13 to 16 minutes, or until the cookies have puffed up and are dry on top. Allow the cookies to cool on the baking sheets. These cookies have a raw flour taste if not baked thoroughly, so it is important to make sure they are cooked all the way through.

6. Make the icing, if using: In a medium bowl, whisk together the icing sugar and hot water until smooth. This might be a little difficult, as you want the icing to be quite thick. If needed, add 1 tablespoon of water to the icing. You are looking for a stiff mixture, not a runny glaze. Divide the icing to make different colours, if desired. Add the gel food colouring one drop at a time, stirring vigorously between each addition, until the desired colour is reached.

7. Using a spoon, spread 1 tablespoon of icing on top of each cookie. Garnish with sprinkles while the icing is still wet and allow the icing to set for 30 to 40 minutes. Store in an airtight container at room temperature for up to 5 days.

Oatmeal Raisin Cookies

Makes ten 4-inch cookies

1 cup raisins

1 cup all-purpose flour

1 teaspoon cinnamon

¾ teaspoon baking soda

½ cup unsalted butter, melted and warm

½ cup granulated sugar

½ cup packed dark brown sugar

½ teaspoon salt

1 large egg, room temperature

1 teaspoon pure vanilla extract

1 cup flaked oats (not quick oats)

There's something about a chewy yet soft and spicy oatmeal cookie bursting with plump raisins that sends you back to your childhood. This cookie brings back all those warm fuzzies for Nickey and her sister Erin, our bakery kitchen manager. It reminds them of a simpler time when they would watch *Leave It to Beaver* with their father while snacking on Dad's Oatmeal Cookies after school. Dad's cookies leaned toward crunchy, but Nickey and Erin learned quickly that chewy and from scratch are much better. An oatmeal cookie is an easy gig, but when you find the perfect recipe you know you have struck nostalgic gold! Flaked oats, as opposed to minute or quick oats, are important here—using a more delicate oat results in a very different cookie. The big oat flakes give you that gooey chew we all look for. You can use any kind of raisins, but if you can find jumbo flame raisins, which are twice the size and plumpness of regular raisins, they add a lovely texture to this cookie.

1. Preheat the oven to 350°F. Line 2 baking sheets with parchment paper or silicone baking mats.

2. In a small bowl, cover the raisins with warm water for 15 to 20 minutes to plump them up.

3. Sift the flour, cinnamon, and baking soda into a small bowl and stir together.

4. In a large bowl, whisk together the melted butter, granulated sugar, brown sugar, and salt until the mixture is smooth and there is no oily film left around the edges.

5. Whisk in the egg and vanilla, adding a little air, until the mixture is smooth and has lightened in colour.

6. Strain the raisins well so there is no excess water. Add the raisins, flour mixture, and oats to the wet ingredients and mix until no dry flour remains. The dough may look a little wet, but it will firm up as the butter cools.

7. Scoop five 3-tablespoon portions of cookie dough onto each baking sheet, leaving ample space between them. Bake, one sheet at a time, for 15 to 18 minutes, or until the cookies are lightly browned all over. For chewier cookies, bake until the centre is risen but a little shiny and wet looking. Allow the cookies to cool on the baking sheets. Store in an airtight container at room temperature for up to 5 days.

Tip: Be careful with the amount of peppermint oil or extract you use. Too much mint may come across as medicinal tasting, so you want to hit that perfect balance. Never pour the extract from the bottle; pour a small amount into a spoon and then add it to your mixture. A little goes a long way, so taste-test before each addition.

Mint Chocolate Crackle Cookies

Rich and fudgy with a refreshing minty intensity, these cookies are gorgeous and decadent. To get that picture-perfect crackle, make sure you roll the cookies completely in granulated sugar before rolling them in icing sugar, then bake them right away. If they sit covered in sugar for too long, the crackle turns into more of a glaze. We love these as minis around the winter holidays, but for everyday snacking make them big to indulge in their fudgy centres. Leave out the mint completely for a chocolate lover's delight. It is important to use bittersweet chocolate for these cookies. We use chocolate with a 71% cocoa content at the bakery. Lower cocoa percentages will lead to a flatter, more spread-out cookie with less structure.

1. Preheat the oven to 350°F. Line 2 baking sheets with parchment paper or silicone baking mats.

2. Make the cookie dough: Sift the flour, cocoa powder, and baking powder into a small bowl and stir together.

3. In the bowl of a stand mixer fitted with the paddle attachment, cream the brown sugar, butter, vanilla, salt, and peppermint oil on medium-high speed for 3 to 4 minutes until fluffy and the sugar is dissolved. Scrape down the sides and bottom of the bowl.

4. Add the eggs and continue to cream on medium-high speed for 2 to 3 minutes until the mixture is pale and smooth. Scrape down the sides and bottom of the bowl.

5. Add the milk and beat on medium-high speed until the mixture is smooth and the milk is fully incorporated. Do not worry if the mixture separates a bit at this point; it will come back together by the end.

6. With the mixer on low speed, slowly pour the melted chocolate into the batter. When you have added all the chocolate, continue to beat on medium-high speed for 2 to 3 minutes until the batter appears to have a pudding texture and the chocolate is fully incorporated. Scrape down the sides and bottom of the bowl.

7. Stir in the flour mixture and chocolate chips and mix on medium-low speed until fully incorporated. Taste for peppermint flavour and add more oil or extract if needed. Be careful, as mint can be quite overwhelming even to mint lovers.

8. Make the coating and finish the cookies: Set up 2 small bowls. Place the granulated sugar in the first bowl and the icing sugar in the second bowl. Scoop a 1½-tablespoon portion of the cookie dough into a rough ball and coat it in the granulated sugar. Then coat it in the icing sugar. Repeat with the remaining dough.

9. Evenly space 13 coated cookies on each baking sheet, leaving ample space between them, and bake immediately as you fill the first sheet. If you let the sugar-covered cookies sit too long at room temperature, the sugar will start to melt and you won't get the same beautiful crackle. Bake, one sheet at a time, for 12 to 15 minutes, or until the cookies are cracked and puffy. Allow the cookies to cool on the baking sheets. These cookies are best enjoyed on the day of baking. Store in an airtight container at room temperature for up to 5 days.

Cookies

1¼ cups all-purpose flour

½ cup cocoa powder

2 teaspoons baking powder

1½ cups packed brown sugar

½ cup unsalted butter, room temperature

2 teaspoons pure vanilla extract

½ teaspoon salt

¼ teaspoon peppermint oil (or 1 teaspoon peppermint extract), more if needed

2 large eggs, room temperature

⅓ cup whole milk, room temperature

8 ounces (225 g) bittersweet chocolate, melted

1 cup semi-sweet chocolate chips

Coating

1½ cups granulated sugar

1½ cups icing sugar

Churro Waffle Cookies

Churro Waffle Cookies

1¾ cups all-purpose flour

⅔ cup granulated sugar

¼ teaspoon baking powder

¼ teaspoon salt

1 cup unsalted butter, melted and
warm

1 teaspoon pure vanilla extract

3 large eggs, room temperature

To finish

1 cup unsalted butter, melted and
warm

3 cups granulated sugar

⅓ cup cinnamon

These cookies are an amazing combination of pound cake meets cookie meets waffle. They have a dense texture that melts in your mouth and just enough spice to balance out the vanilla interior. When we used to make these at our downtown Hamilton Farmers' Market location, people came from across the market to chase the smell. We make quite a few variations on this waffle cookie at the bakery, but this one remains our favourite. It's best enjoyed with a cup of black coffee, but you can dress up this unassuming beauty with some dulce de leche and vanilla ice cream as a fancy dessert, too. Once you have mastered the original, try some variations like lemon poppy seed, toffee chocolate, or birthday party sprinkle.

1. Make the churro waffle cookies: In the bowl of a stand mixer fitted with the paddle attachment, add the flour, sugar, baking powder, and salt. With the mixer on low speed, slowly pour in the melted butter and mix for 2 to 3 minutes, or until fully incorporated.

2. With the mixer on medium-high speed, add the vanilla and then the eggs, one at a time, mixing well between each addition. Scrape down the sides and bottom of the bowl. The batter should be smooth and similar in texture to a cake batter.

3. Increase the speed to high and beat the batter for 7 to 10 minutes, or until you see the colour lighten and the batter start to form stretchy ribbons as it beats. The texture should resemble a thick cake batter. Scrape down the sides and bottom of the bowl and cover with plastic wrap or a wax wrap. Refrigerate for at least an hour or up to 24 hours. The batter will firm up as the butter cools until similar in texture to soft cookie dough.

4. Grease the waffle iron lightly with some canola oil (or other low smoke point oil) and preheat to medium-high. Every waffle maker is different, so try making just one small cookie at a time until you get the heat level right.

5. Using two spoons or a small scoop, drop 1 to 2 tablespoons of the batter into the waffle maker, leaving lots of room between cookies. You should be able to make 3 to 4 cookies at a time. Close the waffle maker and cook for 3 to 4 minutes, adjusting the temperature as needed, until light golden brown. As long as the cookies are cooked through, lighter is better than darker. You could end up with some bitter notes or an overly dry cookie if the exterior is too dark. Transfer the cookies to a wire rack to cool. Repeat with the remaining batter.

6. Finish the cookies: Pour the melted butter into a small bowl big enough to submerge a cookie. In a medium bowl, stir together the sugar and cinnamon.

7. Working quickly, one cookie at a time, dip the baked waffle cookies in the melted butter and then toss them in the cinnamon sugar. The key is to dip the cookies in the butter quickly so that they are fully coated but do not absorb much butter. Once coated in cinnamon sugar, return the cookies to the wire rack to set for 5 to 10 minutes. Store in an airtight container at room temperature for up to 5 days. Leftover cinnamon sugar can be sifted and stored in an airtight container in the refrigerator for up to 3 weeks.

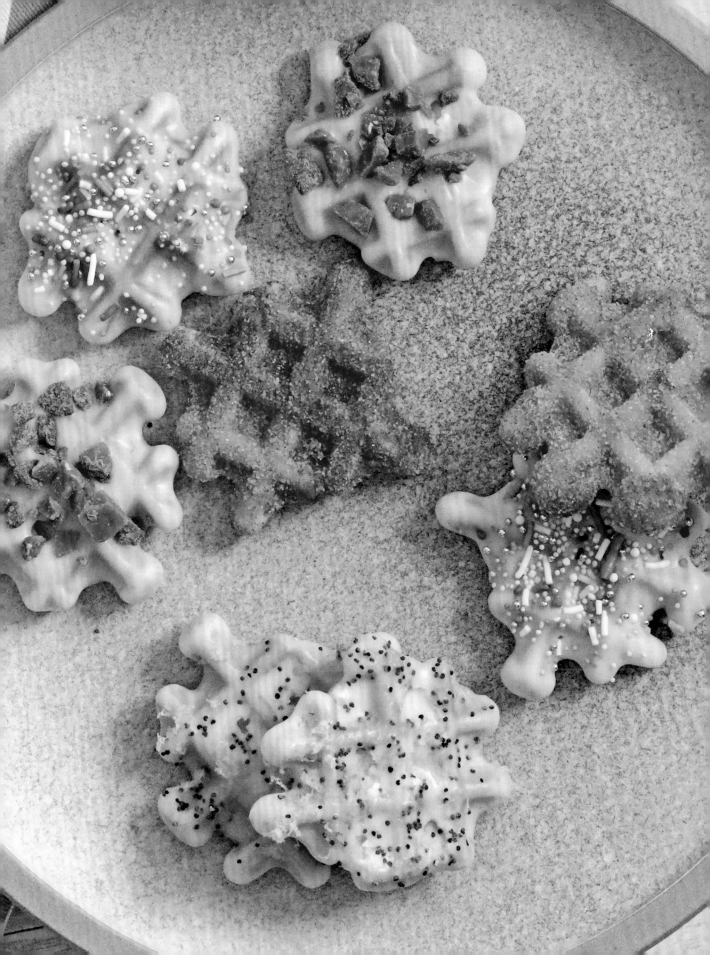

Snickerdoodle Cookies

Cookies

2¾ cups all-purpose flour

2 teaspoons baking powder

1½ cups granulated sugar

1 cup unsalted butter, room
temperature

2 teaspoons pure vanilla extract
or vanilla bean paste

½ teaspoon salt

2 large eggs, room temperature

Coating

2 cups granulated sugar

2 tablespoons cinnamon

A fluffy vanilla interior with a spicy sweet exterior, this cookie screams blankets by the fire and all the cozy comforts of Canadian winters. The cookie itself is a simple soft sugar cookie that highlights the vanilla. The crunchy sugar crust gives texture to the bite but also beautiful sparkle to the plate. If you like, you can mix up the spice in the sugar coating and replace it with your favourite; we love it with pumpkin spice. These cookies always remind us of the Lights of Dundurn Festival we held at the bakery. At the beginning of each December, we would throw a big free party for the neighbourhood to celebrate the arrival of winter. They were magical evenings with imams sharing stories and wisdom, visits from Santa Claus, crafts for kids, face painting, cotton candy, candied peanuts made fresh in front of your eyes, local musicians and dancers, the reading of holiday books, hot apple cider, carnival games, and more. Often we would get snow as the sun set, and when the big fluffy flakes hit our hundreds of twinkle lights, the bakery was breathtaking: a true winter wonderland of sweets and frost-kissed faces.

1. Preheat the oven to 350°F. Line 2 baking sheets with parchment paper or silicone baking mats.

2. Make the cookies: Sift the flour and baking powder into a small bowl and stir together.

3. In the bowl of a stand mixer fitted with the paddle attachment, cream the sugar, butter, vanilla, and salt on medium-high speed until the mixture is pale and fluffy. Scrape down the sides and bottom of the bowl.

4. Add the eggs and continue to cream on medium-high speed for 2 to 3 minutes until the mixture is smooth and has lightened in colour. Scrape down the sides and bottom of the bowl.

5. Stir in the flour mixture and mix on medium-low speed until fully incorporated.

6. Make the coating and finish the cookies: In a medium bowl, mix together the sugar and cinnamon.

7. Scoop 1½-tablespoon portions of the cookie dough, one at a time, into the cinnamon sugar mixture to coat. Evenly space 12 coated cookies on each baking sheet, leaving ample space between them, and bake immediately as you fill the first sheet. If you let the sugar-covered cookies sit too long at room temperature, the sugar will start to melt and you'll get a glaze effect instead of sparkly cinnamon sugar. Bake, one sheet at a time, for 12 to 15 minutes, or until the cookies are cracked and puffy. Allow the cookies to cool on the baking sheets. Store in an airtight container at room temperature for up to 5 days.

Campfire Cookies

Being good Canadians, we of course love camping. Food cooked over a fire always tastes better, and cuddling up around a campfire to trade stories or roast marshmallows has got to be one of the best ways to spend an evening. In our city, we are lucky to be surrounded by easily accessible green spaces and forests. When we feel ourselves overwhelmed by the pressures of running a small business, a session of forest bathing is always the answer. However, sometimes you just cannot get out of the city, so we have got you covered: all the fireside snacks you love in one portable and delicious medium! The salty chips balanced with sweet, gooey marshmallows and crunchy chocolate candies, finished with just of touch of graham cracker crumbs, make these cookies irresistible.

1. Preheat the oven to 350°F. Line 2 baking sheets with parchment paper or silicone baking mats.

2. Sift the flour and baking soda into a small bowl and stir together.

3. In a large bowl, whisk together the melted butter, granulated sugar, brown sugar, and salt until the mixture is smooth and there is no oily film left around the edges.

4. Whisk in the egg and vanilla, adding a little air, until the mixture is smooth and is light in colour.

5. Stir in the flour mixture, chocolate chunks, M&Ms, graham cracker crumbs, and potato chips and mix until no dry flour remains.

6. Scoop five 3-tablespoon portions of cookie dough per baking sheet, leaving ample space between them. Gently press down on the cookies to flatten them to about ¾-inch thickness. Add extra chips to the top of your cookies before baking, if desired.

7. Bake, one sheet at a time, for 13 to 16 minutes, or until the cookies are just starting to look dry on top. Remove from the oven and, working quickly, place 1 or 2 marshmallow pieces on each cookie. Bake the cookies for 2 more minutes until the marshmallow has softened and the cookies are light brown all over. Allow the cookies to cool on the baking sheets. If you feel like your marshmallows are not browned enough after baking, finish them with a kitchen torch. Store in an airtight container at room temperature for up to 5 days.

1½ cups all-purpose flour

½ teaspoon baking soda

½ cup unsalted butter, melted and warm

½ cup granulated sugar

½ cup packed dark brown sugar

½ teaspoon salt

1 large egg, room temperature

1 teaspoon pure vanilla extract

3½ ounces (100 g/½ cup) good-quality chocolate chunks, more for topping if desired

½ cup M&Ms or Smarties

¼ cup graham cracker crumbs

2 ounces (55 g/24 chips) plain ruffle-cut potato chips, more for topping

2 cups marshmallows, cut into 1-inch cubes

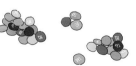

Bacon Chocolate Chunk Cookies

Makes twenty-six 3-inch cookies

1½ cups all-purpose flour

½ teaspoon baking soda

½ pound (225 g) bacon, cooked
and chopped into ½-inch pieces,
fat reserved

6 to 8 tablespoons unsalted
butter, melted and warm

½ cup granulated sugar

½ cup packed dark brown sugar

½ teaspoon salt

1 large egg, room temperature

1 teaspoon pure vanilla extract

1 cup good-quality semi-sweet
chocolate chunks

1 to 2 tablespoons flaky sea salt
(optional)

Let's be honest, everything's better with bacon—real bacon from your local butcher or, even better, bacon cured at home. None of that preservative-laden, moisture-injected grocery store bacon for these cookies, please. Swapping bacon fat for some of the butter in these cookies really gives them a smoky richness that balances so well with the semi-sweet chocolate. If you cannot get enough of that salty and sweet balance, try topping the cookies with flaky sea salt for an extra-salty boost.

1. Preheat the oven to 350°F. Line 2 baking sheets with parchment paper or silicone baking mats.

2. Sift the flour and baking soda into a small bowl and stir together.

3. In a small glass bowl or measuring cup, combine up to 2 tablespoons of the reserved bacon fat with enough melted butter for 8 tablespoons (½ cup) total. If the mixture cools, warm it in the microwave.

4. In a large bowl, whisk together the granulated sugar, brown sugar, salt, and warm butter and bacon fat mixture until smooth and there is no oily film left around the edges.

5. Whisk in the egg and vanilla, adding a little air, until the mixture is smooth and is light in colour.

6. Stir the flour mixture, chocolate chunks, and bacon chunks into the wet ingredients and mix until no dry flour remains. Be careful not to overmix.

7. Scoop thirteen 1½-tablespoon portions of cookie dough onto each prepared baking sheet, leaving ample space between them. Sprinkle the flaky sea salt (if using) over the cookies before baking. Bake, one sheet at a time, for 12 to 15 minutes, or until the cookies are lightly brown and golden brown around the edges. Allow the cookies to cool on the baking sheets. Store in an airtight container at room temperature for up to 5 days.

Gummy Bear Stuffed Cookies

Makes ten 4-inch cookies

Josie's kids, Lily and Finn, are lucky enough to have a mom who owns a bakery and to attend school right across the street from it! Lily and Finn are passionate about cookies and always coming up with new recipe ideas that they think their schoolmates, some of our best customers, will love. Lily really wanted a gummy bear cookie, so we set to work making it happen. As you can imagine, gummy bears are not the easiest ingredient to bake (they just melt). We had to do a lot of experimenting, but the result has become a bakery staple and one of our favourite cookies. This is a great recipe to make with kids, and you can swap any gummy candy for the bears, so get creative and play with your favourite candies. Buy the fancy gummies with better flavour and real fruit juices to elevate this cookie. We use Albanese Gummi Bears in twelve assorted natural flavours.

1½ cups all-purpose flour

½ teaspoon baking soda

½ cup unsalted butter, melted and warm

½ cup granulated sugar

½ cup packed dark brown sugar

½ teaspoon salt

1 large egg, room temperature

1 teaspoon pure vanilla extract

14 ounces (400 g/2 cups) mini rainbow Chipits or chocolate teenies

9 ounces (250 g) gummy bears (at least 70 bears)

1. Preheat the oven to 350°F. Line 2 baking sheets with parchment paper or silicone baking mats.

2. Sift the flour and baking soda into a small bowl and stir together.

3. In a large bowl, whisk together the melted butter, granulated sugar, brown sugar, and salt until the mixture is smooth and there is no oily film left around the edges.

4. Whisk in the egg and vanilla until the mixture is smooth and light in colour.

5. Stir in the flour mixture just until no dry flour remains. The dough may look a little wet, but it will firm up as the butter cools.

6. Using a spoon or your fingers, evenly divide the dough into 10 portions. Roll each portion of dough between your hands into a 1½-inch ball. Refrigerate the balls for 10 to 15 minutes.

7. Place the rainbow chocolate chips in a small bowl big enough to roll dough balls in. When the balls are cold and firm enough to work with (like playdough), flatten one ball at a time in your hands to make a disc. Place 4 gummy bears in the centre of the disc and fold the edges around them. Once the gummy bears are covered and no gummy bits are peeking through the dough, flatten the cookie slightly into a thick disc and (while it is still warm from your hands) roll it immediately in the rainbow chips, completely coating the cookie. If the chips are not sticking, press the cookie into the chips to embed them deeper into the dough.

8. Place 5 cookies, evenly spaced, on each baking sheet. Bake, one sheet at a time, for 15 to 18 minutes, or until the cookies have spread and puffed up. As soon as you remove the cookies from the oven, place 3 gummy bears on top of each cookie. The cookies should still be warm enough to melt the gummy bears just enough to stick to the cookie. If you do not move quickly enough and the bears are not sticking, you can return the cookies to the oven with the bears on top for 1 to 2 minutes to melt the bears a bit. Allow the cookies to cool on the baking sheets. Store in an airtight container at room temperature for up to 5 days.

Bars

Sweet Amy Bars

Amy, one of Josie's best friends, originally came up with the name of our bakery. We were having a hard time finding a name for our business that reflected our dichotomy, was a little playful, and was easy for people to remember. Amy came up with Cake & Loaf at one of our brainstorming sessions and we loved it right away. For the fifth anniversary of the bakery, we developed this bar in her honour to thank her. It is a lot like her: sweet, a little nutty, elegant, unique, and memorable. It has a nutty peanut butter base topped with rich dark chocolate fudge brownie, finished with a beautiful crunchy, sweet brown sugar meringue. It has quite the striking silhouette and is perfect for when you want to impress.

1. Preheat the oven to 350°F. Grease a 9- × 13-inch cake pan with canola oil cooking spray and line with parchment paper.

2. Make the peanut butter cookie base: In a medium bowl, mix together the peanut butter, sugar, peanuts, and eggs. Stir until the mixture is homogeneous and the eggs are fully incorporated. Press the dough evenly into the bottom of the prepared pan.

3. Make the brownie layer: In a large bowl, whisk together the sugar, melted butter, cocoa powder, and salt until the mixture is smooth and there is no oily film left around the edges.

4. Whisk in the eggs and vanilla until the mixture is smooth. Whisk in the buttermilk until the mixture is smooth.

5. Stir in the flour and mix until the batter is smooth and no dry flour remains. Scoop the brownie batter on top of the cookie dough and, using an offset palette knife, spread it evenly over the base. Bake for 50 to 60 minutes, or until a toothpick inserted into the centre of the brownie comes out clean. Cool at room temperature for 2 hours.

6. Remove the brownies from the pan and cut into 12 bars. Use a warm chef's knife and wipe the blade between each cut by dipping it into hot water and drying it on a clean kitchen towel to get nice clean cuts.

7. Make the brown sugar meringue: In a medium bowl over a double boiler, whisk together the egg whites, brown sugar, and lemon juice until the mixture reaches 140°F on a candy thermometer or is warm to the touch and the sugar is dissolved.

8. Transfer the meringue mixture to the bowl of a stand mixer fitted with the whisk attachment and whisk on high speed for 7 to 10 minutes, or until glossy stiff peaks form.

9. Working quickly, spread the meringue over each brownie. Alternatively, you can fill a piping bag fitted with a large No. 824 star tip with meringue and pipe the meringue over each bar for a more refined look. Use a handheld kitchen torch to toast the surface of the meringue. Store in an airtight container at room temperature for up to 5 days.

Peanut Butter Cookie Base

2 cups smooth peanut butter (use sweetened, not natural)
1 cup granulated sugar
1 cup chopped unsalted peanuts
2 large eggs, room temperature

Brownie Layer

2 cups granulated sugar
1 cup unsalted butter, melted and warm
1 cup cocoa powder, sifted
½ teaspoon salt
2 large eggs, room temperature
1 tablespoon pure vanilla extract
½ cup buttermilk, room temperature
1 cup all-purpose flour, sifted

Brown Sugar Meringue

4 large egg whites, room temperature
2 cups lightly packed dark brown sugar
¼ teaspoon lemon juice

Unicorn Bars

Blondie

1 pound (450 g) good-quality
    white chocolate callets or
    white chocolate, chopped
1 cup unsalted butter
4 large eggs, room temperature
⅔ cup granulated sugar
1 tablespoon pure vanilla extract
1 tablespoon vanilla bean paste
1½ teaspoons salt
2½ cups all-purpose flour, sifted
1 cup white chocolate chips
    (or 6 ounces/175 g white
    chocolate, chopped)
1 cup rainbow nonpareil sprinkles

Vanilla Bean Buttercream

½ batch Vanilla Bean Buttercream
    (page 248)

Coloured White Chocolate Ganache

1 batch Coloured White
    Chocolate Ganache (page 255),
    divided into 2 colours of your
    choice

Toppings

2 tablespoons rainbow nonpareil
    sprinkles
2 tablespoons white chocolate
    crisp pearls

Originally developed to celebrate our bakery's fifth anniversary, this bar definitely screams party! Maybe you have a surplus of rainbow sprinkles or maybe you just need a splash of colour to brighten your day. Either way, this bar will bring you pure joy! Weighing in with more than a pound of white couverture chocolate and bursting with coloured sprinkles to finish, these bars rival a once-in-a-lifetime unicorn sighting. We often pull these out for our annual LGBTQ2+ Pride celebrations each June, when we support and raise funds for local initiatives.

1. Preheat the oven to 350°F. Grease a 9- × 13-inch cake pan with canola oil cooking spray and line with parchment paper.

2. Make the blondie: In a medium heat-resistant bowl, melt the white chocolate and butter in the microwave in 30-second intervals, stirring after each interval, until melted and smooth, 1½ to 2 minutes total. (Alternatively, you can use a double boiler to melt the chocolate and butter.) Set aside.

3. In the bowl of a stand mixer fitted with the whisk attachment, whisk together the eggs and sugar on high speed for 6 to 7 minutes until the eggs have doubled in volume and are light in colour. Reduce the speed to low and, with the mixer running, slowly pour in the white chocolate butter mixture. Once the mixture is completely added, increase the speed to medium-high and beat for up to 5 minutes until the mixture is fluffy and smooth. Scrape down the sides and bottom of the bowl.

4. Whisk in the vanilla, vanilla bean paste, and salt until the mixture is smooth. Remove the bowl from the mixer, fold in the flour and chocolate chips, and mix until the batter is smooth and no dry flour remains.

5. Working quickly, fold in the sprinkles and immediately pour the batter into the prepared pan, levelling out the top with a small offset palette knife. If you do not work quickly, the sprinkles can bleed colour into the batter. Bake for 30 to 40 minutes, or until a toothpick inserted into the centre of the bar comes out clean. Cool at room temperature for 1 to 2 hours before icing.

6. Assemble the bars: Using an offset palette knife, spread the vanilla bean buttercream evenly over the cooled bar. Fit two 12-inch piping bags with a No. 3 round tip, then fill each bag with one of the two coloured ganaches. Drizzle the ganache, one colour at a time, over the bar. Create a crosshatch design by drizzling the colours in opposing diagonal zigzag patterns and finish with the sprinkles and crisp pearls. Refrigerate for 20 to 30 minutes to allow the icing to set.

7. Cut the bars using a warm chef's knife by dipping it into hot water and drying it on a clean kitchen towel. Wipe the knife between each cut to get nice clean cuts. Store in an airtight container at room temperature for up to 7 days.

Penthouse Bars

One of our favourite things is taking commercially produced grocery store favourites and making them our own with much better ingredients but flavours that still capture that nostalgia. You might be familiar with the grocery store staple Lofthouse Cookies. They are impossibly soft vanilla cookies topped with garishly bright icing and sprinkles. We still are not sure what chemical magic keeps them soft forever and frankly, we do not want to know. Instead, we have created something better! We love them in classic Cake & Loaf blue but feel free to leave out the colouring for a more sophisticated look or go bright with your own favourite colours. We love that this bar's soft vanilla base gives you the buttery softness you remember but with so much more flavour. Topped with classic icing sugar frosting, it will have you harkening back to your childhood.

1. Preheat the oven to 350°F. Grease a 9- × 13-inch cake pan with canola oil cooking spray and line with parchment paper.

2. Make the cake base: Sift the flour, baking powder, and baking soda into a medium bowl and stir together.

3. In the bowl of a stand mixer fitted with the paddle attachment, beat the cream cheese on medium-high speed until smooth. Scrape down the sides and bottom of the bowl. Add the butter and beat until smooth. Scrape down the sides and bottom of the bowl.

4. Add the sugar and beat on medium-high speed for 3 to 5 minutes until the batter is pale and fluffy. Scrape down the sides and bottom of the bowl.

5. Add the egg and vanilla and continue to beat on medium-high speed for 3 to 5 more minutes until the batter is smooth and fluffy.

6. Reduce the speed to low and add the flour mixture. Increase the speed to medium and mix until the batter is smooth, 1 to 2 minutes. The batter will be quite thick.

7. Scoop the batter into the prepared pan, level it with an offset palette knife, and bake for 20 to 25 minutes, or until a toothpick inserted into the centre of the bar comes out clean. Cool at room temperature for 1 to 2 hours before icing.

8. Finish the bars: Spread the vanilla bean American buttercream evenly over the baked bar. Finish with the sprinkles and gold flake. Refrigerate for 20 to 30 minutes to allow the icing to set.

9. Cut the bars using a warm chef's knife by dipping it into hot water and drying it on a clean kitchen towel. Wipe the knife between each cut to get nice clean cuts. Store in an airtight container at room temperature for up to 7 days.

Cake Base

2½ cups all-purpose flour

1 teaspoon baking powder

½ teaspoon baking soda

8 ounces (225 g/1 cup) cream cheese, room temperature

1 cup unsalted butter, room temperature

1½ cups granulated sugar

1 large egg, room temperature

2 teaspoons pure vanilla extract

Vanilla Bean American Buttercream

1 batch Vanilla Bean American Buttercream (page 245), adding 3 or 4 drops sky blue gel food colouring (optional)

Toppings

2 tablespoons rainbow sprinkles (or sprinkles of your choice)

1 teaspoon edible gold flake

Turtle Brownies

Caramel

1 batch Caramel (page 275), divided (used in the brownie batter and for topping)

Brownies

3 cups granulated sugar

1½ cups cocoa powder, sifted

1½ cups unsalted butter, melted and warm

1 teaspoon salt

3 large eggs, room temperature

1 tablespoon pure vanilla extract

¾ cup buttermilk, room temperature

1½ cups all-purpose flour, sifted

⅔ cup Caramel (recipe above)

1½ cups toasted pecans, chopped

Caramel Chocolate Topping

14 ounces (400 g/2½ cups) caramel chocolate callets or milk chocolate callets or chopped chocolate

½ cup unsalted butter, room temperature

Toppings

1 cup toasted pecans, chopped

½ cup semi-sweet chocolate chips

½ cup Caramel (recipe above)

Discovering caramel chocolate was a game-changer for us. It is chocolate that has been caramelized and is available in a white chocolate or milk chocolate base. It can be difficult to source, but check your local bulk store for coverture caramel chocolate. You can use either variation in this recipe, but we prefer the milk chocolate-based one. This recipe is a little involved, but making your own caramel is worth it. Once you master it, you will wonder why you ever bought something that is so easy to make. There are many versions of turtle brownies out there and frankly, we have never met one we did not like, but we really think that baking the caramel-coated pecans right into the brownie makes all the difference. We hope you agree. Make the caramel a day or more in advance so that it can cool before making the brownies. Toast the pecans needed for the brownie layer and topping in one go at 350°F for ten to fifteen minutes, or until you can smell that amazing nutty fragrance wafting from the oven.

1. Preheat the oven to 350°F. Grease a 9- × 13-inch cake pan with canola oil cooking spray and line with parchment paper.

2. Make the brownies: In a large bowl, whisk together the sugar, cocoa powder, butter, and salt until the mixture is smooth and there is no oily film left around the edges.

3. Whisk in the eggs and vanilla until the mixture is smooth, then whisk in the buttermilk until the mixture is smooth.

4. Stir in the flour and mix until the batter is smooth and no dry flour remains. Scoop the batter into the prepared pan, levelling the top with an offset palette knife.

5. In a small bowl, stir together ⅔ cup of the caramel and 1½ cups of the pecans. Evenly drop teaspoonfuls of caramel pecan mixture over the batter to cover as much surface area as possible. Do not mix it in. Bake for 45 to 60 minutes, or until a toothpick inserted into the centre of the brownie comes out clean. Allow the brownie to cool at room temperature for 1 to 2 hours.

6. Make the caramel chocolate topping: In a medium heat-resistant bowl, melt the caramel chocolate and butter in the microwave in 30-second intervals, stirring vigorously after each interval, until melted and smooth, 1½ to 2 minutes total. Pour over the cooled brownie and spread evenly overtop. Sprinkle 1 cup of the pecans over the wet caramel chocolate.

7. In a small heat-resistant bowl, melt the semi-sweet chocolate chips in the microwave in 30-second intervals, stirring vigorously after each interval, until melted and smooth. Drizzle over the pecans. Allow to set in the fridge for 15 to 20 minutes.

8. Cut the brownies using a warm chef's knife by dipping it into hot water and drying it on a clean kitchen towel. Wipe the knife between each cut to get nice clean cuts. Serve with the remaining ½ cup caramel drizzled on top. Store in an airtight container at room temperature for up to 7 days.

Classic Fudge Brownies

Makes twelve 3-inch square
or 24 triangle bars

This base recipe has lived many different lives, from the Sweet Amy Bars (page 89) to the Turtle Brownies (page 94), because it is amazing and easy to make. It is a decadent addition to more complex desserts like cheesecakes, and when topped with a simple ganache like it is here, it is our go-to solution for chocolate cravings. The absolute key is the cocoa. We use Royal Dutch 22% or 24% cocoa powder, which is one of the darkest and most highly alkalized cocoa powders available. We love the depth of flavour and deep colour it gives our products. Dress up these basic bars by topping them with your favourite candy, dried fruit or nuts, sprinkles, or peanut butter. This base recipe also can be baked as two-bite brownies in mini-muffin cups—just reduce the baking time to ten to twelve minutes.

1. Preheat the oven to 350°F. Grease a 9- × 13-inch cake pan with canola oil cooking spray and line with parchment paper.

2. Make the brownie layer: In a large bowl, whisk together the sugar, cocoa powder, butter, and salt until the mixture is smooth and there is no oily film left around the edges.

3. Whisk in the eggs and vanilla, adding a little air, until the mixture is smooth. Whisk in the buttermilk until the mixture is smooth.

4. Stir in the flour until the batter is smooth and no dry flour remains.

5. Pour the batter into the prepared pan and bake for 25 to 30 minutes, or until a toothpick inserted into the centre of the brownie comes out clean. If you like your brownies extra fudgy, feel free to underbake them a little. Cool at room temperature for 1 to 2 hours.

6. Make the ganache: In a medium heat-resistant bowl, heat the cream and dark chocolate in the microwave in 30-second intervals, stirring vigorously after each interval, until smooth and the chocolate is melted, 1 to 1½ minutes total. Stir the ganache until silky smooth, then pour it over the cooled brownie, evenly spreading it out with an offset palette knife. If you want to add any toppings, sprinkle them over the ganache while it is still wet. Allow to set in the fridge for 15 to 20 minutes.

7. Cut the brownies using a warm chef's knife by dipping it into hot water and drying it on a clean kitchen towel. Wipe the knife between each cut to get nice clean cuts. Store in an airtight container at room temperature for up to 7 days.

Brownie Layer
2 cups granulated sugar
1 cup cocoa powder, sifted
1 cup unsalted butter, melted
   and warm
½ teaspoon salt
2 large eggs
1 tablespoon pure vanilla extract
½ cup buttermilk
1 cup all-purpose flour, sifted

Ganache
⅔ cup whipping (35%) cream
8 ounces (225 g/1⅓ cups) dark
   chocolate callets or chopped
   dark chocolate

Toppings (optional)
1 cup chopped pecans, roasted
   peanuts, chopped M&Ms, Skor
   bits, toasted coconut, or
   sprinkles

Date Bars

Date Filling

2 pounds (900 g) Medjool dates,
  pitted

3 cups water, room temperature

1 teaspoon pure vanilla extract

½ teaspoon salt

Oat Crumble

2 cups all-purpose flour

1 teaspoon cinnamon

1 teaspoon salt

1 teaspoon baking powder

½ teaspoon baking soda

4 cups oat flakes (not quick oats)

1 cup packed dark brown sugar

1½ cups vegan margarine
  (we use Crystal), melted

¼ cup cold water

This was one of the first recipes we developed while we were still working out of Josie's home kitchen. Date bars are omnipresent in Canadian coffee shops, and they really do not vary too much. Oats-heavy crumble sandwiched around stewed, sweetened dates is the norm. We wanted to develop a date bar that was not too sweet and that pleased all our customers, vegan and non-vegan alike. We really love crumble, so we bumped up the traditional ratio of crumble to filling, reduced the sugar, and increased the flavour by keeping the date filling as simple as possible. It has become a customer favourite and has not left the daily menu in more than a decade.

1. Preheat the oven to 350°F. Grease a 9- × 13-inch cake pan with canola oil cooking spray and line with parchment paper.

2. Make the date filling: In a large pot, combine the dates, water, vanilla, and salt and bring to a boil over high heat. Reduce the heat to maintain a low boil and cook, stirring constantly, until all the water is absorbed. Set aside.

3. Make the oat crumble: Sift the flour, cinnamon, salt, baking powder, and baking soda into a large bowl. Add the oat flakes and brown sugar and stir to combine.

4. Add the melted vegan margarine and water to the dry ingredients in the large bowl, and stir until well combined and no dry flour remains.

5. Press half of the oat crumble into the bottom of the prepared pan. (If you like a thicker date bar base, use two-thirds of the crumble mixture.) Using an offset palette knife, spread the date filling evenly over the base. Sprinkle the remaining oat crumble evenly overtop. Bake for 45 to 55 minutes, or until the oat crumble is toasty brown. Cool at room temperature for at least 1 to 2 hours.

6. Cut the bars using a warm chef's knife by dipping it into hot water and drying it on a clean kitchen towel. Wipe the knife between each cut to get nice clean cuts. Store in an airtight container at room temperature for up to 7 days.

OMG Bars

The Milk Calendar, a yearly publication by the Dairy Farmers of Canada, has been gracing kitchen walls for more than forty-six years. Once upon a time, when most of us received daily newspapers on our doorsteps, it was an exciting annual event to receive the new calendar filled with meal ideas for the year. Nickey's mom used to make quite a few recipes from this calendar for her family, including some lifelong faves like Creamy Chicken Soup, Cheddar Quick Bread, and most noteworthy, Domino Cupcakes on special occasions. We have transformed Nickey's favourite Domino Cupcakes into a drool-worthy bar. Rich and moist chocolate cake swirled with vanilla chocolate chip cheesecake and topped with our dreamy cream cheese icing, a dark chocolate ganache drizzle, and dark chocolate crisp pearls take this from milk calendar to extraordinary. You can't help exclaiming "OMG" as you bite into this luscious treat.

1. Preheat the oven to 350°F. Grease a 9- × 13-inch cake pan with canola oil cooking spray and line with parchment paper.

2. Make the chocolate cake: Sift the flour, sugar, cocoa powder, baking soda, and salt into a medium bowl and stir together.

3. In a large bowl, mix together the water, canola oil, and vinegar. Add the dry ingredients to the wet ingredients and stir vigorously until smooth. Pour the batter into the prepared pan.

4. Make the cheesecake filling: In the bowl of a stand mixer fitted with the paddle attachment, beat the cream cheese on high speed for 3 to 4 minutes until smooth. Scrape down the sides and bottom of the bowl. Add the sugar and egg yolks and mix on medium-high speed for 2 to 3 minutes until smooth. Scrape down the sides and bottom of the bowl. Add the chocolate chips and mix just until the chips are evenly distributed.

5. Drop large spoonfuls of the cheesecake filling into the cake batter. Using a butter knife, swirl the two batters together a little. You want to leave distinct areas of cheesecake and chocolate cake batter. Bake for 45 to 60 minutes, or until a toothpick inserted into the centre of the bar comes out clean. Allow to cool at room temperature for 1 to 2 hours before icing.

6. Finish the bars: Spread the dreamy cream cheese icing evenly over the baked bar. Drizzle the ganache over the icing diagonally in a zigzag pattern and sprinkle the crisp pearls overtop. Allow to set in the fridge for 20 to 30 minutes.

7. Cut the bars using a warm chef's knife by dipping it into hot water and drying it on a clean kitchen towel. Wipe the knife between each cut to get nice clean cuts. Store in an airtight container in the refrigerator for up to 7 days.

Chocolate Cake

2¼ cups all-purpose flour
1 cup granulated sugar
⅓ cup cocoa powder
1½ teaspoons baking soda
½ teaspoon salt
1½ cups water, room temperature
¾ cup canola oil
1½ tablespoons white vinegar

Cheesecake Filling

8 ounces (225 g/1 cup) cream
  cheese, room temperature
½ cup granulated sugar
2 large egg yolks, room
  temperature
2 cups semi-sweet chocolate chips

Dreamy Cream Cheese Icing

½ batch Dreamy Cream Cheese
  Icing (page 244)

Dark Chocolate Ganache

1 batch Dark Chocolate Ganache
  (page 254)

Toppings

2 tablespoons dark chocolate
  crisp pearls (we use Callebaut)

Vanilla Bean Nanaimo Bars

Makes twelve 3-inch square or 24 triangle bars

In what seems like another life, Josie worked in mortgages and had the opportunity to travel across the country leading training workshops. One of those journeys took her to Nanaimo, British Columbia, home of the famous Nanaimo bar. This was already one of Josie's favourite desserts, a staple of holiday bar platters and cafés across the country. After conducting extensive research in Nanaimo and visiting every bakery she could find, one thing was clear: no one was using real custard in their bars. Custard powder is what lends most Nanaimo bars their distinctive colour and vanilla custard flavour, but here we have actually used from-scratch pastry cream and vanilla bean. The resulting bar has everything you love about the classic bar but with a custard layer that tastes just like the best room-temperature vanilla ice cream and melts in the mouth. If you are a Nanaimo bar fan, you are going to love these bars, and if the fake vanilla flavour and fluorescent colour has always been a bit of a turn-off for you, it's time to give this Canadian gem another try.

1. Grease a 9- × 13-inch cake pan with canola oil cooking spray and line with parchment paper.

2. Make the base: In a medium pot, melt the butter over medium-low heat. Reduce the heat to low, add the cocoa powder and sugar, and whisk until combined.

3. Break the eggs into a small bowl. While whisking the butter and cocoa mixture over low heat, quickly whisk in the eggs. Increase the heat to medium-low and cook, stirring constantly, for 2 to 3 minutes until the mixture has thickened. Remove from the heat and stir in the graham cracker crumbs, coconut, and walnuts until they are coated in the cocoa mixture. Press the mixture evenly into the bottom of the prepared pan. Set aside.

4. Make the custard layer: In the bowl of a stand mixer fitted with the paddle attachment, cream the butter on high speed until smooth and fluffy. Scrape down the sides and bottom of the bowl. Add the icing sugar, pastry cream, vanilla seeds, vanilla extract, and salt and mix on low speed, increasing to high speed as the icing sugar is mixed in. Beat on high speed for 10 to 12 minutes, or until the mixture is smooth and the icing sugar has lost its gritty texture. It should be similar in texture to room-temperature vanilla ice cream.

5. Spread the custard layer evenly over the prepared base. Using an offset palette knife, smooth it out as flat and level as you can. Cover with plastic wrap or a silicone cover and refrigerate for at least 1 to 2 hours or until firm to the touch. You can refrigerate overnight, if desired.

Base

1 cup unsalted butter

¾ cup cocoa powder, sifted

½ cup granulated sugar

2 large eggs, room temperature

2½ cups graham cracker crumbs

2 cups unsweetened shredded coconut

1 cup walnuts, ground but with some larger chunks

Custard Layer

1 cup unsalted butter, room temperature

4 cups icing sugar

½ cup Pastry Cream (page 274)

1 vanilla bean, seeds scraped (or 1 tablespoon vanilla bean paste)

1 teaspoon pure vanilla extract

¼ teaspoon salt

Dark Chocolate Topping

8 ounces (225 g/1⅓ cups) semi-sweet chocolate callets or chopped semi-sweet chocolate

¼ cup unsalted butter

Continued on next page

*Vanilla Bean Nanaimo Bars
continued*

6. Make the dark chocolate topping: In a medium heat-resistant bowl, melt the chocolate and butter in the microwave in 30-second intervals, stirring vigorously after each interval, until the mixture is smooth and the chocolate is melted, 1 to 1½ minutes total. Pour the topping over the bar and, using a small offset palette knife, spread it evenly over the surface. Clean the knife before the final pass and pull it across the bar horizontally zigzagging from side to side to create ridges in the finish. Refrigerate for 10 to 15 minutes to allow the chocolate to set. Once set, cut the bars right away to avoid cracking the chocolate topping.

7. Cut the bars using a warm chef's knife by dipping it into hot water and drying it on a clean kitchen towel. Wipe the knife between each cut to get nice clean cuts. Store in an airtight container in the refrigerator for up to 9 days.

Snazzy Bars ◗

We invented these bars for one of our favourite employees who happens to be vegan and was always missing out on the fancy treats we make at the bakery. We aim to have a generous vegan selection at all times, but they are often the classic, bestselling options as opposed to some of our more exciting bars. However, this bar is a showstopper—a crunchy almond cookie base topped with fudgy brownie, covered in chewy caramel, and finished with dark chocolate ganache and a candied almond topping.

1. Preheat the oven to 350°F. Grease a 9- × 13-inch cake pan with canola oil cooking spray and line with parchment paper.

2. Make the almond cookie base: Sift the flour, baking powder, baking soda, and salt into a medium bowl and stir together.

3. In a large bowl, whisk together the brown sugar, melted coconut oil, almond milk, and vanilla. Add the flour mixture and the chopped almonds and stir until combined.

4. Press the dough into the bottom of the prepared pan and bake for 15 to 20 minutes, or until the cookie appears dry and golden brown.

5. Meanwhile, make the brownie layer: Sift the flour and baking powder into a medium bowl and stir together.

6. In a large bowl, whisk together the granulated sugar, cocoa powder, melted coconut oil, vanilla, and salt for 2 to 3 minutes until smooth. Slowly whisk in the almond milk, then whisk vigorously until silky smooth.

7. Fold the flour mixture into the wet ingredients and mix well until combined. Spread the brownie batter over the baked almond cookie base and bake for 30 to 35 minutes, or until a toothpick inserted into the centre of the bar comes out clean.

8. Make the almond caramel: In a medium pot, combine the maple syrup, coconut oil, almond butter, cornstarch, vanilla, and salt and stir until the cornstarch is fully incorporated. Cook, stirring often, over medium-low heat, until the caramel is fragrant and bubbly and has reached 230°F on a candy thermometer. Carefully pour the caramel over the baked brownie layer and allow to cool completely.

9. Make the candied almond crunch: Increase the oven temperature to 400°F. Line a baking sheet with parchment paper or a silicone baking mat.

10. In a small bowl, stir together the sliced almonds and maple syrup. Spread evenly over the baking sheet, bake for 5 minutes, and then toss the almonds. Continue baking for 5 to 7 minutes, or until the almonds are dark golden brown. Allow the almonds to cool; the candy coating should harden as they cool. When cool, break the candied almonds into small chunks.

Almond Cookie Base
2 cups all-purpose flour
1 teaspoon baking powder
1 teaspoon baking soda
½ teaspoon salt
1 cup packed dark brown sugar
½ cup coconut oil, melted and warm
¼ cup sweetened almond milk, room temperature
1 tablespoon pure vanilla extract
1 cup sliced almonds, roughly chopped

Brownie Layer
1¾ cups all-purpose flour
1 teaspoon baking powder
2 cups granulated sugar
1 cup cocoa powder
1 cup coconut oil, melted and warm
1 tablespoon pure vanilla extract
1 teaspoon salt
1 cup sweetened almond milk, room temperature

Almond Caramel
1 cup pure maple syrup
¾ cup + 2 tablespoons coconut oil
⅔ cup almond butter
2 tablespoons cornstarch
1 tablespoon pure vanilla extract
½ teaspoon salt

Candied Almond Crunch
1 cup sliced almonds
¼ cup pure maple syrup

Vegan Dark Chocolate Ganache
8 ounces (225 g/1⅓ cups) semi-sweet chocolate callets or chopped semi-sweet chocolate
½ cup sweetened almond milk

Continued on next page

11. When the bar has cooled to room temperature, make the vegan dark chocolate ganache: In a medium heat-resistant bowl, heat the chocolate and almond milk in the microwave in 30-second intervals, stirring after each interval, until the chocolate is melted and the ganache is smooth, 1 to 1½ minutes total. Pour the ganache evenly over the almond caramel layer, smoothing it with an offset palette knife, and then sprinkle the candied almonds overtop. Refrigerate for 1 to 2 hours or overnight to allow everything to firm up before cutting.

12. Cut the bars using a warm chef's knife by dipping it into hot water and drying it on a clean kitchen towel. Wipe the knife between each cut to get nice clean cuts. Store in an airtight container at room temperature for up to 4 days or in the refrigerator for up to 7 days.

White Chocolate Raspberry Almond Bars

Makes twelve 3-inch square or 24 triangle bars

White chocolate tends to be a love it or hate it kind of ingredient but not in this perfectly balanced bar. The tart raspberry and nutty almond richness really work with the sweet creaminess of the white chocolate, and the texture of the white chocolate lends this bar an intense fudginess sometimes missing in blondies. If you can find German bitter almond oil—Bitter-Mandel Aroma is our favourite to use in this recipe instead of almond extract—reduce the amount from 1 teaspoon to ¼ teaspoon, as the oil is very powerful stuff. This bar is also beautiful, with delicate layers and two-tone subtlety. We love this bar in winter because it has a cozy glow about it, but it certainly would be easy to bake all year long.

1. Preheat the oven to 350°F. Grease a 9- × 13-inch cake pan with canola oil cooking spray and line with parchment paper.

2. Make the blondie: In a medium heat-resistant bowl, melt 1 pound (450 g) of the white chocolate and the butter in the microwave in 30-second intervals, stirring after each interval, 1½ to 2 minutes total. (Alternatively, you can use a double boiler to melt the chocolate and butter together.)

3. In the bowl of a stand mixer fitted with the whisk attachment, whisk the eggs and sugar on high speed for 5 to 7 minutes until doubled in volume and light in colour.

4. With the mixer on low speed, slowly pour in the melted white chocolate mixture, then continue to whisk on medium-high speed for 3 to 5 minutes until the mixture is fluffy and smooth.

5. Whisk in the vanilla, almond extract, and salt until smooth. Remove the bowl from the mixer, then fold in the flour and mix until smooth.

6. Pour half of the batter into the prepared pan and bake for 15 to 20 minutes, or until the top is light brown and appears set. Immediately, using an offset palette knife, gently spread the raspberry jam evenly over the hot base.

7. Stir the remaining 1 pound (450 g) white chocolate into the remaining batter in the bowl, then gently spoon it over the jam. Sprinkle the almonds overtop and press them lightly into the batter. Continue baking for 25 to 30 minutes, or until the bar is lightly golden, the almonds are toasted, and the jam bubbles up the sides of the pan. Allow to cool for 1 to 2 hours at room temperature before cutting. If desired, in a small heat-resistant bowl, melt 2 ounces (55 g) white chocolate in the microwave in 30-second intervals, stirring after each interval, 1 minute total. Drizzle it overtop diagonally in a zigzag pattern to finish the bar.

8. Cut the bars using a warm chef's knife by dipping it into hot water and drying it on a clean kitchen towel. Wipe the knife between each cut to get nice clean cuts. Store in an airtight container at room temperature for up to 7 days.

Blondie

2 pounds (900 g) good-quality white chocolate callets or chopped white chocolate, divided
1 cup unsalted butter, room temperature
4 large eggs, room temperature
1 cup granulated sugar
1 tablespoon pure vanilla extract
1 teaspoon almond extract
½ teaspoon salt
2 cups all-purpose flour, sifted
1 cup seedless raspberry jam, room temperature
⅔ cup sliced almonds

Topping (optional)

2 ounces (55 g/¼ cup) good-quality white chocolate callets or chopped white chocolate, for drizzling

Makes twelve 3-inch square or
24 triangle bars

Lemon Bars

Grandma's lemon bars were one of the best parts of Christmas for Josie as a kid. Buttery shortbread crust topped with tart lemon curd and delicately sprinkled with icing sugar. They really were a kind of culinary awakening and one of the first recipes Josie remembers trying on her own. Our lemon bars are based on that original recipe, but we have increased the lemon to shortbread ratio and delivered more lemon flavour. These bars have just the right balance of tart and sweet and are made for lemon lovers! They freeze really well and even taste great right out of the freezer, so do not be afraid to make a batch just for you and freeze the leftovers.

Shortbread Crust

1½ cups unsalted butter,
   room temperature

3 cups all-purpose flour

¾ cup icing sugar

¾ teaspoon salt

Zest of 1 lemon

Lemon Filling

2¼ cups granulated sugar

¼ cup all-purpose flour

6 large eggs, room temperature

Zest of 1 lemon

¾ cup freshly squeezed
   lemon juice

Glaze

½ cup icing sugar

2 tablespoons freshly squeezed
   lemon juice

1. Preheat the oven to 350°F. Grease a 9- × 13-inch cake pan with canola oil cooking spray and line with parchment paper.

2. Make the shortbread crust: In the bowl of a stand mixer fitted with the paddle attachment, cream the butter on medium-high speed until smooth. Scrape down the sides and bottom of the bowl. Add the flour, icing sugar, salt, and lemon zest and continue to beat just until the mixture comes together as a cookie dough.

3. Press two-thirds of the dough into the bottom of the prepared pan. Reserve the remaining dough for topping the bar in step 5. Bake for 20 to 25 minutes, or until the crust is light brown and appears dry.

4. Meanwhile, make the lemon filling: In a medium bowl, whisk together the sugar and flour. Add the eggs and whisk until smooth. Add the lemon zest and juice and whisk until combined.

5. Once the base is baked, immediately pour the lemon filling over the crust through a fine-mesh sieve. Evenly distribute small chunks of the remaining shortbread dough over the filling. Bake for 25 to 30 minutes, or until the shortbread is light golden brown and the filling does not jiggle when you gently shake the pan. Allow to cool in the refrigerator for 1 to 2 hours before finishing.

6. Make the glaze: In a small bowl, whisk together the icing sugar and lemon juice until smooth. Drizzle the glaze diagonally in a zigzag pattern over the bar.

7. Cut the bars using a warm chef's knife by dipping it into hot water and drying it on a clean kitchen towel. Wipe the knife between each cut to get nice clean cuts. Store in an airtight container in the refrigerator for up to 9 days.

Peanut Butter Brownies

Peanut butter and chocolate is one combination we cannot get enough of in baked goods. No matter how you combine these two sweethearts, they always shine. In this recipe, a simple peanut butter cookie dough is nestled into our classic fudge brownie batter. After it bakes and cools, we top it with an easy chocolate American buttercream. If you want to make it extra special, just like we do at the bakery, finish it with candied peanuts and a peanut butter drizzle. However, if that all sounds too intimidating, just serve the freshly baked brownies naked with a tall glass of milk.

1. Preheat the oven to 350°F. Grease a 9- × 13-inch cake pan with canola oil cooking spray and line with parchment paper.

2. Make the brownie batter: In a large bowl, whisk together the sugar, melted butter, cocoa powder, and salt until the mixture is smooth and there is no oily film left around the edges.

3. Whisk in the eggs and vanilla until the mixture is smooth. Whisk in the buttermilk until the mixture is smooth. Stir in the flour and mix until the batter is smooth and no dry flour remains. Set aside.

4. Make the peanut butter batter: In a medium bowl, vigorously mix together the peanut butter, sugar, and eggs until fully incorporated.

5. Scoop the brownie batter into the prepared pan and, using an offset palette knife, spread it evenly. Drop spoonfuls of the peanut butter batter into the brownie batter and knock the pan lightly on the counter so that the peanut butter batter sinks into the brownie batter and the top is level. Do not mix the peanut butter batter into the brownie batter. Bake for 45 to 60 minutes, or until a toothpick inserted into the centre of the brownie comes out clean. Cool at room temperature for 1 to 2 hours.

6. Finish the bars: Spread the chocolate American buttercream evenly over the cooled bar. If desired, in a small heat-resistant bowl, microwave the peanut butter for 30 seconds until melted, then drizzle over the buttercream diagonally in a zigzag pattern. If desired, sprinkle the candied peanuts over the entire bar. Refrigerate for 25 to 30 minutes to let the icing set.

7. Cut the bars using a warm chef's knife by dipping it into hot water and drying it on a clean kitchen towel. Wipe the knife between each cut to get nice clean cuts. Store in an airtight container at room temperature for up to 5 days.

Brownie Batter

2 cups granulated sugar

1 cup unsalted butter, melted and warm

1 cup cocoa powder, sifted

½ teaspoon salt

2 large eggs, room temperature

1 tablespoon pure vanilla extract

½ cup buttermilk, room temperature

1 cup all-purpose flour, sifted

Peanut Butter Batter

2 cups smooth peanut butter (sweetened, not natural)

1 cup granulated sugar

2 large eggs, room temperature

Chocolate American Buttercream

1 batch Chocolate American Buttercream (page 245)

Topping (optional)

½ cup smooth peanut butter (sweetened, not natural), for drizzling

Candied Peanuts (optional)

½ batch Candied Peanuts (page 266)

Chip Crisp Bars

14 ounces (400 g) Vanilla Bean
  Marshmallows (⅓ batch;
  page 272)
1 large bag (20 ounces/585 g)
  plain ruffle-cut potato chips

Homemade marshmallows are much easier than you think! Once you have mastered them, you will look all over for potential marshmallow flavours. Some of our favourites over the years have been passion fruit and mint chocolate chip. In this recipe, we start simple with a basic vanilla marshmallow but if you wish to skip this step, you can definitely replace them with store-bought marshmallows. Once you have tasted homemade marshmallows, though, there is no going back! The salty, crunchy chips combined with the creamy, sweet marshmallow is salty-sweet perfection, but we also add different ingredients depending on the season. Easter brings Mini Egg Chip Crisp Bars, which is a personal favourite of ours, but feel free to fold in a cup or two of any of your favourite candies or chocolates. Make the marshmallows up to six weeks in advance and store in an airtight container at room temperature. Then you will be all set when a craving for these bars strikes.

1. Grease a 9- × 13-inch cake pan generously with canola oil cooking spray and line with parchment paper.

2. In a medium heat-resistant bowl, melt the marshmallow in the microwave in 30-second intervals, stirring after each interval, until melted, 1 to 1½ minutes total.

3. In a large bowl, using a spatula, gently fold the melted marshmallow and potato chips together until the marshmallow is evenly distributed. It will not fully cover the chips, but as long as every chip has some marshmallow on it, you will be fine.

4. Lightly oil or wet your hands. Turn the mixture into the prepared pan and gently press it evenly into the pan, trying to keep the chips as intact as possible. Refrigerate for 25 to 30 minutes, or until firm. Do not keep the bar in the fridge any longer or it will get soggy.

5. Cut the bars using a serrated knife. Wipe the knife between each cut to get nice clean cuts. These bars are best enjoyed on the day of making. Store in an airtight container at room temperature for up to 3 days.

Farmer's Fruit Crumble Bars

We love farmers' markets and are lucky enough to live right in the middle of prime agricultural land teeming with stone fruits, berries, apples, and pears. We get so excited at the bakery, bouncing from season to season using all our favourite local fruits, and this recipe is perfect for just about any of them! Our favourite fruit to use in these bars is peaches, but really any fruit will work as long as it is fresh. These bars are a great balance for some of the heavier chocolate-based bars in this chapter, if you want to have a variety for a spread. They are also perfect for tea or brunch: pretty without effort and show off the jewel tones of the baked fruit.

1. Preheat the oven to 350°F. Grease a 9- × 13-inch cake pan with canola oil cooking spray and line with parchment paper.

2. Make the crumble topping: In a medium bowl, whisk together the brown sugar, melted butter, and salt. Stir in the flour until just combined. Set aside.

3. Make the base: In a small bowl, sift together the flour, baking powder, and salt.

4. In the bowl of a stand mixer fitted with the paddle attachment, beat the icing sugar, butter, and vanilla on medium-high speed until smooth, 2 to 3 minutes. Scrape down the sides and bottom of the bowl. Continue to beat on medium-high speed while adding the eggs, one at a time.

5. Reduce the speed to low and add the flour mixture. Increase the speed to medium-high and mix until the batter is smooth, about 1 to 2 minutes. The batter will be quite thick. Press the batter into the prepared pan.

6. Make the fruit filling: In a medium bowl, mix together the blueberries, brown sugar, and flour. Evenly distribute the fruit filling over the base batter, then sprinkle the crumble topping evenly over the fruit filling. Bake for 50 to 70 minutes, or until a toothpick inserted into the centre of the bar comes out clean. Serve warm or at room temperature.

7. Cut the bars using a serrated knife. Wipe the knife between each cut to get nice clean cuts. Store in an airtight container at room temperature for up to 7 days.

> **Tip:** Swap out the blueberries for the same amount of your favourite fruit. For any type of berries, the fruit can be left whole. If you are using larger fruit like apples or peaches, peel and chop it into 1-inch cubes.

Crumble Topping

1 cup packed brown sugar
¾ cup unsalted butter, melted and warm
½ teaspoon salt
2 cups all-purpose flour

Base

2 cups all-purpose flour
1 teaspoon baking powder
½ teaspoon salt
2 cups icing sugar
1 cup unsalted butter, room temperature
1 teaspoon pure vanilla extract
4 large eggs, room temperature

Fruit Filling

1 pound + 5 ounces (600 g) fresh or frozen wild blueberries
2 tablespoons lightly packed dark brown sugar
¼ cup all-purpose flour

Rocky Road Bars

These bars taste just like rocky road ice cream! We all did a little happy dance in the kitchen the first time our baker, Huong, created this recipe. It really has everything: nutty crunch, rich chocolate, creamy marshmallows, and Rice Krispies bites. The caramel chocolate adds something special, but milk chocolate will do if caramel chocolate is difficult to find. In the first decade of the bakery, we must have tried thousands of recipe variations—always tweaking, always adding to the repertoire. We are so grateful to all the bakers along the way who left their stamp on Cake & Loaf. It is the unique combination of beautiful humans working together creatively over the years that make all these recipes possible.

Vanilla Bean Marshmallows

21 ounces (600 g) Vanilla Bean
   Marshmallows (½ batch;
   page 272), cut into ½-inch cubes

Base

1 cup hazelnut chocolate spread
½ cup unsalted butter, room
   temperature
½ cup whipping (35%) cream,
   room temperature
1½ pounds (675 g/3½ cups)
   semi-sweet chocolate callets or
   chopped chocolate
5 cups Rice Krispies cereal
1½ cups whole almonds, toasted
   and roughly chopped
2½ cups Vanilla Bean
   Marshmallows (recipe above)

Caramel Chocolate Ganache

11 ounces (300 g/1½ cups) milk
   chocolate or caramel chocolate
   callets or chopped chocolate
⅔ cup whipping (35%) cream

Topping

½ cup whole almonds, toasted and
   roughly chopped
1½ cups Vanilla Bean
   Marshmallows (recipe above)
½ cup semi-sweet chocolate chips

1. Grease a 9- × 13-inch cake pan with canola oil cooking spray and line with parchment paper.

2. Make the base: In a medium pot, melt the hazelnut chocolate spread, butter, and cream over low heat, stirring constantly with a heat-resistant spatula, until smooth. Add the semi-sweet chocolate, stirring constantly with a heat-resistant spatula, until the chocolate is melted, making sure to scrape down the sides and bottom of the pot as you stir.

3. In a large bowl, combine the Rice Krispies cereal and almonds. Pour the melted chocolate mixture overtop and, using a silicone spatula, gently fold it into the cereal mixture.

4. Add the 2½ cups of the vanilla bean marshmallows and fold them into the mixture, stirring as little as possible. The heat from the chocolate may melt the marshmallows a bit, but you want to try to keep them as whole as possible. Immediately press the mixture into the prepared pan.

5. Make the caramel chocolate ganache: In a medium heat-resistant bowl, heat the chocolate and cream in the microwave in 30-second intervals, stirring after each interval, until the chocolate is melted and the mixture is smooth, 1 to 2 minutes total.

6. Pour the ganache over the prepared base and spread it out evenly. Sprinkle the chopped almonds, 1½ cups of the vanilla bean marshmallows, and the chocolate chips overtop. Tap the pan gently on your work surface to sink the toppings slightly into the ganache. Refrigerate for 1 hour to allow all the chocolate to set.

7. Cut the bars using a warm chef's knife by dipping it into hot water and drying it on a clean kitchen towel. Wipe the knife between each cut to get nice clean cuts. Store in an airtight container in at room temperature for up to 7 days or in the refrigerator for up to 9 days.

Raspberry Lemonade Bars

Makes twelve 3-inch square or
24 triangle bars

Raspberry Purée

1 pound + 2 ounces (500 g)
    thawed frozen raspberries

Shortbread Crust

1 cup soft vegan margarine
    (we use Crystal)
¾ cup granulated sugar
2½ cups all-purpose flour
¼ cup unsweetened soy milk or
    full-fat canned coconut milk
½ teaspoon salt

Lemonade Filling

1 cup raspberry purée
    (recipe above)
¾ cup cornstarch
½ cup freshly squeezed
    lemon juice (about 3 lemons)
2⅓ cups + 2 tablespoons full-fat
    canned coconut milk
2 cups granulated sugar
Zest of 3 lemons
½ teaspoon salt

We needed a fruity, bright vegan addition that nobody would guess was vegan. We think we have found a winner! This bar tastes just like biting into a summer day, and we love its bright colour. We also make a version with fresh peach purée in place of the raspberry purée that is equally delicious. The best part of working at the farmers market was swapping food with our neighbours. We would share our baked goods with our fellow chefs at other stalls, always eager for feedback and a foodie's two cents on new ideas. In response, we would be gifted a feast of tacos, smoked meats, poke bowls, ramen, and muffuletta sandwiches. These bars and their seasonal variations became a market favourite.

1. Make the raspberry purée: Place the thawed raspberries, with juices, in a large fine-mesh strainer set over a large bowl. Using a silicone spatula or wooden spoon, press the fruit and juices through the strainer. Some small seeds may get through, but that is okay. Set aside.

2. Preheat the oven to 350°F. Grease a 9- × 13-inch cake pan with canola oil cooking spray and line with parchment paper.

3. Make the shortbread crust: In the bowl of a stand mixer fitted with the paddle attachment, cream the vegan margarine and sugar on high speed until light and fluffy, 2 to 3 minutes. Scrape down the sides and bottom of the bowl. Add the flour, milk, and salt and continue beating on medium-high speed until fully incorporated, 1 to 2 minutes.

4. Press the dough evenly into the bottom of the prepared pan and bake for 20 to 25 minutes, or until the crust is light brown, appears dry, and begins to pull away from the sides of the pan.

5. Meanwhile, prepare the lemonade filling: In a small bowl, whisk together the raspberry purée, cornstarch, and lemon juice until the cornstarch is dissolved.

6. In a medium pot, combine the coconut milk, sugar, lemon zest, and salt over medium heat. Slowly heat the mixture, whisking frequently, until the sugar dissolves and any coconut cream melts. When it comes to a boil, stir in the cornstarch mixture and continue stirring while it boils until the mixture thickens and becomes glossy, about 2 minutes.

7. Pour the lemonade filling over the baked crust. Bake for 15 to 20 minutes, or until the filling becomes bubbly around the edges. Allow the bar to cool in the refrigerator for 2 to 3 hours before cutting.

8. Cut the bars using a warm chef's knife by dipping it into hot water and drying it on a clean kitchen towel. Wipe the knife between each cut to get nice clean cuts. Store in an airtight container in the refrigerator for up to 7 days.

Sandwich Cookies

Classic Oreo Sandwich Cookies

Makes 10 sandwich cookies

Our version of the classic Oreo was one of our very first offerings in the shop, and we still get regular requests for it. This is one incredibly rich chocolate cookie snuggled up with a perfectly uncomplicated vanilla bean American buttercream. Really, this is the perfect cookie base for all occasions. Throw some fancy sprinkles on the icing to dress up the cookies for a party. Miniaturize them, add a liqueur ganache centre, and elevate the cookies to cocktail party status. Katie, Josie's sister who worked as our administrator between her social work degrees, claims these as her go-to Cake & Loaf treat. It is the nostalgic quality of the icing for Katie, the way it reminds her of licking birthday cake icing off her fingers as a kid. It has been a privilege to include so many foodie friends and family members in our staff, and you know that with a sister, you will always get honest feedback.

1. Preheat the oven to 350°F. Line 4 baking sheets with parchment paper or silicone baking mats.

2. Make the cookies: Sift the flour, cocoa powder, and baking powder into a medium bowl and stir together.

3. In the bowl of a stand mixer fitted with the paddle attachment, cream the butter, brown sugar, vanilla, and salt on medium-high speed until light and fluffy, about 2 to 3 minutes. Scrape down the sides and bottom of the bowl. Add the eggs, and continue to cream on medium-high speed for 2 to 3 minutes until light and fluffy. Scrape down the sides and bottom of the bowl.

4. Add the milk and beat on medium speed until the mixture is smooth and the milk is fully incorporated, about 2 to 3 minutes. Do not worry if the mixture separates a bit at this point; it will come back together by the end. Scrape down the sides and bottom of the bowl.

5. With the mixer on low speed, slowly pour the melted chocolate into the batter. When you have added all the chocolate, continue to beat on medium-high speed for 2 to 3 minutes until the batter appears to have a pudding texture and the chocolate is fully incorporated. Scrape down the sides and bottom of the bowl. Mix in the flour mixture on low speed until fully incorporated.

6. Scoop five 3-tablespoon portions of the cookie dough onto each prepared baking sheet, leaving ample space between them. Bake, one sheet at a time, for 15 to 18 minutes, or until the cookies are cracked and puffy. Allow the cookies to cool on the baking sheets. They may fall a little while cooling, which is fine.

7. Assemble the sandwich cookies: Fill a piping bag fitted with a No. 824 star tip with the vanilla bean American buttercream. Place half of the cookies, upside down, on a baking sheet. Pipe a thick layer of buttercream onto each cookie, leaving a ¼-inch border of exposed cookie around the outer edge.

8. Place the remaining cookies on top of the iced cookies to form sandwiches. Using even pressure, gently push down on the tops to form a bond with the icing. Store in an airtight container in the refrigerator for up to 4 days.

Chocolate Cookies

1¼ cups all-purpose flour
½ cup cocoa powder
2 teaspoons baking powder
½ cup unsalted butter,
   room temperature
1½ cups packed brown sugar
2 teaspoons pure vanilla extract
½ teaspoon salt
2 large eggs, room temperature
⅓ cup milk, room temperature
8 ounces (225 g) bittersweet
   chocolate, melted

Vanilla Bean American Buttercream

1 batch Vanilla Bean American
   Buttercream (page 245)

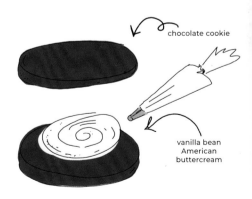

chocolate cookie

vanilla bean American buttercream

Lil Deb Sandwich Cookies

Oat Cookies

2 cups all-purpose flour

1 teaspoon baking soda

1 teaspoon cinnamon

1 cup unsalted butter, melted
   and warm

1 cup granulated sugar

1 cup packed dark brown sugar

1 teaspoon salt

1 teaspoon pure vanilla extract

2 large eggs, room temperature

3 cups quick oats

Vanilla Bean American Buttercream

1 batch Vanilla Bean American
   Buttercream (page 245)

Like the Oatmeal Raisin Cookies (page 72), you know Nickey has something to do with these Lil Debs—she loves her oatmeal cookies! We relish in the challenge of taking store-bought generic products and making them that much better with a fresh, from-scratch approach. This one brings you all the nostalgic flavour of the Little Debbie Oatmeal Creme Pies found in grocery stores. We really wanted to do this cookie justice and had at least three different versions floating around the bakery, ranging in size, chewiness, and degree of crunchiness. We settled on the thickest, softest, and chewiest version for the final cookie sandwich. When we are developing a new product, it may take us several trial runs to find that perfect recipe, but the challenge to create the perfect combination will always ignite a fire in us.

1. Preheat the oven to 350°F. Line 4 baking sheets with parchment paper or silicone baking mats.

2. Make the cookies: Sift the flour, baking soda, and cinnamon into a medium bowl and stir together.

3. In the bowl of a stand mixer fitted with the paddle attachment, beat the melted butter, granulated sugar, brown sugar, salt, and vanilla on medium-high speed until the mixture is smooth and light in colour, about 2 to 3 minutes. Scrape down the sides and bottom of the bowl.

4. Add the eggs and continue to cream on medium-high speed for 2 to 3 minutes until the mixture is light and smooth. Scrape down the sides and bottom of the bowl. Mix in the flour mixture and quick oats on medium-low speed until fully incorporated.

5. Scoop five 3-tablespoon portions of the cookie dough onto each prepared baking sheet, leaving ample space between them. Gently press down on the dough portions to flatten them to about ¾-inch thickness. Bake, one sheet at a time, for 15 to 18 minutes, or until lightly browned all over. Allow the cookies to cool on the baking sheets.

6. Assemble the sandwich cookies: Fill a piping bag fitted with a No. 824 star tip with the vanilla bean American buttercream. Place half of the cookies, upside down, on a baking sheet. Pipe a thick layer of buttercream onto each cookie, leaving a ¼-inch border of exposed cookie around the outer edge.

7. Place the remaining cookies on top of the iced cookies to form sandwiches. Using even pressure, gently push down on the tops to form a bond with the icing. Store in an airtight container in the refrigerator for up to 4 days.

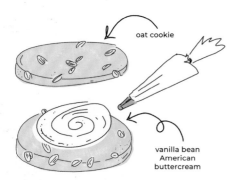

oat cookie

vanilla bean American buttercream

Red Velvet Sandwich Cookies

Sometimes you just want a pretty cookie. We do not often add food colouring to baked goods because it goes against our values to add unnecessary ingredients. However, we do make a few exceptions since life should be as beautiful as it is delicious. These cookies please even red velvet-hating Josie, so you know they are worth trying! Originally, red velvet cake contained no red dye but derived its colour from the chemical interaction of a pH-sensitive antioxidant in cocoa powder and the acid in buttermilk or vinegar. Over the years, and due to some clever marketing by a food colouring company during the Great Depression, it became the norm to expect bright, ruby red velvet products. You can leave out the food colouring and the cookies will still have that signature light milk chocolate taste that balances so perfectly with cream cheese icing.

1. Preheat the oven to 350°F. Line 4 baking sheets with parchment paper or silicone baking mats.

2. Make the cookies: Sift the flour, cocoa powder, and baking soda into a medium bowl and stir together.

3. In a large bowl, whisk together the melted butter, brown sugar, granulated sugar, and salt until the mixture is smooth and there is no oily film left around the edges.

4. Whisk in the eggs, vanilla, and food colouring (if using) until the mixture is light and smooth. Using a silicone spatula, stir in the flour mixture just until it comes together as a dough and no dry flour remains.

5. Scoop five 3-tablespoon portions of the cookie dough onto each baking sheet, leaving ample space between them. Gently press down on the dough portions to flatten them to about ¾-inch thickness. Bake, one sheet at a time, for 15 to 18 minutes, or until the cookies are slightly puffed up and appear dry. Allow the cookies to cool on the baking sheets.

6. Assemble the sandwich cookies: Fill a piping bag fitted with a No. 824 star tip with the dreamy cream cheese icing. Place half of the cookies, upside down, on a baking sheet. Pipe a thick layer of icing onto each cookie, leaving a ¼-inch border of exposed cookie around the outer edge.

7. Place the remaining cookies on top of the iced cookies to form sandwiches. Using even pressure, gently push down the tops to form a bond with the icing. Store in an airtight container in the refrigerator for up to 4 days.

Red Velvet Cookies

3¼ cups all-purpose flour

½ cup cocoa powder

2 teaspoons baking soda

1 cup unsalted butter, melted and warm

1½ cups packed dark brown sugar

½ cup granulated sugar

½ teaspoon salt

3 large eggs

4 teaspoons pure vanilla extract

1 tablespoon red gel food colouring (optional)

Dreamy Cream Cheese Icing

½ batch Dreamy Cream Cheese Icing (page 244)

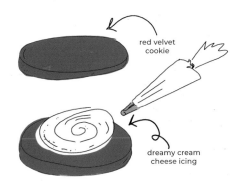

red velvet cookie

dreamy cream cheese icing

Nanaimo Sandwich Cookies

Nanaimo Cookies

1¼ cups all-purpose flour

¾ cup cocoa powder

1 teaspoon baking soda

1 cup unsalted butter, melted
and warm

1 cup granulated sugar

1 cup packed dark brown sugar

½ teaspoon salt

2 large eggs

1½ teaspoons pure vanilla extract

1 cup graham cracker crumbs

1 cup semi-sweet chocolate chips

1 cup walnuts, finely chopped

¾ cup unsweetened shredded
coconut

Bird's Custard American
Buttercream

1 batch Bird's Custard American
Buttercream (page 246)

Dark Chocolate Ganache

1 batch Dark Chocolate Ganache
(page 254)

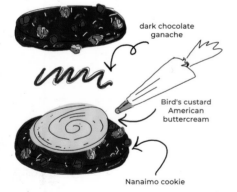

dark chocolate
ganache

Bird's custard
American
buttercream

Nanaimo cookie

Nanaimo is a picturesque city on Vancouver Island, British Columbia, and one hell of a flavour combination. We could eat that coconut, walnut, chocolate, graham cracker, and custard combination all day long. Whenever possible, we invent new ways to get it in our bellies! We do not use Bird's custard powder in our actual Nanaimo bars, but we did find that it was the perfect ingredient here, with the bonus of adding that bright yellow colour to the American buttercream. We originally created these sandwich cookies with a chocolate centre but decided that it dominated the sandwich too much, and we wanted more of the custard icing; just a drizzle of chocolate is enough. These cookies are also quite delicious on their own if you do not want to build the full sandwich.

1. Preheat the oven to 350°F. Line 4 baking sheets with parchment paper or silicone baking mats.

2. Make the cookies: Sift the flour, cocoa powder, and baking soda into a medium bowl and stir together.

3. In a large bowl, whisk together the melted butter, granulated sugar, brown sugar, and salt until the mixture is smooth and there is no oily film left around the edges. Whisk in the eggs and vanilla until the mixture is light and smooth.

4. Using a silicone spatula, stir in the flour mixture, graham cracker crumbs, chocolate chips, walnuts, and coconut and mix until no dry flour remains.

5. Scoop five 3-tablespoon portions of the cookie dough onto each baking sheet, leaving ample space between them. Gently press down on the tops of the dough portions to flatten them to about ¾-inch thickness. Bake, one sheet at a time, for 15 to 18 minutes, or until the cookies are puffy and their tops appear dry. Allow the cookies to cool on the baking sheets.

6. Assemble the sandwich cookies: Fill a piping bag fitted with a No. 824 star tip with the Bird's custard American buttercream. Place half of the cookies, upside down, on a baking sheet. Pipe a thick layer of buttercream onto each cookie, leaving a ¼-inch border of exposed cookie around the outer edge. Using a small piping bag fitted with No. 2 round tip or a parchment paper cone, drizzle the chocolate ganache over the icing in a zigzag pattern.

7. Place the remaining cookies on top of the iced cookies to form sandwiches. Using even pressure, gently push down on the tops to form a bond with the icing. Store in an airtight container in the refrigerator for up to 4 days.

Cookie Assembly Instructions for Filled Sandwich Cookies

These instructions serve as a visual guide (using the Big Skor Sandwich Cookies, page 135) for all the filled sandwich cookies that follow.

1. Place half of the cookies, bottom side up, on a clean baking sheet. Set aside the other cookies. These will be the tops. In the bowl of a stand mixer fitted with the paddle attachment, beat the buttercream until light and fluffy, 7 to 10 minutes. Using a small offset palette knife, smooth 1 tablespoon of the buttercream on the surface of a cookie, leaving a ½-inch border of exposed cookie around the outer edge. This is to prevent the bottom cookie from getting soggy after you add the filling. Repeat to ice the remaining cookies on the baking sheet.

2. Fill a 16-inch piping bag fitted with a No. 824 star tip with the buttercream. Pipe a dam around the outer edge of a bottom cookie to create a well for the filling, leaving a ¼-inch border of exposed cookie around the outer edge. Repeat to pipe dams on the remaining cookies on the baking sheet.

3. If the recipe includes a coating (such as nuts, coconut, or crushed chocolate bars), fill a medium bowl with the coating used in the recipe. Scoop up a palmful of coating ingredients using your dominant hand. Hold the cookie in your opposite hand and, working over the medium bowl to catch any bits that fall, gently push and coat the sides of the icing with the coating while rotating the cookie. Create an even crust around the buttercream border.

4. Fill the well with 2 tablespoons of the filling, being careful not to go above the top of the buttercream border. If you are using chocolate ganache for the filling, reheat it if refrigerated. Place the ganache in a small heat-resistant bowl and heat in the microwave in 15-second intervals, stirring after each interval, until the ganache has a pourable consistency, but not warm enough to melt the buttercream. Add any additional fillings or drizzles as indicated in the recipe.

5. Place the remaining cookies on top of the filled cookies to form sandwiches. Using even pressure, gently push down on the tops to form a bond with the filling.

Big Skor Sandwich Cookies

This might be one of the best recipes we have ever invented. The Skor bits we use at the bakery are not available to home cooks, so you will need to smash the Skor bars yourself. We love this version with its caramel on caramel on caramel layering—it is how we originally envisioned this cookie. If you would like to try the version sold in the bakery, use vanilla bean buttercream instead of caramel buttercream to provide a creamy, less sweet backdrop to the chocolate toffee cookie and the rich, salty caramel centre. This recipe was created by our cake team on the second floor of the bakery, where you can literally taste the sugar in the air. They focus mainly on custom cakes and decorated cookies but are also responsible for our cheesecakes, macarons, trifle cake cups, and sometimes our sandwich cookies. The Big Skor Sandwich Cookies are used to illustrate the step-by-step instructions for filled sandwich cookies on page 132.

1. Preheat the oven to 350°F. Line 4 baking sheets with parchment paper or silicone baking mats.

2. Make the cookies: Sift the flour and baking soda into a medium bowl.

3. In a large bowl, whisk together the melted butter, granulated sugar, brown sugar, and salt until the mixture is smooth and there is no oily film left around the edges. Whisk in the eggs and vanilla until the mixture is smooth and light in colour.

4. Using a spatula, stir in the flour mixture and 2 cups of the crushed Skor chocolate bars and mix until no dry flour remains. The dough may look a little wet, but it will firm up as the butter cools.

5. Scoop five 3-tablespoon portions of the cookie dough onto each baking sheet, leaving ample space between them. Bake, one sheet at a time, for 15 to 18 minutes, or until lightly browned all over. Allow the cookies to cool on the baking sheets.

6. Assemble the sandwich cookies: Place half of the cookies, upside down, on a baking sheet. Spread about 1 tablespoon of the caramel buttercream on each cookie, leaving a ½-inch border of exposed cookie around the outer edge (see instructions on page 132, step 1).

7. Fill a piping bag fitted with a No. 824 star tip with the remaining caramel buttercream. Pipe a thick circle of buttercream around the border of each iced cookie to create a well for the caramel, leaving a ¼-inch border of exposed cookie around the outer edge (see instructions on page 132, step 2).

8. Place 3 cups of the crushed Skor chocolate bars in a medium bowl. Press the crushed chocolate bars into the outside of the iced borders to create a crust (see instructions on page 132, step 3).

9. Fill each well with 2 tablespoons of the caramel. Place the remaining cookies on vtop of the filled cookies to form sandwiches. Using even pressure, gently push down on the tops to form a bond with the filling (see instructions on page 132, steps 4 and 5). Store in an airtight container in the refrigerator for up to 4 days.

Skor Cookies

3 cups all-purpose flour

1 teaspoon baking soda

1 cup unsalted butter, melted and warm

1 cup granulated sugar

1 cup packed dark brown sugar

½ teaspoon salt

2 large eggs

1½ teaspoons pure vanilla extract

2 cups crushed Skor chocolate bars

Caramel

2 batches Caramel (page 275), reserve ¾ cup for the Caramel Buttercream (recipe below)

Caramel Buttercream

½ batch Caramel Buttercream (page 252)

Coating

3 cups crushed Skor chocolate bars

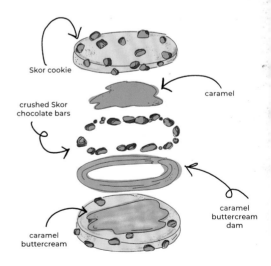

Skor cookie

caramel

crushed Skor chocolate bars

caramel buttercream dam

caramel buttercream

S'mores Sandwich Cookies

S'mores is a popular and much requested flavour combination in the summer. We had a killer s'mores whoopie pie on the menu, but it was messy to eat and we felt that our sandwich cookie lineup was in desperate need of this roasty, toasty chocolate graham mallow masterpiece. In fact, Nickey strongly felt that this gap needed to be filled immediately! She will request a s'mores version of anything—cheesecakes, a marshmallow flavour, on and inside cakes, all over Pop Tarts. When you are the boss, you get your cravings met. It is a fantastic bonus to owning a bakery. This recipe does have several components and may seem a little high maintenance, but you will not regret it as soon as you take that first bite.

1. Preheat the oven to 350°F. Line 4 baking sheets with parchment paper or silicone baking mats.

2. Make the cookies: Sift the all-purpose and whole wheat flours, baking soda, and baking powder into a medium bowl and stir together.

3. In a large bowl, whisk together the melted butter, granulated sugar, brown sugar, and salt until the mixture is smooth and there is no oily film left around the edges. Whisk in the eggs and vanilla until the mixture is smooth and light in colour.

4. Using a spatula, stir in the flour mixture and graham cracker crumbs and mix until no dry flour remains.

5. Scoop five 3-tablespoon portions of the cookie dough onto each baking sheet, leaving ample space between them. Gently press down on the dough portions to flatten them to about ¾-inch thickness. Bake, one sheet at a time, for 15 to 18 minutes, or until lightly browned all over. Allow the cookies to cool on the baking sheets.

6. Assemble the sandwich cookies: Prepare the marshmallow fluff and reheat the milk chocolate ganache if it has been refrigerated. Place half of the cookies, upside down, on a baking sheet. Spread about 1 tablespoon of the marshmallow fluff on each cookie, leaving a ½-inch border of exposed cookie around the outer edge (see instructions on page 132, step 1).

7. Fill a piping bag fitted with a No. 824 star tip with the remaining marshmallow fluff. Pipe a thick circle of marshmallow fluff around the border of each iced cookie to create a well for the ganache, leaving a ¼-inch border of exposed cookie around the outer edge (see instructions on page 132, step 2).

8. Fill each well with 2 tablespoons of the milk chocolate ganache, being careful not to go above the top of the marshmallow border. Place the remaining cookies on top of the filled cookies to form sandwiches. Using even pressure, gently push down on the tops to form a bond with the fillling (see instructions on page 132, steps 4 and 5, skip step 3).

Graham Cookies

1½ cups all-purpose flour
1 cup whole wheat flour
1 teaspoon baking soda
½ teaspoon baking powder
1 cup unsalted butter, melted and warm
1 cup granulated sugar
1 cup packed dark brown sugar
1 teaspoon salt
2 large eggs, room temperature
1½ teaspoons pure vanilla extract
1 cup graham cracker crumbs

Marshmallow Fluff

1 batch Marshmallow Fluff (page 273), made fresh to fill cookies

Milk Chocolate Ganache

3 batches Milk Chocolate Ganache (page 255)

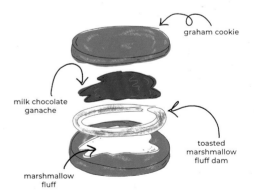

graham cookie

milk chocolate ganache

toasted marshmallow fluff dam

marshmallow fluff

Continued on next page

9. Toast the marshmallow fluff: Turn a baking sheet upside down (ensure the surface is clean) to use as your work surface. Place a sandwich cookie on the baking sheet and, using a small kitchen torch and turning the baking sheet, toast the sides of the marshmallow until evenly golden all around. (Alternatively, you could place the sandwich cookie on a cake turntable, turning it slowly while you toast the marshmallow.) Repeat to finish the sandwich cookies. Store in an airtight container in the refrigerator for up to 4 days.

Cookies and Cream Sandwich Cookies

We love this vegan cookie—it is so delicious and versatile! Our Hamilton Farmers' Market bakers were always coming up with delicious variations for this cookie based on what was available seasonally at the market. We have created this cookie sandwich with a dark chocolate centre, but in the past we have also filled it with vegan caramel, nut butters, jams, and vegan hazelnut chocolate spread. Feel free to dress up the vegan buttercream by adding nut butters or encrust them in chopped nuts or sprinkles. Just like the Classic Oreo Sandwich Cookies (page 125), this recipe lends itself well to miniaturization if you want to elevate it to cocktail party status.

1. Preheat the oven to 350°F. Line 3 baking sheets with parchment paper or silicone baking mats.

2. Make the cookies: In a small bowl, whisk together the water and flaxseed until it starts to thicken, then set aside for 3 to 5 minutes to continue thickening.

3. Sift the flour, cocoa powder, and baking soda into a medium bowl and stir together.

4. In the bowl of a stand mixer fitted with the paddle attachment, beat the sugar, canola oil, soy milk, salt, and vanilla on medium-high speed for 2 to 3 minutes, or until well combined. Scrape down the sides and bottom of the bowl.

5. Add the flaxseed mixture and continue to beat on medium-high speed for 2 to 3 minutes until the mixture is light and smooth. Scrape down the sides and bottom of the bowl. Stir in the flour mixture and chocolate chips on medium-low speed until fully incorporated.

6. Scoop five 3-tablespoon portions of the cookie dough onto each baking sheet, leaving ample space between them. You will need at least 19 cookies total. Gently press on the tops of the dough portions to flatten them to about ¾-inch thickness. Bake, one sheet at a time, for 15 to 18 minutes, or until the tops of the cookies look dry and cracked. Allow the cookies to cool on the baking sheets.

7. Make the vegan cookies and cream buttercream: Place 1 cooled chocolate cookie in a small food processor and blend into crumbs. In the bowl of a stand mixer fitted with the paddle attachment, beat the vegan vanilla bean buttercream on medium-high speed until light and fluffy. Add the cookie crumbs and mix on medium speed just until evenly distributed throughout the icing, 1 to 2 minutes. (Use the buttercream immediately or it will crust quickly.)

8. Assemble the sandwich cookies Place half of the cookies, upside down, on a baking sheet. Spread 1 tablespoon of the buttercream on each cookie, leaving a ½-inch border of exposed cookie around the outer edge (see instructions on page 132, step 1).

Chocolate Cookies

3 tablespoons warm water
1 tablespoon ground flaxseed
2 cups all-purpose flour
¾ cup cocoa powder
1 teaspoon baking soda
2 cups granulated sugar
¾ cup canola oil
¼ cup + 2 tablespoons
  unsweetened soy milk
½ teaspoon salt
2 teaspoons pure vanilla extract
1 cup semi-sweet vegan chocolate
  chips

Vegan Cookies and Cream Buttercream

1 cookie reserved from the
  chocolate cookies (recipe above)
1 batch Vegan Vanilla Bean
  Buttercream (page 247)

Vegan Dark Chocolate Ganache

1 batch Vegan Dark Chocolate
  Ganache (page 257)

chocolate cookie

vegan dark chocolate ganache

vegan cookies and cream buttercream

vegan cookies and cream buttercream dam

Continued on next page

9. Fill a piping bag fitted with a No. 824 star tip with the remaining vegan cookies and cream buttercream. Pipe a thick circle of buttercream onto each iced cookie to create a well for the ganache, leaving a ¼-inch border of exposed cookie around the outer edge. Fill each well with 2 tablespoons of the vegan dark chocolate ganache (see instructions on page 132, steps 2 and 4, skip step 3).

10. Place the remaining cookies on top of the filled cookies to form sandwiches. Using even pressure, gently push down on the tops to form a bond with the filling (see instructions on page 132, step 5). Store in an airtight container in the refrigerator for up to 4 days.

PB Jammer Sandwich Cookies

We took the nostalgic goodness of the Lil Deb and added that childhood favourite combination, peanut butter and jam. The peanut butter oatmeal cookies are truly delicious alone and are also a great base for a trail mix cookie. We love to bake them as minis, add a cup of trail mix, and take them on hikes. However, when combined with creamy peanut butter icing and tart raspberry jam, they are exceptional. This is one of our most requested items at the bakery. Since we bake seasonally and make so many different products, we only have it on the menu once or twice a year. We have been pulled aside multiple times while serving at farmers' markets and asked when people could get their next PB Jammer fix.

1. Preheat the oven to 350°F. Line 4 baking sheets with parchment paper or silicone baking mats.

2. Make the cookies: Sift the flour, baking soda, and baking powder into a small bowl and stir together.

3. In the bowl of a stand mixer fitted with the paddle attachment, cream the butter, granulated sugar, brown sugar, peanut butter, salt, and vanilla on medium-high speed until light and fluffy. Scrape down the sides and bottom of the bowl.

4. Add the eggs and continue to cream on medium-high speed for 2 to 3 minutes, adding a little air, until the mixture is smooth and has lightened in colour. Scrape down the sides and bottom of the bowl. Mix in the flour mixture and quick oats on medium-low speed until fully incorporated.

5. Scoop five 3-tablespoon portions of the cookie dough onto each baking sheet, leaving ample space between them. Gently press down on the dough portions to flatten them to about ¾-inch thickness. Bake, one sheet at a time, for 15 to 18 minutes, or until lightly browned all over. Allow the cookies to cool on the baking sheets.

6. Assemble the sandwich cookies: Place half of the cookies, upside down, on a baking sheet. Spread 1 tablespoon of the peanut butter American buttercream on each cookie, leaving a ½-inch border of exposed cookie around the outer edge (see instructions on page 132, step 1).

7. Fill a piping bag fitted with a No. 824 star tip with the remaining buttercream. Pipe a thick circle of buttercream onto each iced cookie to create a well for the jam filling, leaving a ¼-inch border of exposed cookie around the outer edge (see instructions on page 132, step 2).

8. Fill each well with 2 tablespoons of the raspberry jam. Strain the remaining raspberry jam through a fine-mesh strainer to remove the seeds. Using a small piping bag fitted with a No. 2 round tip or a parchment paper cone, drizzle the seedless raspberry jam over the icing borders in a zigzag pattern (see instructions on page 132, step 4, skip step 3).

9. Place the remaining cookies on top of the filled cookies to form sandwiches. Using even pressure, gently push down on the tops to form a bond with the filling (see instructions on page 132, step 5). Store in an airtight container in the refrigerator for up to 4 days.

Peanut Butter Oat Cookies

1½ cups all-purpose flour
1 teaspoon baking soda
½ teaspoon baking powder
1 cup unsalted butter, room temperature
1 cup granulated sugar
1 cup packed dark brown sugar
1 cup smooth peanut butter (sweetened, not natural)
1 teaspoon salt
2 teaspoons pure vanilla extract
2 large eggs, room temperature
2 cups quick oats

Peanut Butter American Buttercream

1 batch Peanut Butter American Buttercream (page 246)

Filling

2 cups raspberry jam

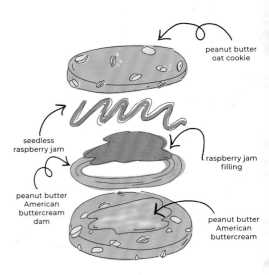

peanut butter oat cookie

seedless raspberry jam

raspberry jam filling

peanut butter American buttercream dam

peanut butter American buttercream

Hazelnut Sandwich Cookies

Hazelnut Chocolate Chunk Cookies

4¼ cups all-purpose flour

2 teaspoons baking powder

1½ teaspoons baking soda

1 teaspoon salt

2 cups granulated sugar

1 cup soft vegan margarine, melted and warm (we use Crystal)

½ cup water, room temperature

2 teaspoons pure vanilla extract

2 teaspoons apple cider vinegar

1 cup semi-sweet chocolate chunks

1 cup toasted and peeled hazelnuts, roughly chopped

Vegan Chocolate Buttercream

1 batch Vegan Chocolate Buttercream (page 248)

Vegan Hazelnut Spread

1 batch Vegan Hazelnut Spread (page 271)

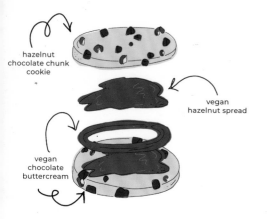

hazelnut chocolate chunk cookie

vegan hazelnut spread

vegan chocolate buttercream

Nutella is a bakery favourite, from our Nutella S'mores Bars to Nutella Stuffed Pretzels. We wanted vegans to share in our love, so we developed a vegan hazelnut chocolate spread, used in the centre of this cookie. It is not quite as creamy as the commercial version, but it also contains zero planet-harming palm oil. You can use this homemade spread to replace Nutella in any of our other recipes. A keen eye might recognize the cookie recipe as the same base used for our Funfetti Sugar Cookies (page 70). To maintain a living-wage workplace, we are constantly looking for cost efficiencies that do not compromise our values. That means when we find a recipe we love, we develop a whole community of recipes around it. That makes training staff easier and requires us to house fewer ingredients but still allows us to make things from scratch in small batches.

1. Preheat the oven to 350°F. Line 4 baking sheets with parchment paper or silicone baking mats.

2. Make the cookies: Sift the flour, baking powder, baking soda, and salt into a medium bowl and stir together.

3. In a large bowl, vigorously whisk together the sugar and melted vegan margarine for 1 to 2 minutes until the mixture is smooth and has lightened in colour. Whisk in the water, vanilla, and apple cider vinegar until the mixture is smooth. This may take a few minutes of stirring, depending on your speed.

4. Stir in the flour mixture, chocolate chunks, and hazelnuts and mix just until combined and no dry flour remains. The dough may look a little wet, but it will firm up as the margarine cools.

5. Scoop six 3-tablespoon portions of the cookie dough onto each baking sheet, leaving ample space between them. Gently press down on the tops of the dough portions to flatten them to about ½-inch thickness. Bake, one sheet at a time, for 15 to 18 minutes, or until the cookies have puffed up and are dry on top.

6. Assemble the sandwich cookies: Place half of the cookies, upside down, on a baking sheet. Spread 1 tablespoon of the vegan chocolate buttercream on each cookie, leaving a ½-inch border of exposed cookie around the outer edge (see instructions on page 132, step 1).

7. Fill a piping bag fitted with a No. 824 star tip with the remaining vegan chocolate buttercream. Pipe a thick circle of buttercream onto each iced cookie to create a well for the vegan hazelnut spread, leaving a ¼-inch border of exposed cookie around the outer edge. Fill each well with 2 to 3 tablespoons of the vegan hazelnut spread (see instructions on page 132, steps 2 and 4, skip step 3).

8. Place the remaining cookies on top of the filled cookies to form sandwiches. Using even pressure, gently push down on the tops to form a bond with the filling (see instructions on page 132, step 5). Store in an airtight container in the refrigerator for up to 4 days.

Tip: Prepare the hazelnuts for both the cookies and the hazelnut spread in advance. Roast the nuts in the oven on a baking sheet for 10 to 15 minutes until you can smell them roasting. Rub the hot nuts between clean kitchen towels to remove the skins.

Lemon Strawberry Sandwich Cookies

Makes 9 sandwich cookies

If you have seen the bakery at Christmastime, you know we love shortbread. We make dozens of different scrumptious variations. This is our summer shortbread baby. Buttery, melt-in-your-mouth shortbread married with bright, freshly made strawberry compote and a gratifying touch of lemon. Use strawberry ice cream instead of buttercream and jam, and you will have an even more delicious summer treat! This recipe makes four-inch cookies, but they would be lovely miniaturized for a tea party or a kid's party. Our strawberry compote contains very little sugar, so the tartness of the strawberries still shines through. If you would like it a little sweeter, you can switch up the fillings with a rainbow of jams to give it that photo-worthy finish.

1. Preheat the oven to 350°F. Line 3 baking sheets with parchment paper or silicone baking mats.

2. Make the cookies: In the bowl of a stand mixer fitted with the paddle attachment, lightly cream the butter and lemon zest at medium-high speed just until the butter is smooth, 1 to 2 minutes. Do not incorporate air into the butter. Scrape down the sides and bottom of the bowl.

3. Add the icing sugar, cornstarch, vanilla, and salt and mix on low speed, increasing to medium-high, until the mixture is smooth and there are no chunks. Scrape down the sides and bottom of the bowl. Add the flour and mix on low speed, increasing to medium-high, until the flour is fully incorporated, without whipping air into the dough.

4. Scoop six 3-tablespoon portions of the cookie dough onto each baking sheet, leaving ample space between them. Gently press down on the tops of the dough portions to flatten them to about ½-inch thickness. Bake, one sheet at a time, for 15 to 18 minutes, or until very lightly browned at the edges. Cool the cookies completely on a wire rack.

5. Assemble the sandwich cookies: Place half of the cookies, upside down, on a baking sheet. Spread 1 tablespoon of the lemon buttercream on each cookie, leaving a ½-inch border of exposed cookie around the outer edge (see instructions on page 132, step 1).

6. Fill a piping bag fitted with a No. 824 star tip with the remaining lemon buttercream. Pipe a thick circle of buttercream onto each iced cookie to create a well for the compote, leaving a ¼-inch border of exposed cookie around the outer edge. Fill each well with 2 tablespoons of the strawberry compote (see instructions on page 132, steps 2 and 4, skip step 3).

7. Place the remaining cookies on top of the filled cookies to form sandwiches. Using even pressure, gently push down on the tops to form a bond with the fillling (see instructions on page 132, step 5). Store in an airtight container in the refrigerator for up to 4 days.

Lemon Shortbread Cookies

2 cups unsalted butter, room temperature
Zest of 2 lemons
1 cup icing sugar
1 cup cornstarch
1 teaspoon pure vanilla extract
½ teaspoon salt
3 cups all-purpose flour

Lemon Buttercream

½ batch Lemon Buttercream (page 253)

Strawberry Compote

1 batch Strawberry Compote (page 258)

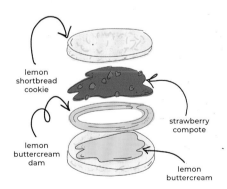

lemon shortbread cookie

strawberry compote

lemon buttercream dam

lemon buttercream

Turtles Sandwich Cookies

Chocolate Pecan Cookies

2¼ cups all-purpose flour

¾ cup cocoa powder

1 teaspoon baking soda

1 cup unsalted butter, melted and warm

1 cup granulated sugar

1 cup packed dark brown sugar

½ teaspoon salt

2 large eggs

1½ teaspoons pure vanilla extract

1 cup caramel or milk chocolate chips

1 cup toasted pecans, roughly chopped

Vanilla Bean Buttercream

½ batch Vanilla Bean Buttercream (page 248), room temperature

Caramel

1 batch Caramel (page 275), room temperature

For assembly

3 cups toasted pecans, roughly chopped

10 pecan halves

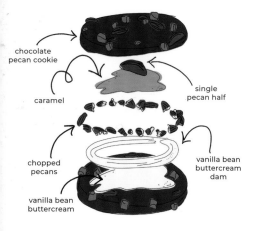

chocolate pecan cookie

caramel

single pecan half

chopped pecans

vanilla bean buttercream dam

vanilla bean buttercream

If you are looking for something that defines sweet indulgence and involves a heavy dose of caramel, chocolate, and pecans, then this sandwich cookie is for you. We took our simple double chocolate cookie and added caramel chips and toasted pecans, creating a perfect vessel to hold our vanilla bean buttercream and a sweet caramel centre. In addition, because we thought it needed more pecans, we put a single perfect pecan half in the centre and then coated the outside of the buttercream in chopped pecans, too. This is the type of cookie that you will find yourself sneaking back to the kitchen for more.

1. Preheat the oven to 350°F. Line 4 baking sheets with parchment paper or silicone baking mats.

2. Make the cookies: Sift the flour, cocoa powder, and baking soda into a medium bowl and stir together.

3. In a large bowl, whisk together the melted butter, granulated sugar, brown sugar, and salt until the mixture is smooth and there is no oily film left around the edges. Whisk in the eggs and vanilla until the mixture is light and smooth.

4. Stir in the flour mixture, caramel or chocolate chips, and 1 cup of the chopped pecans and mix until no dry flour remains.

5. Scoop five 3-tablespoon portions of the cookie dough onto each baking sheet, leaving ample space between them. Gently push down on the tops of the dough portions to flatten them to about ¾-inch thickness. Bake, one sheet at a time, for 15 to 18 minutes, or until the tops of the cookies look dry. Allow the cookies to cool on the baking sheets.

6. Assemble the sandwich cookies: Place half of the cookies, upside down, on a baking sheet. Spread about 1 tablespoon of the vanilla bean buttercream on each cookie, leaving a ½-inch border of exposed cookie around the outer edge (see instructions on page 132, step 1).

7. Fill a piping bag fitted with a No. 824 star tip with the remaining vanilla bean buttercream. Pipe a thick circle of buttercream onto each iced cookie to create a well for the caramel, leaving a ¼-inch border of exposed cookie around the outer edge (see instructions on page 132, step 2).

8. Place 3 cups of the chopped pecans in a medium bowl. Press the pecans into the outside of the iced borders to create a crust (see instructions on page 132, step 3).

9. Fill each well with 2 tablespoons of the caramel. Place one pecan half in the middle of each caramel-filled well. Place the remaining cookies on top of the filled cookies to form sandwiches. Using even pressure, gently push down on the tops to form a bond with the filling (see instructions on page 132, steps 4 and 5). Store in an airtight container in the refrigerator for up to 4 days.

Double Chocolate PB Sandwich Cookies

Rich, deep chocolate flavour and creamy, stick-to-your-mouth peanut butter with a little crunch of peanuts and chocolate chips. You are going to need a glass of milk with this cookie sandwich! You could always add yet another layer of chocolatey peanut butter goodness by sneaking a Reese's Peanut Butter Cup into the centre with the peanut butter. If peanut butter is not your thing, our Hazelnut Chocolate Buttercream (page 251) would work equally well with these cookies.

1. Preheat the oven to 350°F. Line 4 baking sheets with parchment paper or silicone baking mats.

2. Make the cookies: Sift the flour, cocoa powder, and baking powder into a medium bowl and stir together.

3. In the bowl of a stand mixer fitted with the paddle attachment, cream the brown sugar, butter, vanilla, and salt on medium-high speed until the mixture is light and fluffy. Scrape down the sides and bottom of the bowl. Add the eggs and continue to cream on medium-high speed for 2 to 3 minutes until the mixture is light and smooth. Scrape down the sides and bottom of the bowl.

4. Add the milk and beat on medium speed until the mixture is smooth and the milk is fully incorporated. Do not worry if the mixture separates a bit at this point; it will come back together by the end. Scrape down the sides and bottom of the bowl.

5. With the mixer on low speed, slowly pour the melted chocolate into the batter. When all the chocolate has been added, increase the speed to medium-high and continue to beat for 2 to 3 minutes until the batter has a pudding texture and the chocolate is fully incorporated. Scrape down the sides and bottom of the bowl.

6. Mix in the flour mixture, chocolate chips, and 1 cup of the peanuts and mix on low speed until fully incorporated.

7. Scoop five 3-tablespoon portions of the cookie dough onto each baking sheet, leaving ample space between them. Gently press down on the dough portions to flatten them to about ¾-inch thickness. Sprinkle the remaining ¼ cup peanuts on top of half of the cookies. These will be the tops of the cookie sandwiches. Bake, one sheet at a time, for 15 to 18 minutes, or until the cookies are cracked on top and puffy.

8. Assemble the sandwich cookies: Place the cookies without the peanuts on top, upside down, on a baking sheet. Spread about 1 tablespoon of the peanut butter American buttercream on each cookie, leaving a ½-inch border of exposed cookie around the outer edge (see instructions on page 132, step 1).

9. Fill a piping bag fitted with a No. 824 star tip with the remaining peanut butter American buttercream. Pipe a circle of buttercream onto the iced cookies to create a well for the peanut butter, leaving a ¼-inch border of exposed cookie around the outer edge. Fill the well of each cookie with 2 tablespoons of peanut butter (see instructions on page 132, steps 2 and 4, skip step 3).

10. Place the peanut-topped cookies on top of the filled cookies to form sandwiches. Using even pressure, gently push down on the tops to form a bond with the filling (see instructions on page 132, step 5). Store in an airtight container at room temperature for up to 6 days.

Double Chocolate Peanut Cookies

1¼ cups all-purpose flour

½ cup cocoa powder

2 teaspoons baking powder

1½ cups packed brown sugar

½ cup unsalted butter, room temperature

2 teaspoons pure vanilla extract

½ teaspoon salt

2 large eggs

⅓ cup 2% milk

8 ounces (225 g/1¼ cups) bittersweet dark chocolate, melted

2 cups semi-sweet chocolate chips

1¼ cups roasted unsalted peanuts, roughly chopped, divided

Peanut Butter American Buttercream

1 batch Peanut Butter American Buttercream (page 246)

Filling

1¼ cups smooth peanut butter (sweetened, not natural)

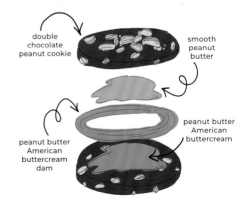

double chocolate peanut cookie

smooth peanut butter

peanut butter American buttercream

peanut butter American buttercream dam

Whiskey Cowboy Sandwich Cookies

Cowboy Cookies

2 cups all-purpose flour

1 teaspoon baking soda

1 teaspoon cinnamon

1 cup unsalted butter, melted

1 cup granulated sugar

1 cup packed dark brown sugar

1 teaspoon salt

1 teaspoon pure vanilla extract

2 large eggs

3 cups quick oats

1 cup milk chocolate chips

½ cup dried cranberries

½ cup roasted pecans, roughly chopped

½ cup unsweetened shredded coconut

Milk Chocolate Whiskey Ganache

7 ounces (200 g/1 cup) milk chocolate callets or chopped milk chocolate

½ cup whipping (35%) cream

¼ cup whiskey

Vanilla Bean Buttercream

½ batch Vanilla Bean Buttercream (page 248)

Coating

3 cups unsweetened shredded coconut, toasted

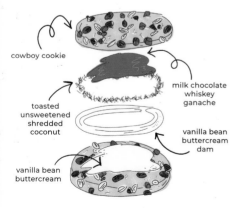

cowboy cookie

milk chocolate whiskey ganache

toasted unsweetened shredded coconut

vanilla bean buttercream dam

vanilla bean buttercream

We had never really pictured ourselves attending the Canadian Country Music Awards until they came to Hamilton, Ontario, a few years ago and we were asked to design desserts to celebrate the nominees. We developed this sandwich cookie to celebrate Brett Kissel, nominated for the Fans' Choice Award. A whiskey-infused chocolate ganache centre is surrounded by vanilla bean buttercream with toasted coconut and sandwiched between two chewy oatmeal cookies studded with cranberries, pecans, and milk chocolate chunks. Brett turned out to be a great person and thanked us graciously for the dessert. He even ended up ordering a cake from us that made it into a music video! We were invited to the awards and given VIP access with a few employees, which was incredibly fun. We even got up close and personal with the queen of country music, Shania Twain, on the red carpet.

1. Preheat the oven to 350°F. Line 4 baking sheets with parchment paper or silicone baking mats.

2. Make the cookies: Sift the flour, baking soda, and cinnamon into a medium bowl and stir together.

3. In the bowl of a stand mixer fitted with the paddle attachment, cream the melted butter, granulated sugar, brown sugar, salt, and vanilla on medium-high speed until the mixture is light and fluffy. Scrape down the sides and bottom of the bowl. Add the eggs and continue to cream on medium-high speed for 2 to 3 minutes until the mixture is light and smooth. Scrape down the sides and bottom of the bowl.

4. With the mixer on medium-low speed, mix in the flour mixture, quick oats, chocolate chips, cranberries, pecans, and coconut until fully incorporated.

5. Scoop five 3-tablespoon portions of the cookie dough onto each baking sheet, leaving ample space between them. Gently press down on the tops of the dough portions to flatten them to about ¾-inch thickness. Bake, one sheet at a time, for 15 to 18 minutes, or until lightly browned all over. Allow the cookies to cool on the baking sheets.

6. Make the milk chocolate whiskey ganache: In a medium heat-resistant bowl, heat the chocolate and cream in the microwave in 30-second intervals, stirring vigorously after each interval, until all the chocolate is melted, 1 to 1½ minutes total. Add the whiskey and stir until the ganache is smooth and glossy.

7. Assemble the sandwich cookies: Place half of the cookies, upside down, on a baking sheet. Spread about 1 tablespoon of the vanilla bean buttercream on each cookie, leaving a ½-inch border of exposed cookie around the outer edge (see instructions on page 132, step 1).

8. Fill a piping bag fitted with a No. 824 star tip with the remaining vanilla bean buttercream. Pipe a thick circle of buttercream onto the iced cookies to create a well for the ganache, leaving a ¼-inch border of exposed cookie around the outer edge (see instructions on page 132, step 2).

9. Place the 3 cups of coconut in a medium bowl. Press the coconut into the outside of the iced borders to create a crust (see instructions on page 132, step 3).

10. Fill each well with 2 tablespoons of the ganache. Place the remaining cookies on top of the filled cookies to form sandwiches. Using even pressure, gently push down on the tops to form a bond with the filling (see instructions on page 132, steps 4 and 5). Store in an airtight container in the refrigerator for up to 4 days.

Cheesecakes

Vanilla Bean Cheesecake

Cheesecake was not really something we offered at the bakery until the Cheesecake Queen, Helen, arrived on the scene. She truly changed the entire game when it came to creating the perfect balance required in cheesecakes. Creating a core recipe is what we all strive for as professional bakers; all the rest is just delicious additions. Starting with Josie's high school cheesecake recipe and using her decades of experience as a baker, Helen created the perfect cheesecake base. She passed on her knowledge to our cake team, and they will happily scrape that bowl numerous times to yield the most amazing cheesecake batter ever. Making and baking cheesecake batter is a labour of love but worth every ounce of high-maintenance deliciousness.

This recipe is the base for most of the cheesecakes in this section. Make sure your cream cheese is very soft before you begin. If not, microwave it for 30 seconds to warm it up. You can top this vanilla base cheesecake with any of our compotes or ganaches. See Icings, Buttercreams, and Fillings (page 241) to make it your own.

1. Preheat the oven to 350°F. Grease a 6-inch round cake pan or springform pan with canola oil cooking spray and line the bottom and sides with separate pieces of parchment paper. (If you are using a springform pan, wrap the outside bottom and sides with tin foil to make it watertight.)

2. Make the graham crumb base: Press the graham crumb mixture evenly into the bottom of the prepared pan. Using even pressure, flatten the mixture with the bottom of a dry measuring cup. Bake for 10 to 15 minutes until lightly browned.

3. Reduce the oven temperature to 300°F.

4. Make the cheesecake filling: In the bowl of a stand mixer fitted with the paddle attachment, beat the cream cheese on high speed until smooth and no lumps remain. Using a silicone spatula, scrape down the sides and bottom of the bowl.

5. Sift the sugar and flour over the cream cheese and beat on medium-high speed just until smooth and fully combined. Do not overmix. Scrape down the sides and bottom of the bowl.

6. Add the eggs and vanilla and beat just until smooth and combined. Do not overbeat. It is important to keep air bubbles to a minimum. Scrape down the sides and bottom of the bowl.

7. Add the cream and beat just until fully incorporated.

8. Pour the batter over the graham crust. Carefully knock the bottom of the pan on the counter 8 to 10 times to remove any air bubbles. The bubbles will float to the top. Set the cake or springform pan in the centre of a deep baking pan and place in the oven. Carefully pour boiling water into the baking pan to come a third of the way up the sides of the cake or springform pan. Bake for 60 to 75 minutes. Do not open the oven door during the baking time. The cheesecake is done when it looks nearly set and only a small circle in the centre appears when the pan is jiggled slightly. The centre will firm up during the cooling time. Cool completely, then cover with plastic wrap and place in the refrigerator overnight.

Makes one 6-inch cheesecake, serves 10 to 14

Graham Crumb Base

½ batch Graham Crumb Base (page 264)

Cheesecake Filling

1½ pounds (675 g/3 cups) cream cheese, room temperature
¾ cup granulated sugar
2 tablespoons all-purpose flour
3 large eggs, room temperature
1 teaspoon pure vanilla extract
½ cup whipping (35%) cream, room temperature

Continued on next page

9. Decorate the cheesecake: If baked in a cake pan, invert the cheesecake onto a clean plate and gently tap the bottom of the pan until the cheesecake slides out. Remove the parchment paper from the cheesecake and place the cake right side up. If baked in a springform pan, remove the sides of the pan and the parchment paper. Place the cheesecake on a serving plate or 8-inch round cake board. Serve plain or with desired toppings. Store, with toppings, in an airtight container in the refrigerator for up to 2 days. Store, without toppings, in an airtight container in the refrigerator for up to 2 weeks or in the freezer for up to 2 months.

Variation

Mini Cheesecakes: Preheat the oven to 300°F. Line two 12-cup muffin pans with paper or silicone cupcake liners. Fill each muffin cup with 1 heaping tablespoon of graham crumb mixture and press into the bottom corners and base. Using a large spoon or an ice cream scoop, fill the muffin cups three-quarters full with cheesecake filling. Bake for 12 to 15 minutes, or until the cheesecakes have domed slightly.

Chocolate Cheesecake

Makes one 6-inch cheesecake, serves 10 to 14

This chocolate cheesecake is the perfect classic counterpart to our vanilla bean cheesecake. A bittersweet couverture chocolate always works as the best anchor for desserts you know you will be dressing up with sweeter toppings and ganaches. This is the go-to birthday party cake for Josie's family gatherings. They prefer its rich, creamy texture to a cake with sweet icings. In Icings, Buttercreams, and Fillings (page 241), we have included a number of fruit compotes, ganaches, and toppings to create your own spin-offs and turn heads with this basic chocolate cheesecake.

Graham Crumb Base

½ batch Graham Crumb Base
   (page 264)

Cheesecake Filling

3 cups cream cheese, room
   temperature
¾ cup granulated sugar
2 tablespoons all-purpose flour
3 large eggs, room temperature
1 teaspoon pure vanilla extract
½ cup whipping (35%) cream,
   room temperature
7 ounces (200 g/1 cup) semi-sweet
   chocolate callets or chopped
   semi-sweet chocolate

1. Preheat the oven to 350°F. Grease a 6-inch round cake pan or springform pan with canola oil cooking spray and line the bottom and sides with separate pieces of parchment paper. (If you are using a springform pan, wrap the outside bottom and sides with tin foil to make it watertight.)

2. Make the graham crumb base: Press the graham crumb mixture evenly into the bottom of the prepared pan. Using even pressure, flatten the mixture with the bottom of a dry measuring cup. Bake for 10 to 15 minutes until lightly browned.

3. Reduce the oven temperature to 300°F.

4. Make the cheesecake filling: In the bowl of a stand mixer fitted with the paddle attachment, beat the cream cheese on high speed until smooth and no lumps remain. It is important to start this recipe with smooth cream cheese. Using a silicone spatula, scrape down the sides and bottom of the bowl.

5. Sift the sugar and flour over the cream cheese and beat on medium-high speed just until smooth and fully combined. Do not overmix. Scrape down the sides and bottom of the bowl.

6. Add the eggs and vanilla and beat until smooth and combined. Do not overbeat. It is important to keep air bubbles to a minimum. Scrape down the sides and bottom of the bowl.

7. Add the cream and beat until fully incorporated.

8. In a medium heat-resistant bowl, melt the chocolate in the microwave in 30-second intervals, stirring vigorously after each interval, until smooth. Using a spatula, add 1 cup of the cheesecake batter to the chocolate and mix until thoroughly combined. This will prevent the formation of chocolate lumps, creating a smooth texture. Add the chocolate mixture to the mixing bowl with the remaining vanilla cheesecake batter. Beat for 1 minute on medium speed, scrape down the sides and bottom of the bowl, and beat again for 1 minute, until no vanilla streaks remain.

Continued on next page

Chocolate Cheesecake continued

9. Pour the batter over the graham crust. Carefully knock the bottom of the pan on the counter 8 to 10 times to remove any air bubbles. The bubbles will float to the top. Set the cake or springform pan in the centre of a deep baking pan and place in the oven. Carefully pour boiling water into the baking pan to come a third of the way up the sides of the cake or springform pan. Bake for 60 to 75 minutes. Do not open the oven door during the baking time. The cheesecake is done when it looks nearly set and only a small circle in the centre appears when the pan is jiggled slightly. The centre will firm up during the cooling time. Cool completely, then cover with plastic wrap and place in the refrigerator overnight.

10. Decorate the cheesecake: If baked in a cake pan, invert the cheesecake onto a clean plate and gently tap the bottom of the pan until the cheesecake slides out. Remove the parchment paper from the cheesecake and place the cake right side up. If baked in a springform pan, remove the sides of the pan and the parchment paper. Place the cheesecake on a serving plate or 8-inch round cake board. Serve plain or with desired toppings. Store, with toppings, in an airtight container in the refrigerator for up to 2 days. Store, without toppings, tightly covered or in an airtight container in the refrigerator for up to 2 weeks or in the freezer for up to 2 months.

Cinnamon Apple Caramel Crumble Cheesecake

Makes one 9-inch cheesecake, serves 12 to 16

When a hint of sweater weather and a certain fall crispness is in the air, our minds go immediately to pumpkin spice doughnuts and this cheesecake. We bake this cheesecake in a 9-inch pan because we want more surface area to cover in cinnamon apple topping, crumble, and caramel drizzle. There is more cinnamon apple compote hidden inside the vanilla bean cheesecake for added deliciousness! Join the festive fall party any time of year with this cheesecake.

1. Make the cheesecake: Prepare the vanilla bean cheesecake as instructed on page 157, steps 1 to 7, using a 9-inch pan instead of a 6-inch pan and using 1 batch of graham crumb base instead of ½ batch.

2. Pour half of the cheesecake filling over the prepared graham crust. Carefully spoon 2 cups of the cinnamon apple compote over the filling to form a middle layer. Do not mix in. Pour the remaining cheesecake fillling over the compote. Store the remaining cinnamon apple compote in an airtight container in the refrigerator until needed in step 5.

3. Carefully knock the bottom of the pan on the counter 8 to 10 times to remove any air bubbles. The bubbles will float to the top. Set the cake pan or springform pan in the centre of a deep baking pan and place in the oven. Carefully pour boiling water into the pan to come a third of the way up the sides of the cake or springform pan. Bake for 60 to 75 minutes. Do not open the oven door during the baking time. The cheesecake is done when it looks nearly set and only a small circle in the centre appears when the pan is jiggled slightly. The centre will firm up during the cooling time. Cool completely, then cover with plastic wrap and place in the refrigerator overnight.

4. Bake the brown sugar oat crumble: Preheat the oven to 350°F. Spread the crumble in a single layer on a baking sheet lined with parchment paper or a silicone baking mat. Bake for 10 to 15 minutes or until golden brown. Set aside to cool.

5. Decorate the cheesecake: If baked in a cake pan, invert the cheesecake onto a clean plate and gently tap the bottom of the pan until the cheesecake slides out. Remove the parchment paper from the cheesecake and place the cake right side up. If baked in a springform pan, remove the sides of the pan and the parchment paper. Place the cheesecake on a serving plate or 10-inch round cake board. Store covered in the refrigerator for up to 4 days. When ready to serve, using a spoon, spread the remaining cinnamon apple compote on top of the cheesecake to meet the edge. Evenly sprinkle the baked crumble over the entire surface of the compote. Using a spoon, drizzle the caramel over the entire cheesecake.

Vanilla Bean Cheesecake
1 batch Vanilla Bean Cheesecake (page 157), with modifications in step 1 at left

Cinnamon Apple Compote
1 batch Cinnamon Apple Compote (page 260)

Brown Sugar Oat Crumble
1 batch Brown Sugar Oat Crumble (page 260)

Caramel
½ batch Caramel (page 275)

Pecan Butter Tart Cheesecake

Makes one 6-inch cheesecake, serves 10 to 14

Vanilla Bean Cheesecake

1 batch Vanilla Bean Cheesecake (page 157), with modifications at right

Butter Tart Custard

1 cup packed brown sugar

⅔ cup maple syrup

4 large eggs, room temperature and lightly beaten

1 cup toasted pecan halves, chopped

½ cup raisins, plumped in warm water and drained

2 tablespoons unsalted butter, melted

1 teaspoon pure vanilla extract

Caramel

⅔ batch Caramel (page 275)

For assembly

½ cup toasted pecan halves

Creating a baked good that marries two favourite desserts is always something we appreciate. Our maple syrup butter tarts are well loved, and we usually stick to classic walnuts or raisins when we make them at the bakery, but for this cheesecake we change it up with pecans and raisins. The ooey-gooey, super-sweet, nutty flavour is balanced by our vanilla bean cheesecake in this snuggle session. The butter tart filling is poured directly over the graham cracker crust, creating a luscious, fudge-like caramelized maple base layer for the vanilla cheesecake on top. With additional butter tart filling on top, you could say the cheesecake is getting the best hug of its life. This cake is lovely served with a scoop of vanilla ice cream.

1. Start making the vanilla bean cheesecake: Prepare the vanilla bean cheesecake as instructed on page 157, steps 1 to 3.

2. Make the butter tart custard: In a medium saucepan, combine the brown sugar, maple syrup, eggs, 1 cup of the pecans, raisins, butter, and vanilla. Whisk together well and bring to a boil over high heat. Reduce the heat to medium-low and, stirring frequently with a wooden spoon, keep on a low boil until the mixture thickens, about 5 minutes. Pour three-quarters of the custard over the prepared graham crust, smoothing it with a small offset palette knife. Fully cool the remaining custard, then store covered in the refrigerator until needed in step 5.

3. Continue making the cheesecake: Prepare the vanilla bean cheesecake as instructed on page 157, steps 4 to 8.

4. Decorate the cheesecake: If baked in a cake pan, invert the cheesecake onto a clean plate and gently tap the bottom of the pan until the cheesecake slides out. Remove the parchment paper from the cheesecake and place the cake right side up. If baked in a springform pan, remove the sides of the pan and the parchment paper. Place the cheesecake on a serving plate or 8-inch round cake board.

5. In a small bowl, combine the remaining butter tart custard with the caramel and mix together. Spoon the mixture over the top of the cheesecake and, using the back of the spoon, spread it out to meet the edge of the cheesecake. Sprinkle with the ½ cup pecan halves. Store in an airtight container in the refrigerator for up to 4 days.

Tips: This cheesecake does not travel well with the meringue topping. If making this for an event, top with the lemon curd and meringue just before serving.

Use a cake turntable when toasting the meringue to toast every nook and cranny of the meringue while turning the cake.

Lemon Meringue Cheesecake

For every staff birthday, we ask the staff member what they would like and then make them a meal. Some people request complete feasts like roast beef with Yorkshire puddings, roasted vegetables, and all the trimmings. Some prefer something sweeter. No matter the request, we all gather in the kitchen to sing happy birthday and share in their meal. Most years, Nickey has requested a lemon meringue cheesecake for her birthday meal. The bright, tart lemon curd cuts perfectly through the creamy richness of the cheesecake, and the sweet, airy meringue topping balances it all out. This is the perfect centrepiece for any celebration, with its impressive height and cloud of meringue on top.

1. Make the cheesecake: Prepare the vanilla bean cheesecake as instructed on page 157, steps 1 to 7.

2. In a small bowl, mix the lemon zest and juice until combined. Add the lemon mixture to the cheesecake batter and, using a spatula, stir until the lemon is evenly distributed throughout the batter. Pour the batter over the prepared graham crust. Carefully knock the bottom of the pan on the counter 8 to 10 times to remove any air bubbles. The bubbles will float to the top. Set the cake or springform pan in the centre of a deep baking pan and place in the oven. Carefully pour boiling water into the baking pan to come a third of the way up the sides of the cake or springform pan. Bake for 60 to 75 minutes. Do not open the oven door during the baking time. The cheesecake is done when it looks nearly set and only a small circle in the centre appears when the pan is jiggled slightly. The centre will firm up during the cooling time. Cool completely, then cover with plastic wrap and place in the refrigerator overnight.

3. Decorate the cheesecake: If baked in a cake pan, invert the cheesecake onto a clean plate and gently tap the bottom of the pan until the cheesecake slides out. Remove the parchment paper from the cheesecake and place the cake right side up. If baked in a springform pan, remove the sides of the pan and the parchment paper. Place the cheesecake on a serving plate or 8-inch round cake board.

4. Fill a piping bag fitted with a No. 806 round tip with the meringue. Pipe a dam around the top edge of the cheesecake, leaving a ½-inch border of exposed cheesecake around the outer edge. Fill the centre with 1 to 1½ cups of the lemon curd. Using a small offset palette knife, evenly spread the curd to meet the edges of the meringue. Using a large silicone spatula, dollop the remaining meringue over the curd. Smooth the meringue out in a dome, trying not to mix it with the curd. Connect the smoothed-out meringue on top with the meringue dam to create a seal, ensuring the curd does not ooze out.

5. Texture the meringue in your preferred way. You can either keep it smooth or add a twist. Spikes, swirls, or graceful lines can be made using a palette knife, a toothpick, or the bottom of a spoon. Using a mini kitchen torch, evenly toast the surface of the meringue.

6. Serve immediately, as the meringue tends to weep over time. Store leftovers in an airtight container in the refrigerator for up to 3 days.

Makes one 6-inch cheesecake, serves 10 to 14

Lemon Cheesecake
1 batch Vanilla Bean Cheesecake (page 157, steps 1 to 7)
Zest of 1 lemon (about 1 tablespoon)
Juice of 2 lemons (about ¼ cup)

Meringue
2 batches Meringue (page 265)

Lemon Curd
½ batch Lemon Curd (page 270)

Double Chocolate Brownie Cheesecake

Makes one 6-inch cheesecake, serves 10 to 14

Double Chocolate Cheesecake

1 batch Chocolate Cheesecake (page 159, steps 1 to 7)

7 ounces (200 g/1 cup) white chocolate chips

Dark Chocolate Ganache

2 batches Dark Chocolate Ganache (page 254)

Classic Fudge Brownies

½ batch Classic Fudge Brownies (page 97; see headnote for baking instructions)

Milk Chocolate Ganache

1 batch Milk Chocolate Ganache (page 255)

For assembly

1 tablespoon white chocolate crisp pearls

1 tablespoon milk chocolate crisp pearls

This cheesecake is a chocoholic's dream, developed just for this book! One sliver-size slice of this cheesecake will vanquish your chocolate craving in an instant. Nickey wanted to give all of you chocolate lovers something special, so she laid out all her chocolate options and set to work playing with combinations. Starting with that decadent double chocolate cheesecake base and the milk and dark chocolate ganaches, she decided to play off our classic fudge brownies and chop them up as a topping with some crisp pearls for crunch. She was not shy about the height of this cheesecake either, as it is a towering salute to all things chocolate; just make sure it will fit in your fridge! You can make a full batch of the Classic Fudge Brownies (page 97) or the half-batch required for this cheesecake. If making a half-batch, use an eight-inch square baking pan and reduce the baking time to fifteen to twenty-five minutes.

1. Make the cheesecake: Prepare the chocolate cheesecake as instructed on page 159, steps 1 to 7.

2. Stir the white chocolate chips into the chocolate cheesecake batter. Pour the batter over the prepared graham crust. Carefully knock the bottom of the pan on the counter 8 to 10 times to remove any air bubbles. The bubbles will float to the top. Set the cake or springform pan in the centre of a deep baking pan and place in the oven. Carefully pour boiling water into the pan to come a third of the way up the sides of the cake or springform pan. Bake for 60 to 75 minutes. Do not open the oven door during the baking time. The cheesecake is done when it looks nearly set and only a small circle in the centre appears when the pan is jiggled slightly. The centre will firm up during the cooling time. Cool completely, then cover with plastic wrap and place in the refrigerator overnight.

3. Decorate the cheesecake: If baked in a cake pan, invert the cheesecake onto a clean plate and gently tap the bottom of the pan until the cheesecake slides out. Remove the parchment paper from the cheesecake and place the cake right side up. If baked in a springform pan, remove the sides of the pan and the parchment paper. Place the cheesecake on a serving plate or 8-inch round cake board.

4. In a small heat-resistant bowl, reheat the dark chocolate ganache in the microwave in 10-second intervals, stirring after each interval, until the ganache is melted with no lumps and fluid enough to spread and flatten out to give a smooth finish. Do not overheat the ganache. Pour ¾ cup of the ganache in the centre of the cake and, using an offset palette knife, smooth it out to the edge until the ganache begins to drip over the edge to form decorative chocolate drips.

5. Cut the classic fudge brownies into 2-inch chunks and stack them on top of the dark chocolate ganache, starting at the edge and building into the middle of the cheesecake, keeping a ¼-inch gap around the edge. Keep adding layers of brownie chunks until you are satisfied with your tower.

6. In a small heat-resistant bowl, reheat the milk chocolate ganache in the microwave in 10-second intervals, stirring after each interval. Using a spoon or piping bag, drizzle the milk chocolate and remaining dark chocolate ganaches over the brownie chunks in a zigzag pattern. Sprinkle with the white and milk chocolate crisp pearls. Store in an airtight container in the refrigerator for up to 4 days.

Lemon Mascarpone No-Bake Cheesecake Pie

Makes one 9-inch cheesecake, serves 8 to 12

Unbelievably creamy with a bright, tart lemon finish, this pie is a perfect balance of richness and zesty citrus. The sunshine yellow of the lemon curd will bring light and warmth to any table, but we love this pie best served for dessert just when everyone thinks they might be full. There is no annoying pastry to worry about, and if you have the lemon curd and mascarpone made in advance, it is quite quick to assemble. We were pleasantly surprised to learn how easy it was to make our own mascarpone cheese. You can use store-bought mascarpone here, but if you have the time to plan a week ahead, we strongly encourage you to make the mascarpone yourself.

1. Preheat the oven to 350°F.

2. Make the graham crumb crust: Firmly and evenly press the graham crumb base mixture into the bottom and all the way up the sides of a 9-inch pie plate to form a pie shell. Bake for 10 to 15 minutes until light golden brown.

3. Make the mascarpone layer: In the bowl of a stand mixer fitted with the paddle attachment, beat the mascarpone, 2 tablespoons of the lemon curd, vanilla, and salt on medium-high speed for 2 to 3 minutes until smooth. Spoon the mixture into the cooled baked pie shell and smooth it flat with a small offset palette knife or the back of a spoon.

4. Spoon the remaining 2 cups lemon curd on top of the mascarpone layer and smooth it flat with a small offset palette knife or the back of a spoon. Allow the pie to set in the refrigerator for 10 to 15 minutes.

5. Spoon the whipped cream around the outer edge of the pie for a rustic finish or fill a 12-inch piping bag fitted with a No. 825 star tip and finish the pie by piping a star swirl border around the outer edge (see Piping Styles on page 242).

6. Make the sugared lemon zest: In a small bowl, rub together the lemon zest and sugar and sprinkle it over the whipped cream for a little sparkle. Store covered at room temperature for 1 day or in the refrigerator for up to 6 days.

Graham Crumb Base
1 batch Graham Crumb Base
   (page 264)

Mascarpone Layer
⅔ pound (300 g/1¼ cups)
   Homemade Mascarpone
   (page 269) or store-bought
2 cups + 2 tablespoons Lemon
   Curd (page 270), divided
1 teaspoon pure vanilla extract
¼ teaspoon salt

Whipped Cream
1 batch Whipped Cream
   (page 275)

Sugared Lemon Zest
Zest of ½ lemon
2 tablespoons granulated sugar

Cakes

Cake Assembly Instructions

Use these instructions as a guide to assemble any cake you make in this book. Practice definitely makes perfect when stacking and masking cakes, and the process can be a little challenging at first. Take your time and note that any cake can be masked in the rustic buttercream finish, skipping the ganache and other toppings if you are a novice cake decorator and want to start with the basics. Be sure to refer to the cake recipe you are building and to the recipe illustration for stacking order. Some cakes require a plain centre layer, whereas others have fillings in each layer. The recipe will indicate which stacking method to use.

PREPARE THE CAKE LAYERS

1. When the cake layers have fully cooled, remove the parchment paper from the bottoms. Using a serrated knife, trim the domes off the top of the cake layers to make them flat and level with the bottom of the layers. Keep your knife level while cutting (see photo A). Save the cake domes to use for cake crumbs for decorating the sides of cakes. For most cakes, cut the cake layers in half horizontally, making four layers of cake total (see photo B). Use the cake halves with a flat-baked bottom for the bottom and top layers of your cake and the halves with two cut sides for the centre layers.

    Note that some cakes are baked as individual layers and only need to have their domes trimmed (see photo C).

STACK THE CAKE

2. In the bowl of a stand mixer fitted with the paddle attachment, beat the room-temperature buttercream on medium-high speed for about 10 minutes to remove any large bubbles, creating light and fluffy texture. You will rebeat the buttercream several times during cake assembly, so keep your mixer and paddle attachment handy. Fill a 16-inch piping bag fitted with a No. 804 round tip with 2 cups of buttercream. As you stack your cake, following the method in the cake recipe, moisten the entire surface of each cake layer with up to 4 tablespoons of Simple Syrup (page 267) using a pastry brush. The simple syrup adds extra moisture and flavour to the cake. Note that chocolate-based cakes do not require simple syrup, as they are already moist enough (see photo D).

3. a. **SIMPLE STACKING METHOD:** Stack as you go for cakes filled only with buttercream or firm fillings.

    Place the bottom layer, cut side up, on an 8-inch round cake board or serving plate and moisten with simple syrup (see photo E). Using even pressure, pipe a buttercream dam around the top edge of the cake layer (see photo F). As indicated in the recipe, evenly sprinkle or spoon any fillings onto the cake layer. Using an offset palette knife, spread semi-solid fillings outward until they meet the edge of the buttercream dam. Place ½ cup of buttercream over the toppings and/or fillings in the well. Using an offset palette knife, spread out and smooth the buttercream just until it meets the edge of the dam (see photo G). For layers with a buttercream bullseye pattern, pipe the dam, then pipe a smaller buttercream circle in the centre of each cake layer to create a bullseye. Pipe the bullseye cavities full of the second buttercream or filling to create a filled bullseye (see photo H). Place the second cake layer with two cut sides on top of the buttercream layer. Repeat this process for the second and third cake layers using the fillings indicated in the recipe. Place the remaining flat-baked bottom cake layer, cut side down, so you have a smooth, flat surface for the top of your cake.

OR

b. **COLD STACKING METHOD:** Ice the cake layers individually and then stack chilled layers to stabilize cakes filled with compotes, curds, or soft spreads. This will prevent the fillings from leaking out during stacking.

Lay out three 8-inch round cake boards or plates. Place a cake layer, cut side up, on each cake board or plate and brush each with Simple Syrup (page 267), if using a vanilla-based cake (skip the simple syrup if using a chocolate-based cake). Set aside the remaining cake layer with only one cut side for the top layer of the stacked cake. Place 1 tablespoon of buttercream on each cake layer and, using a step pallete knife, spread out and smooth the buttercream over the entire surface of the cakes (see photo I). This creates a barrier to seal in the fillings and stop them from seeping into the soft cake. Follow the method in the cake recipe you are building, since each cake has slightly different buttercream patterns.

Using even pressure, pipe a buttercream dam, bullseye, or centre dot pattern as instructed in the cake recipe on all three cake layers. To pipe a bullseye, pipe a dam around the outer edge of the cake layer. Pipe a smaller circle in the centre of each cake layer, maintaining space between both buttercream circles and inside the small circle to form cavities for the filling (see photo H). To pipe a centre dot pattern, pipe a dam around the outer edge of the cake layer and then pipe a solid buttercream dot in the centre of the cake layer to the same height as the dam (see photo J). Fill the cavities created by your piped buttercream with curd, fruit compote, or a combination of cream and compote for the cake you are assembling. Using a step pallete knife, evenly spread and smooth out the add-ins to meet the top edge of the buttercream dam walls you have created. Do not overfill the cavities. Place the three iced cake layers, uncovered, in the refrigerator to harden for 30 minutes. When the filled cake layers are hardened, stack the layers by lifting them off the plates or cake boards with a large palette knife and using your hand on the side to stabilize them (refer to the recipe illustration for stacking order). Place the reserved top cake layer, cut side down, on top of the cake and pat down with light pressure to attach it.

CRUMB COAT

4. If you are making a vanilla-based cake, use a pastry brush to moisten the entire surface of the top cake layer with up to 4 tablespoons of Simple Syrup (page 267; see photo K). Clean the edge of the cake board with a damp kitchen towel to remove excess crumbs. Place the cake on a turntable. In the bowl of a stand mixer fitted with the paddle attachment, beat the buttercream on medium-high speed for about 10 minutes, until light and fluffy. Scoop about ¼ cup of buttercream on top of the cake. Using a step palette knife, with even pressure, spread out and lightly coat the top of the cake with a layer of buttercream. Begin to cover the sides of the cake in a thin, flat coating of buttercream while turning the turntable, flattening and removing excess buttercream. You will have a thin coating with some exposed cake areas; you should be able to see some of the cake through the icing (see photo L). Clean the cake board, removing any buttercream splatter and crumbs. This crumb coat captures all the crumbs and will give the cake a nice clean finish when the second layer of buttercream is applied. Place the cake in the refrigerator to harden for at least 15 minutes.

Continued on next page

MASK THE CAKE

5. In the bowl of a stand mixer fitted with the paddle attachment, beat the remaining buttercream on medium-high speed until light and fluffy, about 10 minutes. This will release large bubbles, while aerating finer bubbles, which makes it easier to achieve a smooth buttercream finish. Remove the cake from the refrigerator and place it on a turntable. Place ¼ cup of buttercream on top of the cake. Using a step palette knife, spread and smooth the icing ¼-inch thick over the top surface of the cake (see photo M). Cover the sides of the cake with additional buttercream, flattening it to ¼-inch thick while turning the turntable to create smooth sides. The icing from the sides will peak and push over the top of your cake, creating a wall (see photo N). Wipe the palette knife clean on a damp kitchen towel and complete masking the cake with one of the following finishes.

6. a. **FLAT FINISH:** For a simple, clean look or to encrust cake sides completely with toppings, like coconut, use a flat finish. Hold the edge of a clean palette knife parallel to the side of the cake and apply even pressure as you rotate the cake smoothly to give the sides of the cake an extra-smooth finish. Wipe the palette knife clean between passes and continue to smooth the buttercream until you are happy with the results (see photo O).

   OR

   b. **RUSTIC FINISH:** Intentionally a little messy and unrefined, this is the easiest way to finish the sides of a cake. Use the tip of a palette knife to push the buttercream back and forth in different directions to create a rough and patchy, textured buttercream finish. You can smooth the top of the cake flat as described in step 7 or finish the top of the cake with the same rustic finish as the sides (see photo P).

   OR

   c. **HORIZONTAL LINES:** Starting at the bottom edge of the cake, place the tip of a pallete knife against the cake horizontally. Slowly turn the turntable, pulling the palette knife up the cake to create horizontal lines on the side of the cake. You can space out the lines as much or as little as you would like. Experiment and flatten the buttercream out again until you find your desired look (see photo Q).

7. To finish the top of the cake, flatten the wall of buttercream creating a sharp edge by pulling a palette knife from the outside in toward the centre of the cake. Continue with this technique until you have a smooth, level top, cleaning the palette knife between each pass (see photo R). Clean the edges of the cake board with a clean, damp kitchen towel, removing any buttercream splatter and crumbs.

DECORATE THE CAKE

8. Fill a medium bowl with cake crumbs or toppings according to the cake recipe. Carefully balance the masked cake on the cake board in your non-dominant hand. Scoop a handful of cake crumbs or sprinkles with your other hand. Working over the bowl, carefully bring your palm to the bottom edge of the cake and pat the crumbs or sprinkles onto the soft buttercream, creating a decorative edge (see photo S). To completely encrust the sides of the cake with toppings, continue scooping handfuls of toppings and move your way up the sides of the cake. Completely cover the sides of the cake and then carefully create a ½-inch border on the top edge of the cake, creating a round topping frame and leaving a 5-inch round plain buttercream centre on top of the cake (see photo T). Place the cake, uncovered, in the refrigerator to set for 30 minutes.

9. Finish the top of the cake as indicated in the recipe. To add a ganache top, in a small heat-resistant bowl, reheat the ganache in the microwave in 15-second intervals, stirring after each interval. The ganache should be melted with no lumps and fluid enough to give a smooth finish to achieve the drip effect but not warm enough to melt the buttercream. Do not overheat the ganache. Have a clean step palette knife ready to use. Place the cake on the turntable and pour the ganache in the centre of the cake. With the tip of the step palette knife touching the centre of the ganache, angle the pallete knife down with the back handle lifted away and up from the cake at the back. Keeping the tip of the pallete knife positioned in the centre of the cake, slowly turn the turntable and begin to lower and flatten the angle of the palette knife to meet the top edge of the cake as you smooth out the ganache. Stop when the ganache begins to drip over the edge of the cake to form decorative chocolate drips (see photo U). Place the cake in the refrigerator to set for 10 minutes. The ganache should be firm to the touch.

10. To add a decorative buttercream border, in the bowl of a stand mixer fitted with the paddle attachment, beat the remaining buttercream for a final time on medium-high speed until light and fluffy, about 5 minutes. Fill a piping bag fitted with a No. 804 round tip, or the tip specified in the recipe, with buttercream. Pipe a border around the outer edge of the cake top, leaving about ½ inch of space from the edge of the cake. See Piping Styles on page 242 for different styles to use. We prefer a round reverse shell border (see photo V). Decorate with sprinkles or assorted decorative toppings according to the recipe (see photo W).

Vanilla Cake

Makes two 6-inch round cakes,
serves 8 to 12

2½ cups all-purpose flour
2¼ teaspoons baking powder
1 teaspoon salt
2 cups granulated sugar
4 large eggs, room temperature
¾ cup canola oil
1 tablespoon pure vanilla extract
1 tablespoon vanilla bean paste
1 cup buttermilk, room
   temperature

There are many different versions of vanilla cake, and we might have tested them all over the last decade of recipe development. It is a tough job tasting all that cake, but we think it has been worth it. This oil-based cake stays moist longer than butter-based cakes and comes together with very little effort. The combination of vanilla extract and vanilla bean paste gives this cake a deep, rich vanilla flavour that tastes great all on its own. It is the base used for most of the vanilla-based cake recipes in this chapter, including some delicious swirled variations in the Marble Cake (page 195) and Maple Walnut Cinnamon Swirl Cake (page 201). For a classic vanilla stacked cake with vanilla buttercream, try our Birthday Party Cake (page 183) and omit the sprinkles.

If you are looking for a simple dessert or teatime treat, serve one of these cakes sprinkled lightly with icing sugar and topped with edible flowers or a dollop of fresh whipped cream and fresh berries for a stunning and easy finish.

1. Preheat the oven to 350°F. Grease two 6-inch round cake pans with canola oil cooking spray and line the bottoms with parchment paper circles.

2. Sift the flour, baking powder, and salt into a medium bowl and, using a whisk, blend until thoroughly combined.

3. In the bowl of a stand mixer fitted with the whisk attachment, combine the sugar, eggs, canola oil, vanilla extract, and vanilla bean paste. Whip on high speed until the mixture is pale in colour and has reached the ribbon stage, 12 to 15 minutes. You will know the mixture has reached the ribbon stage when you lift the whisk and the mixture drops back into the bowl in long ribbons.

4. Add half of the dry ingredients to the wet ingredients and whip on medium speed until almost fully incorporated, less than 1 minute. Scrape down the sides and bottom of the bowl. Add the buttermilk and whip on medium-high speed just until combined. Scrape down the sides and bottom of the bowl.

5. Add the remaining dry ingredients and whip just until combined. Scrape down the sides and bottom of the bowl. Whip a final time on medium-high speed until smooth, about 1 minute. Do not overmix, as doing so may deflate the air bubbles.

6. Divide the batter evenly between the prepared pans and, using a small offset palette knife, smooth out the tops. Bake for 50 to 70 minutes, or until a toothpick inserted into the centres of the cakes comes out clean. Allow the cakes to cool in the pans on a wire rack for 20 minutes. Remove the cakes from the pans, leaving the parchment paper circles on the bottoms, and cool completely on the wire rack. Once the cakes are cool, wrap them tightly in plastic wrap and store at room temperature for up to 3 days.

Chocolate Cake

Makes two 6-inch round cakes, serves 8 to 12

Make sure you source the best cocoa you can for this cake. We use a Royal Dutch 22% or 24% cocoa powder for deep chocolate flavour. The batter will be quite liquid, which can be surprising, but we promise it will yield a super-moist cake. We love this cake because it stays moist for days and gives great stability for stacking layers. If stacking cakes seems intimidating, bake the cake in a 9- × 13-inch pan for forty to fifty-five minutes and, once cool, drizzle it with a double batch of any of the chocolate ganaches for a simple and delicious finish. This is the base cake for the Caramel Chocolate Skor Cake (page 184) and Hazelnut Crunch Cake (page 187; baked in three pans).

2 cups all-purpose flour

2 cups granulated sugar

¾ cup cocoa powder, sifted

2 teaspoons baking soda

1 teaspoon salt

1 cup buttermilk, room temperature

1 cup canola oil

2 large eggs, room temperature

1 tablespoon pure vanilla extract

1 cup boiling water

1. Preheat the oven to 350°F. Grease two 6-inch round cake pans with canola oil cooking spray and line the bottoms with parchment paper circles.

2. In the bowl of a stand mixer, combine the flour, sugar, cocoa powder, baking soda, and salt. Using a hand whisk, blend until thoroughly combined.

3. Return the bowl to a stand mixer fitted with the whisk attachment. Add the buttermilk, canola oil, eggs, and vanilla and whip on medium speed until well combined. Scrape down the sides and bottom of the bowl.

4. With the mixer on low speed, carefully and slowly add the boiling water to the cake batter in a steady stream. Increase the speed slowly to medium and whip the batter until well combined and smooth, about 2 minutes. Scrape down the sides and bottom of the bowl. Whip a final time on medium speed for 30 seconds.

5. Divide the batter evenly between the prepared pans. Bake for 70 to 80 minutes, or until a toothpick inserted into the centres of the cakes comes out clean. Allow the cakes to cool in the pans on a wire rack for 20 minutes. Remove the cakes from the pans, leaving the parchment paper circles on the bottoms, and cool completely on the wire rack. Once the cakes are cool, wrap them tightly in plastic wrap and store at room temperature for up to 5 days.

Birthday Party Cake

Makes one 6-inch round 4-layer cake, serves 8 to 12

The Birthday Party Cake has quickly become an iconic product for us, familiar to any fan of the bakery with its signature Cake & Loaf blue tone and rainbow sprinkles. This is the go-to cake for any vanilla lover. Vanilla cake filled with creamy vanilla buttercream may be a little basic, but it is also familiar and approachable, perfect for when you do not know what to serve a crowd. This recipe has evolved over the years, as we have as a bakery, to a tested and true, dependable favourite and has been a part of many parties near and far. We always recommend this cake for birthdays, as it hits the spot for those craving light flavour with a fun whimsy that screams *party*.

1. Trim the domes off the top of the baked vanilla cake layers. Cut the cake layers in half horizontally to make 4 layers total (see instructions on page 174, step 1).

2. Stack the vanilla cake, using the simple stacking method, with the vanilla bean buttercream on an 8-inch cake board or serving plate, using up to 4 tablespoons of the simple syrup to moisten each cake layer. Add 2 tablespoons of rainbow sprinkles topped with ½ cup buttercream to each filling layer (see instructions on page 174, steps 2 and 3a).

3. Crumb coat the top and sides of the stacked cake with a thin layer of buttercream and place the cake, uncovered, in the refrigerator for 15 minutes (see instructions on page 175, step 4).

4. Mask the chilled cake with buttercream using a horizontal line finish (see instructions on page 176, steps 5, 6c, and 7).

5. Using your hand, gently pat ½ cup of rainbow sprinkles onto the soft buttercream around the bottom edge of the cake to create a decorative border. Place the cake, uncovered, in the refrigerator for 30 minutes (see instructions on page 176, step 8).

6. Reheat the blue ganache to a pourable consistency in the microwave. Pour the ganache in the centre of the cake, spreading it outwards with a palette knife to the edges of the cake and allowing it to overflow onto the sides. Place the cake, uncovered, in the refrigerator for 10 minutes, or until the ganache is firm to the touch (see instructions on page 177, step 9).

7. Finish the cake by piping a round reverse shell border (see Piping Styles on page 242) of buttercream around the edge of the cake top, leaving ½ inch of exposed ganache around the outer edge. Sprinkle the piped buttercream border with 1 tablespoon of rainbow sprinkles, the white chocolate crisp pearls, and the gold flakes (see instructions on page 177, step 10).

8. The finished cake is best enjoyed at room temperature on the day it is assembled but can be covered and stored in the refrigerator for up to 4 days. Remove the cake from the refrigerator and let sit at room temperature for 5 to 8 hours before serving.

Vanilla Cake
1 batch Vanilla Cake (page 180)

Simple Syrup
1 batch Simple Syrup (page 267)

Vanilla Bean Buttercream
1 batch Vanilla Bean Buttercream (page 248)

Blue Ganache
1 batch Blue Ganache (page 256)

For assembly
1 cup rainbow nonpareil sprinkles
2 tablespoons white chocolate crisp pearls
1 teaspoon edible gold flakes

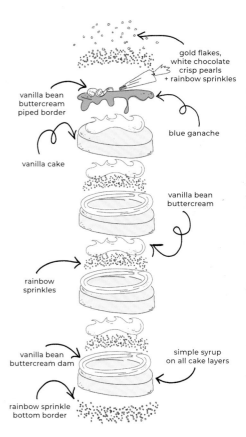

gold flakes, white chocolate crisp pearls + rainbow sprinkles

vanilla bean buttercream piped border

blue ganache

vanilla cake

vanilla bean buttercream

rainbow sprinkles

vanilla bean buttercream dam

simple syrup on all cake layers

rainbow sprinkle bottom border

Makes one 6-inch round 4-layer cake, serves 8 to 12

Caramel Chocolate Skor Cake

Chocolate Cake

1 batch Chocolate Cake (page 181)

Caramel Buttercream

1 batch Caramel Buttercream (page 252; adjust to use 1¼ cups Caramel in the buttercream; reserve the remaining ¼ cup for topping)

Chocolate Cake Crumbs

1 batch chocolate Cake Crumbs (page 268)

Dark Chocolate Ganache

1 batch Dark Chocolate Ganache (page 254)

For assembly

¾ cup crushed Skor chocolate bars

¼ cup Caramel, reserved (see above)

This is a customer favourite and our go-to chocolate cake flavour at the bakery. Our chocolate cake is incredibly moist and keeps very well without drying out for days. This cake takes our soft dark chocolate cake layers and contrasts them with the sweet crunch of almond toffee and the creamy depth of caramel buttercream to bring you to a completely different chocolate cake experience. Do not be alarmed by how liquid the batter appears; we promise it will bake up beautifully. If you like, you can even swap out the boiling water in the chocolate cake for hot coffee for an even deeper chocolate flavour.

1. Trim the domes off the top of the baked chocolate cake layers. Cut the cake layers in half horizontally to make 4 layers total (see instructions on page 174, step 1).

2. Stack the chocolate cake, using the simple stacking method, with the caramel buttercream on an 8-inch cake board or serving plate, adding ¼ cup of crushed Skor bars topped with ½ cup buttercream to each of the first and third filling layers. The second layer requires only buttercream (see instructions on page 174, steps 2 and 3a).

3. Crumb coat the top and sides of the stacked cake with a thin layer of the buttercream and place the cake, uncovered, in the refrigerator for 15 minutes (see instructions on page 175, step 4).

4. Mask the chilled cake with the buttercream using a horizontal line finish (see instructions on page 176, steps 5, 6c, and 7).

5. Using your hand, gently pat the chocolate cake crumbs into the soft buttercream around the bottom edge of the cake to create a decorative border. Place the cake, uncovered, in the refrigerator for 30 minutes (see instructions on page 176, step 8).

6. Reheat the dark chocolate ganache to a pourable consistency in the microwave. Pour the ganache in the centre of the cake, spreading it outwards with a palette knife to the edges of the cake and allowing it to overflow onto the sides. Place the cake, uncovered, in the refrigerator for 10 minutes, or until the ganache is firm to the touch (see instructions on page 177, step 9).

7. Finish the cake by piping a round reverse shell border (see Piping Styles on page 242) of buttercream around the edge of the cake top, leaving ½ inch of exposed ganache around the outer edge. Sprinkle the piped buttercream border with the remaining ¼ cup crushed Skor bars (see instructions on page 177, step 10). Using a spoon or piping bag, drizzle the top of the cake in a crosshatch pattern with the reserved ¼ cup caramel.

8. The finished cake is best enjoyed at room temperature on the day it is assembled but can be covered and stored in the refrigerator for up to 4 days. Remove the cake from the refrigerator and let sit at room temperature for 5 to 8 hours before serving.

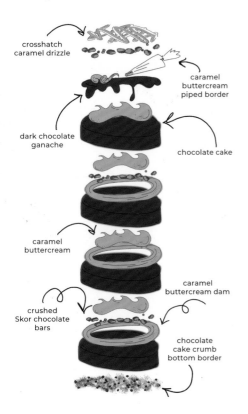

crosshatch caramel drizzle

caramel buttercream piped border

dark chocolate ganache

chocolate cake

caramel buttercream

caramel buttercream dam

crushed Skor chocolate bars

chocolate cake crumb bottom border

Hazelnut Crunch Cake

An obsession with macarons among our bakers turned into a random experiment to create larger macaron discs and led to this crunchy chocolate masterpiece. The final recipe for the meringue discs is slightly different from a macaron—a little more stable and delivering a bigger crunch factor—but the overall flavour is the same. We love how the tender chocolate cake contrasts with the crunchy discs, all lovingly wrapped in luscious hazelnut chocolate spread and creamy icing. This cake has presence and is perfect for special celebrations.

1. Make the meringue discs: Position a rack in the middle of the oven. Preheat the oven to 250°F. Using a permanent marker, draw two 5-inch circles on a sheet of parchment paper. This is your template for piping the meringues. Place the sheet of parchment, marker side down, on a baking sheet. Set aside.

2. Sift the ground almonds and ¼ cup of the sugar into a medium bowl and stir together. Add the cornstarch and whisk together. Set aside.

3. Place a 16-inch piping bag fitted with a No. 806 round tip in an empty tall cup. Fold the top edge of the piping bag over the lip of the cup to form a pocket for the meringue batter. This will help stabilize the piping bag while it is being filled.

4. In the bowl of a stand mixer fitted with the whisk attachment, beat the egg whites to soft peaks on high speed, about 1 minute or less. Decrease the speed to medium-low and gradually add the remaining 1 cup sugar. Add the salt and continue beating on medium-high speed until glossy medium stiff peaks form. Do not overbeat. If the meringue is too dry, the mixture will not hold its shape.

5. Using a spatula, transfer half of the meringue into the almond mixture and carefully fold it in. When almost completely combined, carefully fold in the remaining meringue. Fill the prepared piping bag with the meringue. Using even pressure, pipe the meringue within the circles drawn on the prepared parchment sheet, starting in the centre and spiralling out to fill the circles.

6. Bake for 45 to 60 minutes, or until lightly browned all over. The meringue discs should be completely dry, with a dry, crunchy centre. Tap the tops and listen for a hollow sound. Cool the meringue discs completely on a wire rack for 15 to 20 minutes before removing them from the parchment paper. Do not attempt to remove the paper until fully cooled; this will avoid breakage of the discs. If you are not using the meringue discs immediately, store them separated by parchment paper in an airtight container at room temperature for up to 7 days.

7. Assemble the cake: Trim the domes off the tops of the 3 baked chocolate cake layers but do not cut the layers in half horizontally (see instructions on page 174, step 1).

Makes one 6-inch round 3-layer cake, serves 8 to 12

Meringue Discs (makes two 5-inch round discs)
⅔ cup + 1 tablespoon finely ground almonds
1¼ cups granulated sugar, divided
2 tablespoons cornstarch
5 large egg whites, room temperature
Pinch of salt

Chocolate Cake
1 batch Chocolate Cake (page 181; baked in 3 pans and baking time reduced to 45 to 60 minutes)

Hazelnut Chocolate Buttercream
1 batch Hazelnut Chocolate Buttercream (page 251)

Chocolate Cake Crumbs
1 batch chocolate Cake Crumbs (page 268)

Milk Chocolate Ganache
1 batch Milk Chocolate Ganache (page 255)

For assembly
¾ cup hazelnut chocolate spread or Vegan Hazelnut Spread (page 271)
2 to 3 tablespoons hazelnuts, toasted, peeled, and cut in half
2 tablespoons milk chocolate crisp pearls

Continued on next page

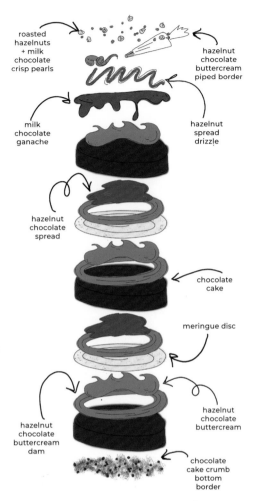

roasted hazelnuts + milk chocolate crisp pearls

hazelnut chocolate buttercream piped border

milk chocolate ganache

hazelnut spread drizzle

hazelnut chocolate spread

chocolate cake

meringue disc

hazelnut chocolate buttercream

hazelnut chocolate buttercream dam

chocolate cake crumb bottom border

8. Stack the cake using the simple stacking method. Place a cake layer, cut side up, on an 8-inch cake board or serving plate. Pipe a hazelnut chocolate buttercream dam around the top edge of the cake layer and fill the well with ½ cup of buttercream. Place a meringue disc in the centre of the buttercream layer. Pipe a buttercream dam around the outside edge of the disc. Fill the well with ¼ cup of the hazelnut chocolate spread. Place a second cake layer on top and repeat to build the layer as done with the first layer, finishing with a buttercream dam and hazelnut chocolate spread. Place the final cake layer, cut side down, on top (see instructions on page 174, steps 2 and 3a).

9. Crumb coat the top and sides of the stacked cake with a thin layer of the buttercream. Place the cake in the refrigerator for 15 minutes so that the crumb coat can firm up (see instructions on page 175, step 4).

10. Mask the chilled cake with the buttercream using a horizontal line finish (see instructions on page 176, steps 5, 6c, and 7).

11. Using your hand, gently pat the chocolate cake crumbs into the soft buttercream around the bottom edge of the cake to create a decorative border. Place the cake in the refrigerator for 30 minutes (see instructions on page 176, step 8).

12. Reheat the milk chocolate ganache to a pourable consistency in the microwave. Pour the ganache in the centre of the cake, spreading it outwards with a palette knife to the edges of the cake and allowing it to overflow onto the sides. Place the cake in the refrigerator for 10 minutes, or until the ganache is firm to the touch (see instructions on page 177, step 9).

13. In a small heat-resistant bowl, heat the remaining ¼ cup hazelnut chocolate spread in the microwave for 15 to 30 seconds, just until it is a pourable consistency. Using a spoon or piping bag, drizzle the hazelnut chocolate spread over the top of the cake in a zigzag pattern.

14. Using a piping bag fitted with a No. 825 tip, finish the cake by piping a star swirl border (see Piping Styles on page 242) of buttercream around the edge of the cake top, leaving ½ inch of exposed ganache around the outer edge. Sprinkle the piped buttercream border with the toasted hazelnuts and milk chocolate crisp pearls (see instructions on page 177, step 10).

15. The finished cake is best enjoyed at room temperature on the day it is assembled but can be covered and stored in the refrigerator for up to 4 days. Remove the cake from the refrigerator and let sit at room temperature for 5 to 8 hours before serving.

Tip: If necessary, trim the meringue discs using a serrated bread knife. They need to be slightly smaller than the 6-inch cake so they will not bulge out the side.

Loaded Carrot Cake

Makes one 6-inch round 4-layer cake, serves 8 to 12

Loaded with spices, lots of fresh carrots, pineapple, coconut, pecans, and plump raisins, this is carrot cake done right. Every bakery should have a good carrot cake at its core, and Nickey will stand behind this cake forever and always. Raisins are an often-misunderstood ingredient but do not skip them; these ones are plumped in pineapple juice, and we promise you will not even recognize them for what they once were. The Dreamy Cream Cheese Icing (page 244) is extra creamy and not too sweet, a perfect partner for this flavourful cake. In fact, it is practically health food with all those carrots and nuts and fruit, so what are you waiting for?

Note that we use four cake pans to allow this heavy batter to expand properly while baking.

1. Preheat the oven to 350°F. Grease four 6-inch round cake pans with canola oil cooking spray and line the bottoms with parchment paper circles.

2. Make the carrot cake: In a small heat-resistant bowl, heat the reserved pineapple juice for 1 minute in the microwave. Add the raisins to the pineapple juice and let sit to plump up, 10 to 15 minutes.

3. Sift the flour, cinnamon, nutmeg, pumpkin spice, baking soda, baking powder, and salt into a medium bowl and stir together.

4. In the bowl of a stand mixer fitted with the paddle attachment, combine the brown sugar, eggs, canola oil, and vanilla and beat on medium-high speed until the sugar is dissolved, up to 5 minutes. Test by rubbing a bit of the mixture between 2 fingertips. It should feel smooth, not gritty.

5. Strain the raisins and discard the pineapple juice. Add the raisins along with the grated carrots, drained crushed pineapple, chopped pecans, and flaked coconut and beat on medium-low speed until combined, less than a minute. Using a spatula, scrape down the sides and bottom of the bowl. Add the dry ingredients to the bowl and beat until the batter is combined and the dry ingredients are fully incorporated, 1 to 2 minutes. Do not overmix.

6. Divide the batter evenly among the prepared pans and, using a small offset palette knife, smooth out the tops. Bake all 4 cakes at the same time, spacing out the pans on the same rack for even baking, for 20 to 30 minutes, or until a toothpick inserted into the centres of the cakes comes out clean. Allow the cakes to cool in the pans on a wire rack for 20 minutes. Remove the cakes from the pans, leaving the parchment paper circles on the bottoms, and cool completely on the wire rack.

7. Assemble the cake: Trim the domes off the top of the baked carrot cake layers but do not cut the layers in half horizontally (see instructions on page 174, step 1).

Carrot Cake
1 cup canned crushed pineapple, drained and juice reserved
½ cup raisins
1½ cups all-purpose flour
1 tablespoon cinnamon
1 tablespoon freshly grated or ground nutmeg
2 teaspoons Pumpkin Spice (page 267)
1½ teaspoons baking soda
¼ teaspoon baking powder
¼ teaspoon salt
1½ cups packed brown sugar
3 large eggs, room temperature
¼ cup canola oil
½ teaspoon pure vanilla extract
2½ cups grated peeled carrots
¾ cup pecans, roughly chopped
½ cup sweetened flaked coconut

Simple Syrup
1 batch Simple Syrup (page 267)

Dreamy Cream Cheese Icing
1 batch Dreamy Cream Cheese Icing (page 244)

Maple Candied Pecans
½ batch Maple Candied Pecans (page 266)

For assembly
3 cups unsweetened shredded coconut, toasted
2 tablespoons white chocolate crisp pearls

Continued on next page

Loaded Carrot Cake continued

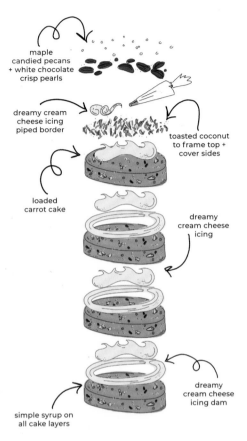

maple candied pecans + white chocolate crisp pearls

dreamy cream cheese icing piped border

toasted coconut to frame top + cover sides

loaded carrot cake

dreamy cream cheese icing

dreamy cream cheese icing dam

simple syrup on all cake layers

8. Stack the cake, using the simple stacking method, with the dreamy cream cheese icing on an 8-inch cake board or serving plate, using up to 4 tablespoons of simple syrup to moisten each cake layer. Pipe an icing dam around the top edge of each cake layer and fill each well with ½ cup of the icing. There are no additional fillings inside the layers for this cake (see instructions on page 174, steps 2 and 3a).

9. Crumb coat the top and sides of the stacked cake with a thin layer of icing. Place the cake in the refrigerator for 15 minutes so that the crumb coat can firm up (see instructions on page 175, step 4).

10. Mask the chilled cake with icing using a flat finish (see instructions on page 176, steps 5, 6a, and 7).

11. Using your hand, pat the toasted coconut into the soft icing, completely covering the sides of the cake in toasted coconut. Carefully create a ½-inch border on the top edge of the cake with the coconut, creating a round topping frame and leaving a 5-inch round plain icing centre on top of the cake (see instructions on page 176, step 8).

12. Finish the cake by piping a round reverse shell border (see Piping Styles on page 242) of icing around the edge of the cake top where the toasted coconut meets the plain icing. Sprinkle the piped icing border with maple candied pecans and white chocolate crisp pearls (see instructions on page 177, step 10). Place the cake, uncovered, in the refrigerator for 30 minutes to allow the cream cheese icing to firm up.

13. The finished cake is best enjoyed at room temperature on the day it is assembled but can be covered and stored in the refrigerator for up to 4 days. Remove the cake from the refrigerator and let sit at room temperature for 2 hours before serving.

Red Velvet Beet Cake

Makes one 6-inch round 4-layer cake, serves 8 to 12

When we first arrived on the baking scene, we felt there was a huge gap in delicious vegan baking, especially in the cake department. This recipe started as an experimental cupcake recipe for a friend's baptism party. We were skeptical at first, but the earthiness of the beets playing off the sweetness of the cake and slight bitterness of cocoa, as well as the bright natural red tone, made for one heavenly cake when paired with our sweet vegan buttercream. If you are not looking to keep the dessert completely vegan, we suggest trying the cake with our Dreamy Cream Cheese Icing (page 244), the way it was originally conceived. That is our personal favourite, and to this day Nickey will sneak some of the beet cake cut-offs and slather them with our Dreamy Cream Cheese Icing when she thinks no one is looking.

Note that we use four cake pans to allow this heavy batter to expand properly while baking.

1. Preheat the oven to 350°F. Grease four 6-inch round cake pans with canola oil cooking spray and line the bottoms with parchment paper circles.

2. Make the cake: In the bowl of a stand mixer fitted with the whisk attachment, sift the flour, cocoa powder, baking powder, and salt and whisk on low speed for 30 seconds to combine.

3. In a blender or food processor, combine the drained beets and ⅔ cup of the reserved beet liquid. Blend for 5 to 7 minutes, scraping down the sides at least twice, until the mixture is silky smooth. Add the sugar, canola oil, lemon juice, and vanilla and blend until smooth. Scrape down the sides as necessary.

4. Pour the wet ingredients on top of the dry ingredients in the bowl of the stand mixer. Using the whisk attachment, start on low speed to moisten the mixture and then whip on high speed, about 2 minutes, until the batter is smooth and airy. Scrape down the sides and bottom of the bowl. Whip a final time on medium speed for 30 seconds.

5. Divide the batter evenly among the prepared pans and, using a small offset palette knife, smooth out the tops. Bake all 4 cakes at the same time, spacing out the pans on the same rack for even baking, for 30 to 45 minutes, or until a toothpick inserted into the centres of the cakes comes out clean. Allow the cakes to cool in the pans on a wire rack for 20 minutes. Remove the cakes from the pans, leaving the parchment paper circles on the bottoms, and cool completely on the wire rack.

6. Prepare the vegan vanilla bean buttercream just before assembling the cake because it forms a crust on the surface quite quickly. If you are leaving it in the mixing bowl briefly, cover it with a damp kitchen towel.

7. Assemble the cake: Trim the domes off the tops of the 4 baked red velvet beet cake layers but do not cut the layers in half horizontally (see instructions on page 174, step 1).

Red Velvet Beet Cake

1½ cups all-purpose flour

½ cup + 2 tablespoons cocoa powder

1 tablespoon baking powder

½ teaspoon salt

2 cans (14 ounces/398 mL each) sliced or whole beets packed in water, drained and liquid reserved

1¼ cups granulated sugar

⅔ cup canola oil

½ cup lemon juice

2 teaspoons pure vanilla extract

Simple Syrup

1 batch Simple Syrup (page 267)

Vegan Vanilla Bean Buttercream

1 batch Vegan Vanilla Bean Buttercream (page 247)

Red Velvet Beet Cake Crumbs

1 batch red velvet beet Cake Crumbs (page 268)

Continued on next page

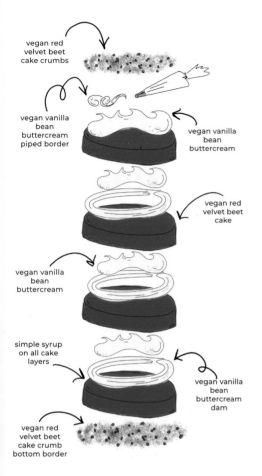

vegan red velvet beet cake crumbs

vegan vanilla bean buttercream piped border

vegan vanilla bean buttercream

vegan red velvet beet cake

vegan vanilla bean buttercream

simple syrup on all cake layers

vegan vanilla bean buttercream dam

vegan red velvet beet cake crumb bottom border

8. Stack the cake, using the simple stacking method, with the vegan vanilla bean buttercream on an 8-inch cake board or serving plate, using up to 4 tablespoons of simple syrup to moisten each cake layer. Pipe a buttercream dam around the top edge of each cake layer and fill each well with ½ cup of the buttercream. There are no additional fillings inside the layers for this cake (see instructions on page 174, steps 2 and 3a).

9. Crumb coat the top and sides of the stacked cake with a thin layer of buttercream and place the cake, uncovered, in the refrigerator for 15 minutes (see instructions on page 175, step 4).

10. Mask the chilled cake with buttercream using a rustic finish (see instructions on page 176, steps 5, 6b, and 7).

11. Reserve 1 tablespoon of the red velvet beet cake crumbs for the top of the cake. Using your hand, gently pat the remaining cake crumbs into the soft buttercream around the bottom edge of the cake to create a decorative border. Place the cake, uncovered, in the refrigerator for 30 minutes (see instructions on page 176, step 8).

12. Using a piping bag fitted with a No. 825 tip, finish the cake by piping a star swirl border (see Piping Styles on page 242) of buttercream around the edge of the cake top, leaving ½ inch of exposed buttercream at the outer edge. Sprinkle the piped buttercream border with the reserved 1 tablespoon of cake crumbs (see instructions on page 177, step 10).

13. The finished cake is best enjoyed at room temperature on the day it is assembled but can be covered and stored in the refrigerator for up to 4 days. Remove the cake from the refrigerator and let sit at room temperature for 5 to 8 hours before serving.

> **Tip:** This vegan icing is a little temperamental. If you are having any troubles with the finishing touches, you can try rewhipping the icing in the bowl of a stand mixer fitted with the paddle attachment or fill a cup that is tall enough to fit the step palette knife with hot water. Dip the knife in the hot water, pat it dry on a clean kitchen towel, and smooth out the icing. This will allow you a little more time to work with the icing, as the heat helps with smoothing and manipulating the icing.

Marble Cake

Makes one 6-inch round 4-layer cake, serves 8 to 12

If you cannot choose between classic vanilla and chocolate cake, we suggest our marble cake—the best of both worlds. This is a beautiful slice of cake to serve to your guests—vanilla with a kiss of chocolate swirl—and you will be pleasing both team chocolate and team vanilla at the same time. Vanilla bean buttercream and chocolate buttercream share the spotlight evenly through all three layers of filling, and the exterior is vanilla bean buttercream with poured dark chocolate ganache to balance it out perfectly. This is also the ideal base to create your own custom cake flavour. Add your own fruit filling, curds, favourite candy, local specialty chocolate, or puddings to the filling layers instead of the chocolate buttercream.

1. Make the marble cake: Prepare the vanilla cake batter as instructed on page 180, steps 1 to 5.

2. In a medium bowl, whisk together the sifted cocoa powder and canola oil to a smooth consistency. Add 2 cups of the vanilla cake batter to the cocoa mixture and mix until smooth. This is your chocolate batter.

3. Divide the vanilla batter evenly between the prepared cake pans and, using a small offset palette knife, smooth out the tops. Divide the chocolate batter between the pans by pouring circles of chocolate batter on the surface of the vanilla batter. Using a butter knife, swirl the 2 batters by pulling through and folding in the chocolate batter. Do not overmix; you want the marbling to stand out. Bake for 50 to 70 minutes, or until a toothpick inserted into the centres of the cakes comes out clean. Allow the cakes to cool in the pans on a wire rack for 20 minutes. Remove the cakes from the pans, leaving the parchment paper circles on the bottoms, and cool completely on the wire rack.

4. Make the chocolate buttercream: In the bowl of a stand mixer fitted with the paddle attachment, beat the full batch of vanilla bean buttercream on medium-high speed until light and fluffy, 5 to 10 minutes. Transfer 2 cups of the buttercream to a small bowl. Add the melted chocolate and sifted cocoa powder to the small bowl and, using a hand whisk, vigorously whisk until fully incorporated. Fill a 16-inch piping bag fitted with a No. 804 round tip with the chocolate buttercream. Fill another 16-inch piping bag fitted with a No. 804 round tip with the vanilla bean buttercream.

5. Assemble the cake: Trim the domes off the tops of the baked marble cake layers. Cut the cake layers in half horizontally (see instructions on page 174, step 1).

6. Stack the marble cake, using the simple stacking method, on an 8-inch cake board or serving plate, using up to 4 tablespoons of simple syrup to moisten each cake layer. For each filling layer, pipe a bullseye pattern of vanilla bean buttercream, then pipe the bullseye cavities full of chocolate buttercream (see instructions on page 174, steps 2 and 3a).

Marble Cake
1 batch Vanilla Cake (page 180, steps 1 to 5)
⅓ cup cocoa powder, sifted
2 tablespoons canola oil

Simple Syrup
1 batch Simple Syrup (page 267)

Vanilla Bean Buttercream
1 batch Vanilla Bean Buttercream (page 248), reserve 2 cups for Chocolate Buttercream (see below)

Chocolate Buttercream
2 cups Vanilla Bean Buttercream, reserved (see above)
3 ounces (85 g) bittersweet chocolate, melted and room temperature
1½ teaspoons cocoa powder, sifted

Chocolate Cake Crumbs
1 batch chocolate Cake Crumbs (page 268)

Dark Chocolate Ganache
1 batch Dark Chocolate Ganache (page 254)

For assembly
1 tablespoon white chocolate crisp pearls
1 tablespoon dark chocolate crisp pearls

Continued on next page

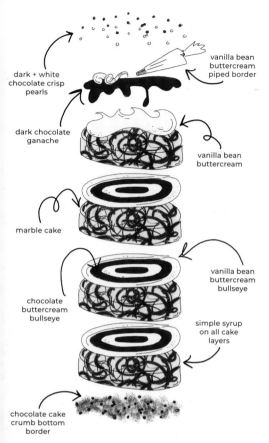

dark + white chocolate crisp pearls

vanilla bean buttercream piped border

dark chocolate ganache

vanilla bean buttercream

marble cake

vanilla bean buttercream bullseye

chocolate buttercream bullseye

simple syrup on all cake layers

chocolate cake crumb bottom border

7. Crumb coat the top and sides of the stacked cake with the vanilla bean buttercream. Place the cake in the refrigerator for 15 minutes so that the crumb coat can firm up (see instructions on page 175, step 4).

8. Mask the chilled cake with the vanilla bean buttercream using a horizontal line finish (see instructions on page 176 steps 5, 6c, and 7).

9. Using your hand, gently pat the chocolate cake crumbs into the soft buttercream around the bottom edge of the cake to create a decorative border. Place the cake in the refrigerator for 30 minutes (see instructions on page 176, step 8).

10. Reheat the dark chocolate ganache to a pourable consistency in the microwave. Pour the ganache in the centre of the cake, spreading it outwards with a palette knife to the edges of the cake and allowing it to overflow onto the sides. Place the cake in the refrigerator for 10 minutes, or until the ganache is firm to the touch (see instructions on page 177, step 9).

11. Finish the cake by piping a round reverse shell border (see Piping Styles on page 242) of vanilla bean buttercream around the edge of the cake top, leaving ¼ inch of exposed ganache around the outer edge. Sprinkle the piped buttercream border with the white and dark chocolate crisp pearls (see instructions on page 177, step 10).

12. The finished cake is best enjoyed at room temperature on the day it is assembled but can be covered and stored in the refrigerator for up to 4 days. Remove the cake from the refrigerator and let sit at room temperature for 5 to 8 hours before serving.

Lemonlicious Cake

Makes one 6-inch round 4-layer cake, serves 8 to 12

Zesty, bright, and loaded with lemon life, our Lemonlicious Cake has remained a popular staple at the bakery. It started as a vanilla sponge cake, evolved into a butter-based vanilla cake, and then morphed into the lemon vanilla cake we offer today. Farm fresh eggs, freshly squeezed lemon juice, and lemon zest bring this cake to another level. Seek out farm fresh, free-range eggs and notice the difference a beautiful natural yolk tone can impart to your baking. You will want to make sure you make the Candied Lemon Peel a few days in advance so it has a chance to dry out properly. The other components can be made ahead or on the same day. Lemon curd is a very versatile ingredient to have on hand, so consider a double batch. Josie likes to eat it with a spoon like pudding given the chance, but it is also delicious with yogurt or vanilla ice cream.

Lemon Vanilla Cake

1 batch Vanilla Cake (page 180), adding the zest of 2 lemons with the vanilla in step 3

Simple Syrup

1 batch Simple Syrup (page 267), lemon variation

Lemon Buttercream

1 batch Lemon Buttercream (page 253)

Lemon Curd

½ batch Lemon Curd (page 270)

Vanilla Cake Crumbs

1 batch vanilla Cake Crumbs (page 268)

White Chocolate Ganache

1 batch White Chocolate Ganache (page 255)

Candied Lemon Peel

1 batch Candied Lemon Peel (page 271)

For assembly

2 tablespoons white chocolate crisp pearls

1. Trim the domes off the top of the baked lemon vanilla cake layers. Cut the cake layers in half horizontally. Reserve one cake layer with a flat uncut side for the top of the cake (see instructions on page 174, step 1).

2. Stack the cake using the cold stacking method. Place each of the other 3 cake layers, cut side up, on an 8-inch plate or cake board and moisten them with the lemon simple syrup. Using a step pallete knife, spread 1 tablespoon of the lemon buttercream on each cake layer to create a barrier to stop the lemon curd from seeping into the cake. Pipe a bullseye pattern of buttercream on the bottom and one centre cake layer and fill the cavities with 1 cup of the curd per layer. On the third cake layer, pipe a buttercream dam and fill the well with ½ cup of the buttercream. Place all 3 cake layers in the refrigerator, uncovered, to firm up for 30 minutes. Stack the chilled cake layers starting with the bottom layer, which has an uncut bottom and a bullseye top, followed by the plain buttercream layer and then the second bullseye layer. Top with the reserved cake layer, cut side down. Using a pastry brush, moisten the entire surface of the top cake layer with 4 tablespoons of the lemon simple syrup (see instructions on page 174, step 2 and 3b).

3. Crumb coat the top and sides of the stacked cake with the buttercream. Place the cake in the refrigerator for 15 minutes so that the crumb coat can firm up (see instructions on page 175, step 4).

4. Mask the cake with the buttercream using a horizontal line finish (see instructions on page 176, steps 5, 6c, and 7).

5. Using your hand, gently pat the vanilla cake crumbs into the soft buttercream around the bottom edge of the cake to create a decorative border. Place the cake in the refrigerator for 10 minutes (see instructions on page 176, step 8).

6. Reheat the white chocolate ganache to a pourable consistency in the microwave. Pour the ganache in the centre of the cake, spreading it outwards with a palette knife to the edges of the cake and allowing it to overflow onto the sides. Place the cake in the refrigerator for 10 minutes, or until the ganache is firm to the touch (see instructions on page 177, step 9).

Continued on next page

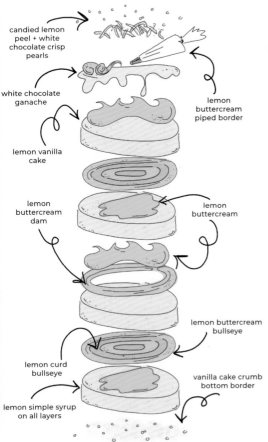

candied lemon peel + white chocolate crisp pearls

white chocolate ganache

lemon vanilla cake

lemon buttercream dam

lemon buttercream piped border

lemon buttercream

lemon buttercream bullseye

lemon curd bullseye

vanilla cake crumb bottom border

lemon simple syrup on all layers

7. Finish the cake by piping a round reverse shell border (see Piping Styles on page 242) of buttercream around the edge of the cake top, leaving ¼ inch of exposed ganache around the outer edge. Sprinkle the piped buttercream border with the candied lemon peel and white chocolate crisp pearls (see instructions on page 177, step 10).

8. The finished cake is best enjoyed at room temperature on the day it is assembled but can be covered and stored in the refrigerator for up to 4 days. Remove the cake from the refrigerator and let sit at room temperature for 5 to 8 hours before serving.

> **Tip:** Use any extra lemon curd that you did not put in the cake by plating it with the cake slices. You can never have too much zesty bright lemon curd!

Maple Walnut Cinnamon Swirl Cake

Maple syrup is one of our favourite ingredients to play with at the bakery and a wonderful local sugar substitute. We love to use amber or dark maple syrup in all our baking since it has a much more intense maple flavour. Growing up, a common school trip for our bakers and us was visiting the sugar shacks. We all feel a certain nostalgic connection to that liquid gold. Walnuts and maple is a natural pairing, with a vanilla-cinnamon swirl cake that is reminiscent of fresh baked cinnamon buns. Finished with cinnamon maple candied walnuts and a fresh drizzle of maple syrup. this cake will please any maple lover.

1. Make the cinnamon swirl vanilla cake: Prepare the vanilla cake batter as instructed on page 180, steps 1 to 5.

2. In a medium bowl, whisk together the brown sugar, cinnamon, and milk to a smooth consistency. Add 2 cups of the vanilla cake batter and mix until smooth. This is your cinnamon batter.

3. Divide the vanilla batter evenly between the prepared cake pans and, using a small offset palette knife, smooth out the tops. Divide the cinnamon batter between the pans by pouring circles of cinnamon batter on the surface of the vanilla batter. Using a butter knife, swirl the 2 batters by pulling through and folding in the cinnamon batter. Do not overmix; you want the marbling to stand out. Bake for 50 to 70 minutes, or until a toothpick inserted into the centres of the cakes comes out clean. Allow the cakes to cool in the pans on a wire rack for 20 minutes. Remove the cakes from the pans, leaving the parchment paper circles on the bottoms, and cool completely on the wire rack.

4. Make the maple walnut spread: In a small bowl, combine ¾ cup of the maple candied walnuts and the maple syrup and let them sit at room temperature for 20 to 30 minutes to make a thick and chunky spread. The mixture will thicken as it sits.

5. Assemble the cake: Trim the domes off the top of the baked cinnamon swirl vanilla cake layers. Cut the cake layers in half horizontally to make 4 layers total (see instructions on page 174, step 1).

6. Stack the cake, using the simple stacking method, with the maple buttercream on an 8-inch serving plate or cake board using up to 4 tablespoons of maple simple syrup to moisten each cake layer. For the first and third filling layers, pipe a buttercream dam around the edge of the cake layers and spoon half of the maple walnut spread in the centre of each well. Using a palette knife, spread the maple walnut spread until it meets the edge of the buttercream dam, then top with ½ cup of the buttercream. The second layer requires only buttercream (see instructions on page 174, steps 2 and 3a).

7. Crumb coat the top and sides of the stacked cake with a thin layer of buttercream and place the cake, uncovered, in the refrigerator for 15 minutes (see instructions on page 175, step 4).

Makes one 6-inch round 4-layer cake, serves 8 to 12

Cinnamon Swirl Vanilla Cake

1 batch Vanilla Cake
  (page 180, steps 1 to 5)
3 tablespoons packed brown
  sugar
1 tablespoon cinnamon
1 tablespoon 2% milk, room
  temperature

Simple Syrup

1 batch Simple Syrup (page 267),
  maple variation

Maple Buttercream

1 batch Maple Buttercream
  (page 252)

Maple Candied Walnuts

1 batch Maple Candied Walnuts
  (page 266)

Maple Walnut Spread

¾ cup Maple Candied Walnuts
  (recipe above), chopped
  semi-fine
2 tablespoons grade A
  dark maple syrup

For assembly

¼ cup grade A dark maple syrup

Continued on next page

Maple Walnut Cinnamon Swirl
Cake continued

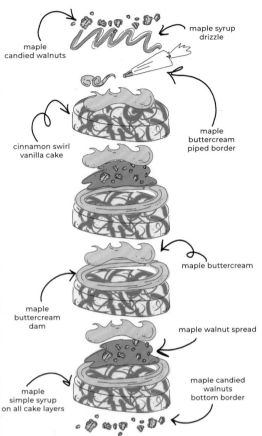

maple candied walnuts

maple syrup drizzle

cinnamon swirl vanilla cake

maple buttercream piped border

maple buttercream

maple buttercream dam

maple walnut spread

maple simple syrup on all cake layers

maple candied walnuts bottom border

8. Mask the chilled cake with buttercream using the horizontal line finish (see instructions on page 176, steps 5, 6c, and 7).

9. Using your hand, gently pat ½ cup of the maple candied walnuts into the soft buttercream around the bottom edge of the cake to create a decorative border. Place the cake, uncovered, in the refrigerator for 30 minutes (see instructions on page 176, step 8).

10. Finish the cake by piping a round reverse shell border (see Piping Styles on page 242) of buttercream around the edge of the cake top, leaving ½ inch of exposed buttercream at the outer edge. Sprinkle the piped buttercream border with the remaining ¼ cup maple candied walnuts (see instructions on page 177, step 10).

11. The finished cake is best enjoyed at room temperature on the day it is assembled but can be covered and stored in the refrigerator for up to 4 days. Remove the cake from the refrigerator and let sit at room temperature for 5 to 8 hours before serving. Before serving, using a spoon or a piping bag, drizzle the top of the cake in a zigzag pattern with the ¼ cup maple syrup.

Peach Mascarpone Cake

Makes one 6-inch round 4-layer cake, serves 8 to 12

When Josie announced her engagement, Nickey was obviously her go-to cake baker for her wedding day. Tasked with creating a unique custom flavour, Nickey cycled through her cake flavour catalogue. Nothing was jumping out until the two sat down to brainstorm together. Josie suggested a mascarpone filling, and Nickey jumped in with peaches. Vanilla cake was the obvious choice, and they settled on adding some cinnamon to Josie's grandma's canned peaches for a touch of warm spice. The wedding cake was a four-tier towering square masterpiece with a sage green flat iced buttercream finish and dark chocolate brown handcrafted damask detail pieces. We cannot recall if there was even a slice left at the end of the night, which is highly unlikely since it was a delicious marriage of flavours, but we were too busy creating memories to care.

Vanilla Cake
1 batch Vanilla Cake (page 180)

Simple Syrup
1 batch Simple Syrup (page 267)

Vanilla Bean Buttercream
1 batch Vanilla Bean Buttercream
(page 248)

Peach Compote
1 batch Peach Compote (page 259)

Mascarpone Filling
½ batch Mascarpone Filling
(page 270)

1. Trim the domes off the top of the baked vanilla cake layers. Cut the cake layers in half horizontally. Reserve one cake layer with a flat uncut side for the top of the cake (see instructions on page 174, step 1).

2. Stack the cake using the cold stacking method. Place each of the other 3 cake layers, cut side up, on an 8-inch plate or cake board and moisten them with up to 4 tablespoons of the simple syrup per layer. Spread 1 tablespoon of the vanilla bean buttercream on each cake layer to seal the cake so that the peach compote does not soak into the cake. Pipe a buttercream dam and a centre dot on each cake layer. Fill the area between each dam and dot with a thin layer (¼ cup) of the peach compote and top it with ⅓ cup of the mascarpone filling, flattening the filling to meet the centre dot and the dam walls. For this cake, all 3 filling layers are the same. Place the 3 iced cake layers in the refrigerator, uncovered, to firm up for 30 minutes Stack the chilled cake layers starting with the bottom layer, which has an uncut bottom, followed by the 2 centre layers. Top with the reserved cake layer, cut side down. Using a pastry brush, moisten the entire surface of the top cake layer with 4 tablespoons of the simple syrup (see instructions on page 174, steps 2 and 3b).

3. Crumb coat the cake with the buttercream. Place the cake in the refrigerator for 15 minutes so that the crumb coat can firm up (see instructions on page 175, step 4).

4. Mask the chilled cake with buttercream using the rustic finish (see instructions on page 176, steps 5, 6b, and 7).

5. The finished cake is best enjoyed at room temperature on the day it is assembled but can be covered and stored in the refrigerator for up to 4 days. Remove the cake from the refrigerator and let sit at room temperature for 5 to 8 hours before serving. Before serving, spoon the remaining peach compote over the top of the cake.

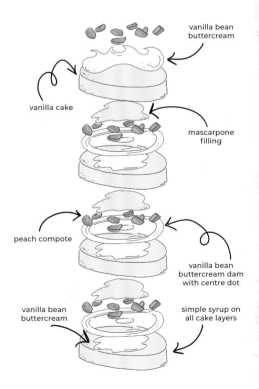

vanilla bean buttercream

vanilla cake

mascarpone filling

peach compote

vanilla bean buttercream dam with centre dot

vanilla bean buttercream

simple syrup on all cake layers

Raspberry White Chocolate Cake

Makes one 6-inch round 4-layer cake, serves 8 to 12

Raspberry. White chocolate. Vanilla cake. Swiss meringue buttercream. All of the ingredients that Nickey's husband, Alex, craves in any shape or form. This may stem from his love of our White Chocolate Raspberry Almond Bars (page 109) that we release for the winter holiday season. Our cake team took it upon themselves to create a cake to appease his request, and this creation was born. Raspberry buttercream bursting with raspberry jam, surrounding vanilla cake with two layers focused on white chocolate chunks and a third on raspberry jam. Raspberry white chocolate ganache tops this raspberry dream, and a raspberry drizzle gives it that final punch to send this cake over the edge.

1. Make the raspberry buttercream: In the bowl of a stand mixer fitted with the paddle attachment, beat the full batch of vanilla bean buttercream for 5 to 10 minutes until light and fluffy.

2. Transfer 3 cups of the vanilla bean buttercream to a medium bowl. Add the raspberry jam and, using a hand whisk, vigorously whisk until fully incorporated. Fill a 16-inch piping bag fitted with a No. 804 round tip with the raspberry buttercream.

3. Assemble the cake: Trim the domes off the top of the baked vanilla cake layers. Cut the cake layers in half horizontally. Reserve one cake layer with a flat uncut side for the top of the cake (see instructions on page 174, step 1).

4. Stack the cake using the cold stacking method. Place each of the other 3 cake layers, cut side up, on an 8-inch plate or cake board and moisten them with the raspberry simple syrup. Using a step pallete knife, spread 1 tablespoon of the raspberry buttercream on each cake layer. Pipe a raspberry buttercream dam on the bottom and one centre cake layer and fill each well with 2 tablespoons of the white chocolate and ½ cup of the raspberry buttercream. Pipe a bullseye pattern of raspberry buttercream on the remaining centre cake layer and fill the bullseye cavities with 1 cup of the raspberry jam. Place all 3 cake layers in the refrigerator, uncovered, to firm up for 30 minutes. Stack the chilled cake layers starting with the bottom layer, which has an uncut bottom, followed by the bullseye layer and then the second white chocolate and raspberry buttercream layer. Top with the reserved cake layer, cut side down. Using a pastry brush, moisten the entire surface of the top cake layer with 4 tablespoons of the raspberry simple syrup (see instructions on page 174, steps 2 and 3b).

5. Crumb coat the top and sides of the stacked cake with the vanilla bean buttercream. Place the cake in the refrigerator for 15 minutes so that the crumb coat can firm up (see instructions on page 175, step 4).

6. Mask the cake with the vanilla bean buttercream using a horizontal line finish (see instructions on page 176, steps 5, 6c, and 7).

7. Using your hand, gently pat the vanilla cake crumbs into the soft buttercream around the bottom edge of the cake to create a decorative border. Place the cake in the refrigerator for 10 minutes (see instructions on page 176, step 8).

Vanilla Cake
1 batch Vanilla Cake (page 180)

Simple Syrup
1 batch Simple Syrup (page 267), raspberry variation

Vanilla Bean Buttercream
1 batch Vanilla Bean Buttercream (page 248), reserve 3 cups for Raspberry Buttercream (see below)

Raspberry Buttercream
3 cups Vanilla Buttercream, reserved (see above)
½ cup raspberry jam

Vanilla Cake Crumbs
1 batch vanilla Cake Crumbs (page 268)

Raspberry White Chocolate Ganache
1 batch Raspberry White Chocolate Ganache (page 257)

For assembly
1¼ cups raspberry jam
3 ounces (85 g/½ cup) white chocolate callets or chopped good-quality white chocolate
2 tablespoons white chocolate crisp pearls

Continued on next page

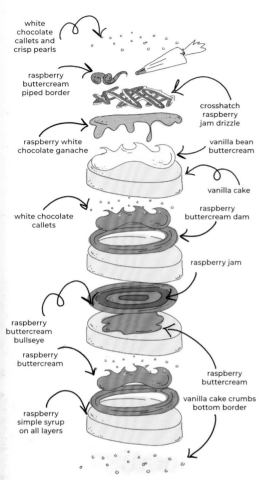

white chocolate callets and crisp pearls

raspberry buttercream piped border

crosshatch raspberry jam drizzle

raspberry white chocolate ganache

vanilla bean buttercream

vanilla cake

white chocolate callets

raspberry buttercream dam

raspberry jam

raspberry buttercream bullseye

raspberry buttercream

raspberry buttercream

raspberry simple syrup on all layers

vanilla cake crumbs bottom border

8. Reheat the raspberry white chocolate ganache to a pourable consistency in the microwave. Pour the ganache in the centre of the cake, spreading it outwards with a palette knife to the edges of the cake and allowing it to overflow onto the sides. Place the cake in the refrigerator for 10 minutes, or until the ganache is firm to the touch (see instructions on page 177, step 9).

9. Using a spoon or a piping bag, drizzle the top of the cake in a crosshatch pattern with the remaining ¼ cup raspberry jam.

10. Finish the cake by piping a round reverse shell border (see Piping Styles on page 242) of raspberry buttercream around the edge of the cake top, leaving ¼ inch of exposed ganache around the outer edge. Sprinkle the piped buttercream border with the remaining white chocolate callets and the white chocolate crisp pearls (see instructions on page 177, step 10).

11. The finished cake is best enjoyed at room temperature on the day it is assembled but can be covered and stored in the refrigerator for up to 4 days. Remove the cake from the refrigerator and let sit at room temperature for 5 to 8 hours before serving.

Tip: For a less sweet alternative, use our Raspberry Compote (page 259) in place of the raspberry jam to fill the cake layers.

Tarts and Pies

Maple Syrup Butter Tarts

Makes twelve 3-inch butter tarts

As good Canadians, we are serious about butter tarts. We have travelled from coast to coast to try butter tarts from all over the country, and a few things are clear. Maple syrup makes the best butter tarts, butter pastry is key whether it is a short crust or traditional pastry, and no one can agree on raisins or walnuts. We get into debates with customers all the time over walnuts versus raisins. Do you prefer the traditional sweet softness of raisins or the more modern nutty crunch of walnuts? Our very first front-of-house employee and one of Josie's best friends, Amanda, advocates for pecans. She will tell you our butter tarts are almost as good as the ones her Scottish paternal grandmother made with unimaginably flaky pastry and chopped pecans. It is hard to compete with grandmas in the baking arena, but we think this recipe will help you try.

Butter Pastry

1½ batches Butter Pastry
(page 262)

Butter Tart Filling

1 cup packed dark brown sugar

2 teaspoons cornstarch

¼ cup unsalted butter, melted and
room temperature

3 large eggs, room temperature

1 cup pure maple syrup

1 teaspoon pure vanilla extract

½ teaspoon salt

¾ cup chopped toasted walnuts or
pecans, raisins, chocolate chips,
or coconut

1. Preheat the oven to 400°F. Generously grease a 12-cup muffin pan with canola oil cooking spray.

2. Prepare the tart shells: Roll out the butter pastry dough to about ⅛-inch thickness. Cut out twelve 5-inch circles of dough. Press the dough circles into the muffin cups, forming walls that extend about ¾ inch above the rims of the muffin cups. Place the muffin pan in the refrigerator while you make the filling to allow the pastry to relax and firm up a bit.

3. Make the filling: In a medium bowl, whisk together the brown sugar and cornstarch. Whisk in the melted butter. Add the eggs and continue whisking until the mixture is smooth and there is no oily film left around the edges.

4. Whisk in the maple syrup, vanilla, and salt until fully incorporated.

5. Remove the muffin pan from the refrigerator and add 1 tablespoon of the addition of your choice to each tart shell. Pour the maple syrup filling over top, filling each tart shell level with the pan, leaving about ¾-inch headspace of pastry for the filling to bubble up as it cooks. Bake for 35 to 40 minutes, or until the filling has puffed up above the tart and the pastry is deep golden brown. The filling will settle as it cools. Using a small offset palette knife, remove the tarts from the pan immediately, so they do not stick to the pan as they cool. Allow to cool before serving, as the sugar filling is very hot. Store in an airtight container at room temperature for up to 4 days.

Pineapple Sour Cherry Tarts

Makes twelve 3-inch tarts

Butter Pastry

2 batches Butter Pastry
  (page 262)

Fruit Filling

3 cups fresh pineapple, peeled,
  cored, and cut into ½-inch cubes
1 cup frozen or fresh pitted sour
  cherries
⅓ cup packed brown sugar
¼ cup cornstarch
1 teaspoon pure vanilla extract
½ teaspoon salt

Egg Wash

1 egg
1 tablespoon water, room
  temperature

The combination of fresh pineapple and sour cherries was one of necessity at first. A case of accidental abundance that led to a delicious discovery! Make sure to use nice ripe pineapple; do not try to substitute canned pineapple or it just will not be the same. We usually use frozen sour cherries, but fresh cherries would be delicious too. We love the way ideas like this evolve in the bakery kitchen. Someone announces an idea, and we spend the whole shift throwing improvements back and forth across the kitchen. Then someone creates a couple of different versions for us all to try and the delicious creative cycle continues, with everyone tasting and weighing in with feedback. Finally, we settle on the most delicious version—and this tart was born.

1. Preheat the oven to 400°F. Generously grease a 12-cup muffin pan with canola oil cooking spray. Line a baking sheet with parchment paper.

2. Prepare the tart shells: On a lightly floured work surface, roll out the butter pastry dough to about ⅛-inch thickness. Cut out twelve 5-inch circles of dough. Press the dough circles into the muffin cups. Using a sharp paring knife, cut 12 pineapple-shaped pieces (stars or circles are cute, too) from the pieces of rolled-out dough left around your circle cut-outs. Use the paring knife to add texture to the decorative pieces. Transfer the pieces to the prepared baking sheet, then place the muffin pan and baking sheet in the refrigerator for 10 to 15 minutes to allow the pastry to relax and firm up a bit.

3. Make the fruit filling: In a large bowl, using a spatula, mix together the pineapple, cherries, brown sugar, cornstarch, vanilla, and salt until no dry cornstarch or sugar remains.

4. Using a large spoon, pack the fruit filling into the tart shells. Arrange the fruit to fill all corners of the tart; the fruit will decrease in volume as it cooks, and you do not want to end up with a half-filled tart. Top the tarts with the decorative pieces.

5. Make the egg wash: In a small bowl, whisk together the egg and water. Using a pastry brush, brush the tops of the tart crusts and decorative pieces with the egg wash.

6. Place the muffin pan on a baking sheet to catch any filling that bubbles over. Bake for 15 minutes at 400°F. Reduce the oven temperature to 350°F and bake for another 20 to 30 minutes, or until the fruit juice has bubbled up and the crust is golden brown. To double-check doneness, insert a knife into the centre of a tart. If the liquid on the knife is clear, the tarts are done. Store in an airtight container at room temperature for up to 6 days.

> **Tip:** To make these tarts vegan, use Vegan Pastry (page 263) in lieu of the Butter Pastry and omit the egg wash. The fruit filling is already vegan.

Tip: To make pumpkin cut-out decorations, use the already rolled-out dough left over after cutting out your circles. If needed, you can reroll the dough, but every time you do so it will get less flaky. Using a knife or small pumpkin cookie cutter, cut out 12 dough pieces. Place them on a baking sheet lined with parchment paper, then place the baking sheet in the refrigerator for 15 to 20 minutes so that the dough does not shrink during baking. Brush the decorative pieces with egg wash and bake with the tart shells at 400°F for 15 to 20 minutes until golden brown and flaky.

Classic Pumpkin Tarts

Makes 12 tarts

When we first dreamed of owning a bakery, we imagined maybe making a couple of dozen pumpkin pies for Thanksgiving weekend. We spent weeks testing and tasting to get just the right balance of spicy and sweet to play off the butter pastry. The bourbon is optional, but we think it adds the perfect nutty note to these tarts. The pumpkin filling is on the sweet side, so feel free to reduce the brown sugar to ½ cup for a more pumpkin-forward variation. By our ninth Thanksgiving, we were pumping out hundreds of pumpkin pies over the holiday weekend, all with hand-rolled shells and small batches of filling. On one particularly memorable Thanksgiving weekend, three of our four ovens broke down at the last minute. We were devastated. People were depending on us! Thanks to the very generous offer of a neighbouring business, we were able to load a couple hundred pies onto rolling racks and wheel them up the street at 2 a.m. to bake them. We will never forget carefully pushing rolling racks filled with pies uphill on an empty city street in the middle of the night, laughing at how absurd it was the whole time.

1. Preheat the oven to 400°F. Generously grease a 12-cup muffin pan with canola oil cooking spray.

2. Prepare the tart shells: On a lightly floured work surface, roll out the butter pastry dough to about ⅛-inch thickness. Cut out twelve 5-inch circles of dough. Press the dough circles into the muffin cups. (Use the rolled pastry from around the circles if making pumpkin cut-out decorations; see Tip.) Place the muffin pan in the refrigerator for 15 to 20 minutes to allow the pastry to relax and firm up a bit.

3. Blind-bake the tart shells: Line each shell with a parchment paper square and fill with ½ cup dried beans. Bake for 20 to 25 minutes, or until the edges of the shells are golden brown. Remove the parchment paper and beans. Allow the pie shell to cool completely on a wire rack.

4. Make the filling: Reduce the oven temperature to 325°F. In a large bowl, whisk together the pumpkin purée, brown sugar, eggs, pumpkin spice, and salt until the brown sugar is dissolved and the spice is evenly distributed. Add the cream, bourbon (if using), and vanilla and continue whisking until smooth.

5. Pour the filling into the tart shells and bake for 30 to 35 minutes, or until the filling jiggles in the centre just slightly when the muffin pan is shaken.

6. If desired, let the tarts cool and top them with whipped cream. Fill a 12-inch piping bag fitted with a No. 824 star tip with the whipped cream and pipe a medium rosette in the centre of each tart (see Piping Styles on page 242). Top each rosette with a baked pumpkin cut-out, if using (see Tip).

7. These tarts are best enjoyed on the day of baking. Store in an airtight container at room temperature for 1 day or in the refrigerator for up to 4 days.

Butter Pastry

2 batches Butter Pastry
   (page 262)

Filling

1 can (14 ounces/398 mL) pure
   pumpkin purée
¾ cup packed brown sugar
2 large eggs, room temperature
1 tablespoon Pumpkin Spice
   (page 267)
¼ teaspoon salt
¾ cup whipping (35%) cream
1 tablespoon bourbon (optional)
1 teaspoon pure vanilla extract

Whipped Cream (optional)

1 batch Whipped Cream
   (page 275)

Lemon Meringue Pie

Makes one 9-inch pie,
serves 6 to 8

Spying that lemon meringue pie in a glass dome on the counter at a Tim Hortons back in the late 1980s always had little Nickey smacking her lips. She never did get a slice at the coffee shop, but after much begging, grocery-store meringue pies made their way to her kitchen table. Something always felt like it was missing, though. Either the lemon filling was too gummy or chemical tasting or the meringue tasted like lumpy packing foam or was just overly sweet. When her passion for baking from scratch was ignited, only then did Nickey truly experience a real lemon meringue pie—nothing can beat homemade. We have worked hard to find just the right balance of zest, juice, and sweetness in this version, and we hope this pie brings you much joy. In the bakery we strain out the zest at the last minute before filling the pie shell, but at home Josie leaves it in; it is really a personal preference.

1. Preheat the oven to 400°F.

2. Prepare the crust: On a lightly floured work surface, roll out the butter pastry dough into an 11- to 12-inch circle about ⅛ inch thick (depending on the depth of the pie plate). Fold the dough in half to lift it without stretching and gently unfold it in a 9-inch pie plate. Gently press the dough into the sides and bottom of the plate, making sure not to stretch the dough. Trim the dough as needed and crimp the edges of the pastry. Place the pie plate in the refrigerator to allow the pastry to relax and firm up a bit, at least 15 minutes.

3. Blind-bake the crust: Line the shell with parchment paper and fill it with about 3 cups of dried beans or pie weights. Bake for 20 to 25 minutes, or until the crust is a deep golden brown. Remove the parchment paper and beans or pie weights. Allow the pie shell to cool completely on a wire rack.

4. Make the lemon filling: In a large pot over high heat, bring 1⅓ cups of the water, sugar, and butter to a rolling boil. Boil for 1 full minute, then remove from the heat.

5. In a large bowl, stir together the remaining ½ cup water, cornstarch, and egg yolks until the cornstarch is fully dissolved. Add the hot water mixture, ¼ cup at a time, to the bowl, stirring constantly. Stir in the lemon zest and ⅔ cup lemon juice. Pour the mixture back into the pot and return it to a boil, stirring constantly, over medium-high heat. Reduce the heat to medium-low to maintain a low boil, stirring constantly and scraping the bottom of the pot well, for 4 to 5 minutes, or until the mixture has thickened and the cornstarch has cooked clear.

6. If you do not want zest in the pie filling, strain the filling through a fine-mesh sieve into the prebaked pie crust. Otherwise, simply pour the filling into the prebaked crust. Place in the fridge for 2 to 3 hours until completely cool. Any leftover filling makes a delicious pudding.

7. When the pie is cool, prepare the meringue and evenly spread it over the top of the pie. If desired, you can add swirls of meringue using a palette knife, toothpick, or spoon. Using a mini kitchen torch, toast the top of the meringue to finish. Store, covered, at room temperature for 1 day or in the refrigerator for up to 4 days.

Butter Pastry

1 batch Butter Pastry (page 262)

Lemon Filling

1⅓ cups + ½ cup water, room
   temperature, divided
1½ cups granulated sugar
2 tablespoons unsalted butter
½ cup cornstarch
5 egg yolks, room temperature
Zest and juice of 5 lemons (you
   will need ⅔ cup juice)

Meringue

3 batches Meringue (page 265)

Fruit Crumble Pie

Makes one 9-inch pie,
serves 6 to 8

We do not add very much sugar to our fruit pies at the bakery. In our opinion, the sweetness of the crumble should contrast with the natural tartness of the fruit. Even with quite sour fruits like rhubarb, we prefer to balance things out with a sweeter fruit like apple or strawberry in lieu of more sugar. Almost any kind of fruit will work in this recipe, just prepare it as needed by peeling, coring, and/or cubing. For larger fruits like apple, rhubarb, peach, or pear, we usually cut them into ½-inch cubes. For berries, just remove the stems and keep them whole, unless they are very large and you prefer to cut them in half. It is also nice to swap out the brown sugar in the fruit filling with an alternative like honey or maple syrup for a more complex flavour. We use the same all-butter pastry in all our pies, and we hand-roll every single shell at the bakery. Nickey's sister Erin, our talented kitchen manager, has developed impressive arm muscles and is unmatched in her rolling technique and speed. Every holiday, she oversees the rolling of hundreds of hand-rolled pie shells and keeps everyone's spirits up with her positivity when our bodies start to complain.

Butter Pastry
1 batch Butter Pastry (page 262)

Fruit Filling
1¾ pounds (790 g) peeled and
    chopped fruit or whole berries
    (4 heaping cups)
¼ cup cornstarch
¼ cup packed brown sugar
1 teaspoon cinnamon
1 teaspoon pure vanilla extract
¼ teaspoon salt

Brown Sugar Oat Crumble
1 batch Brown Sugar Oat
    Crumble (page 260)

1. Preheat the oven to 400°F.

2. Prepare the crust: On a lightly floured work surface, roll out the butter pastry dough into an 11- to 12-inch circle about ⅛ inch thick (depending on the depth of the pie plate). Fold the dough in half to lift it without stretching and gently unfold it in a 9-inch pie plate. Gently press the dough into the sides and bottom of the plate, making sure not to stretch the dough. Trim the dough as needed and crimp the edges of the pastry. Place the pie plate in the refrigerator to allow the pastry to relax and firm up a bit, at least 15 minutes.

3. Make the fruit filling: In a large bowl, mix together the fruit, cornstarch, brown sugar, cinnamon, vanilla, and salt until no dry cornstarch or sugar remains. Taste to make sure you are happy with the sweetness and flavour. Generally, fruit will get a little sweeter when cooked. Adjust the salt, sugar, vanilla, or cinnamon to your taste, if desired.

4. Spoon the fruit filling into the prepared crust. Sprinkle evenly with the brown sugar oat crumble. You do not want to be able to see any fruit, just crumble. Place the pie on a baking sheet and bake for 15 minutes at 400°F. Reduce the oven temperature to 350°F and bake for another 45 to 60 minutes, or until the fruit juice bubbles up and the crust is golden brown. To double-check doneness, insert a knife into the centre of the pie. If the liquid on the knife is clear, this means the cornstarch is properly cooked and the pie is done. Allow the pie to cool slightly and serve warm. Store, covered, at room temperature for up to 3 days or in the refrigerator for up to 7 days.

> **Tip:** To make a vegan version of this pie, use Vegan Pastry (page 263) instead of the Butter Pastry and Vegan Shortbread Crumble (page 261) instead of the Brown Sugar Oat Crumble. The fruit filling is already vegan.

Coconut Cream Pie

Makes one 9-inch pie,
serves 6 to 8

Butter Pastry

1 batch Butter Pastry (page 262)

Coconut Filling

3⅔ cups full-fat canned
    coconut milk
1 cup granulated sugar
1 cup unsweetened
    shredded coconut
1⅓ cups whole milk,
    room temperature
4 eggs, room temperature
⅔ cup cornstarch
1 tablespoon pure vanilla extract
½ teaspoon salt

Whipped Cream

2 batches Whipped Cream
    (page 275)

For assembly

¼ cup sweetened flaked coconut,
    toasted

The first complicated recipe Nickey ever attempted, as a kid in her mother's kitchen, was a coconut cream pie. She managed to make a lumpy, somewhat burnt homemade coconut custard filling and a passable, if slightly burnt shortening crust. Although it might not seem like a success, that pie sparked a passion and started a deeper understanding of the baking method for Nickey, and she learned not to ignore the essential instruction to stir the custard constantly as it cooks! Coconut cream is still her favourite pie. This version features coconut on coconut, with a rich coconut milk and shredded coconut filling finished with fluffy whipped cream and even more toasted coconut, all nestled in flaky butter pastry. Any filling that does not fit in your crust makes an excellent snack for the baker—try it mixed with some semi-sweet chocolate chips and chopped almonds for an Almond Joy flavour.

1. Preheat the oven to 400°F.

2. Prepare the crust: On a lightly floured work surface, roll out the butter pastry dough into an 11- to 12-inch circle about ⅛ inch thick (depending on the depth of the pie plate). Fold the dough in half to lift it without stretching and gently unfold it in a 9-inch pie plate. Gently press the dough into the sides and bottom of the plate, making sure not to stretch the dough. Trim the dough as needed and crimp the edges of the pastry. Place the pie plate in the refrigerator to allow the pastry to relax and firm up a bit, at least 15 minutes.

3. Blind-bake the crust. Line the pie shell with parchment paper and fill it with about 3 cups of dried beans or fill it with pie weights. Bake for 20 to 25 minutes, or until the crust is a deep golden brown. Remove the parchment paper and beans or pie weights. Allow the pie shell to cool completely on a wire rack.

4. Make the coconut filling: In a large pot over high heat, bring the coconut milk, sugar, and shredded coconut to a rolling boil, stirring frequently with a whisk. Boil for 1 full minute, then remove from the heat.

5. In a large bowl, combine the whole milk, eggs, cornstarch, vanilla, and salt and whisk until the cornstarch is fully dissolved. Temper the egg mixture by adding the hot coconut mixture, ¼ cup at a time, stirring constantly. Pour the mixture back into the pot and return it to a boil over medium-high heat, whisking constantly. Reduce the heat to medium and keep on a low boil, stirring constantly for 2 to 3 minutes, or until the mixture has thickened.

6. Pour the filling into the prebaked pie crust. Place in the refrigerator for 2 to 3 hours until completely cool. Any leftover filling makes a delicious pudding.

7. Spoon the whipped cream over the top of the pie for a rustic finish or fill a 16-inch piping bag fitted with a No. 825 star tip and finish the pie by piping lines of star swirl border across the pie to cover the whole surface (see Piping Styles on page 242). Sprinkle with the cooled toasted coconut. This pie is best enjoyed on the day of baking. Store, covered, at room temperature for 1 day or in the refrigerator for up to 6 days.

Lime Cream Pie

Makes one 9-inch pie, serves 6 to 8

The perfect marriage of bright, tart lime and creamy-smooth sweetness, this pie is love at first bite. You are going to adore the silky texture of this pie, which is similar to that of cheesecake but without the heaviness of cream cheese. It is also a beautiful pie, easy to dress up for a party or celebration. It has a lovely subtle green tone that really shines with some freshly zested lime peel as a garnish. We also make a meringue-topped version and a bar version of this pie at the bakery, so feel free to play with your own variations. This pie recipe is as easy as it comes. No fussy pastry. Just zest, mix, pour, and bake!

1. Preheat the oven to 350°F.

2. Prepare the graham crumb crust: Firmly and evenly press the graham crumb mixture into the bottom and all the way up the sides of a 9-inch pie plate to form a pie crust. Bake for 10 to 15 minutes until light golden brown.

3. Make the lime filling: In the bowl of a stand mixer fitted with the whisk attachment, whisk together the egg yolks and lime zest on high speed for 4 to 5 minutes until pale in colour. Add the condensed milk and continue to whisk on high speed for 4 to 5 minutes until the mixture has thickened. Slowly whisk in the lime juice until the mixture is smooth and homogeneous.

4. Pour the filling into the prebaked pie shell and bake for 15 to 20 minutes, just until the top looks dry and the filling looks almost set, with a slight jiggle. Let the pie cool to room temperature, then refrigerate for at least 1 hour before topping it with whipped cream.

5. Spoon the whipped cream around the outer edge of the pie. Alternatively, fill a piping bag fitted with a No. 804 star tip with the whipped cream and pipe a border (we use a rosette border; see Piping Styles on page 242).

6. Make the sugared lime zest: In a small bowl, combine the sugar and lime zest. Rub the sugar and zest together with your fingers and sprinkle over the whipped cream border for a little sparkle. This pie is best enjoyed on the day of baking. Store, covered, at room temperature for 1 day or in the refrigerator for up to 6 days.

Graham Crumb Crust
1 batch Graham Crumb Base
 (page 264)

Lime Filling
5 large egg yolks,
 room temperature
Zest of 6 limes
1¾ cups sweetened
 condensed milk
1 cup lime juice

Whipped Cream
1 batch Whipped Cream
 (page 275)

Sugared Lime Zest
2 tablespoons granulated sugar
Zest of ½ lime

Butterscotch Skor Pie

Makes one 9-inch pie,
serves 8 to 12

Chocolate Graham Crumb Crust

1 batch Chocolate Graham
   Cracker Base (page 264)

Butterscotch Filling

1½ cups packed dark brown sugar
1 can (12 ounces/354 mL)
   evaporated milk, chilled
   overnight in the fridge
¼ teaspoon salt

Ganache

⅔ cup whipping (35%) cream
8 ounces (225 g/1⅓ cups)
   semi-sweet chocolate callets or
   chopped semi-sweet chocolate

For assembly

¾ cup crushed Skor chocolate bars
   or Skor Chipits

If you have a sweet tooth, then this luscious and decadent chocolate beauty is for you. Make sure to use a dark chocolate you love for the ganache; it will make all the difference. This recipe seems so simple at first, but the key is to watch the mixture as you whisk it. It will get voluminous and thick as it whips—until it starts to fall. Do not walk away while it is mixing or you will miss the moment it stops gaining volume and starts to collapse. Chilling the evaporated milk overnight before making the pie is also key. We learned that the hard way after a couple of failed attempts.

1. Preheat the oven to 375°F.

2. Prepare the chocolate graham crumb crust: Firmly and evenly press the graham crumb mixture into the bottom and all the way up the sides of a 9-inch pie plate to form a pie crust. Bake for 10 minutes, or until the crust has puffed up slightly and appears dry.

3. Make the butterscotch filling: In the bowl of a stand mixer fitted with the whisk attachment, whip the brown sugar, chilled evaporated milk, and salt on high speed for 10 to 15 minutes until light and airy. Watch the mixture carefully and stop whipping when it stops increasing in volume. If you whip for too long, the mixture will fall.

4. Pour the mixture into the prebaked pie shell and bake for 10 to 15 minutes, or until the filling looks semi-firm and dry on top but still has quite a jiggle if you shake the pie plate gently. The filling will firm up as it cools. Let the pie cool to room temperature, then refrigerate for at least 2 hours before topping with the ganache and crushed Skor chocolate bars. You want the butterscotch layer to be firm.

5. Make the ganache: In a medium heat-resistant bowl, melt the chocolate and cream in the microwave in 30-second intervals, vigorously stirring after each interval, until smooth and the chocolate is melted. Stir the ganache until silky smooth. Spoon 3 tablespoons of the ganache into a small bowl and set aside. Pour the remaining ganache over the baked pie, spreading the ganache with a pallete knife, if needed, to cover the entire surface of the pie.

6. Sprinkle the crushed Skor chocolate bars over the wet ganache forming a 3-inch border of crushed chocolate bars around the edge of the pie.

7. Using a fork or a small parchment cone, drizzle the reserved ganache over the crushed Skor chocolate bars for a decorative touch. Place the pie in the refrigerator for 20 to 30 minutes to set the ganache. Store, covered, at room temperature for 1 day or in the refrigerator for up to 6 days.

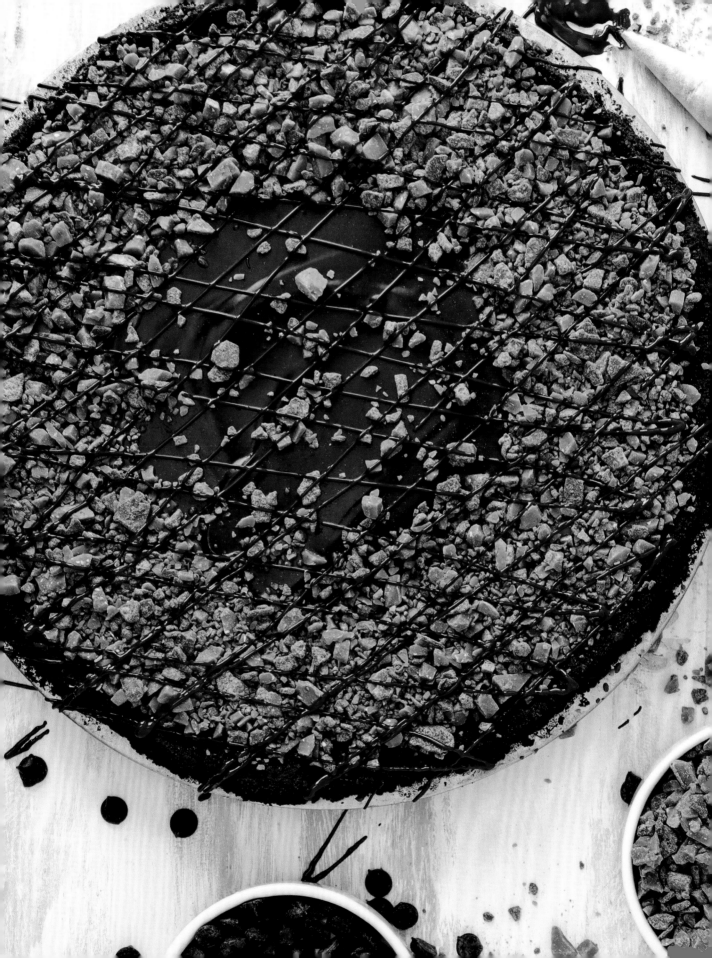

Peach Shortbread Crumble

Makes one 9-inch round crumble, serves 6 to 8

Crumbles are a great way to get that buttery, fruity pie goodness with very little effort, because they have no crust. We have used our vegan crumble here, but you could easily swap it out for the Brown Sugar Oat Crumble (page 260) or Mum's Shortbread Crumble (page 261). The fruit filling remains the same whether you are keeping this crumble vegan or not. Baking crumble has to be one of the best smells in the world, and pulling this jewel-toned beauty out of the oven is sure to impress any lucky eater. We love serving crumbles in a glass dish so you can see the beautiful fruit through the sides of the dish.

1. Preheat the oven to 375°F.

2. Make the fruit filling: In a large bowl, mix together the peaches, cornstarch, brown sugar, cinnamon, vanilla, and salt until no dry cornstarch or sugar remains. Taste to check the sweetness and flavour. Generally, fruit will get a little sweeter when cooked. Adjust the salt, sugar, vanilla, or cinnamon to your taste, if desired.

3. Spoon the fruit filling into a 9-inch round pie plate and sprinkle evenly with the vegan shortbread crumble. You do not want to be able to see any fruit, just crumble. Place the pie plate on a baking sheet to catch any filling that bubbles over. Bake for 45 to 60 minutes, or until the fruit juice bubbles up and the crumble is golden brown. To double-check doneness, insert a knife into the centre of the crumble. If the liquid on the knife is clear, this means the cornstarch is properly cooked and the crumble is done. Allow the crumble to cool slightly and serve warm. Store, covered, at room temperature for up to 3 days or in the refrigerator for up to 7 days.

> **Tip:** Almost any kind of fruit will work in this crumble, just prepare it as needed by peeling, coring, and/or cubing. For larger fruits like apple, rhubarb, or pear, we usually cut them into 1-inch cubes. For berries, just remove the stems and keep them whole, unless they are very large and you prefer to cut them in half.

Fruit Filling

1¾ pounds (790 g) peeled and sliced peaches (5 cups)

¼ cup cornstarch

¼ cup packed brown sugar

1 teaspoon cinnamon

1 teaspoon pure vanilla extract

½ teaspoon salt

Vegan Shortbread Crumble

1 batch Vegan Shortbread Crumble (page 261)

Cookie Monster Pie

Cookie Crumb Crust

1½ batches Chocolate Chunk
   Cookies (page 65), portioned
   with a ½-ounce scoop and
   baked for 9 to 11 minutes, or
   two ⅔-pound (300 g) bags
   store-bought chocolate chip
   cookies, divided
¼ cup unsalted butter, melted
   and cooled

Chocolate Filling

1 cup whipping (35%) cream
½ cup whole milk
10 ounces (285 g) semi-sweet
   chocolate callets or chopped
   solid chocolate
2 large eggs, room temperature
2 tablespoons granulated sugar
¼ teaspoon salt

Whipped Cream

1 batch Whipped Cream
   (page 275)

For assembly

¼ cup dark chocolate curls

So many of our recipes were invented to make the best of mistakes. This nod to everyone's favourite blue monster is one of our finest. We all have our little blunders, and we are not immune. We hate to see food go to waste, so we always try to find a delicious solution, if possible. Once, we overbaked a batch of chocolate chip cookies and a genius employee suggested we make pie bases out of the rock-hard cookies. We have made this pie ever since with properly baked cookies too, but if you are baking the cookies just for this recipe, you might want to bake them for an extra two or three minutes to dry them out a touch. Do not be afraid to make a little extra of the chocolate filling, as it makes an amazing pudding snack.

1. Set aside 14 chocolate chunk cookies for garnish.

2. Preheat the oven to 375°F.

3. Make the cookie crumb crust: In a food processor, pulse the remaining chocolate chunk cookies into coarse crumbs, being careful not to overmix and melt the chocolate. You need 4 cups of crumbs.

4. In a medium bowl, mix together the cookie crumbs and melted butter until well mixed. Firmly and evenly press the crumb mixture into the bottom and sides of a 9-inch pie plate to form a pie crust. Bake for 10 to 15 minutes until the edges are golden brown. Allow the crust to cool completely on a wire rack.

5. Make the chocolate filling: In a large pot, bring the cream and milk to a simmer over medium heat, stirring frequently. When you see steam dancing across the top of the dairy, remove the pot from the heat and stir in the chocolate until melted.

6. Whisk in the eggs, sugar, and salt until the mixture is smooth. Return the pot to the stove over low heat and cook, stirring constantly, for 7 to 8 minutes, or until the filling has thickened slightly to a thin pudding texture.

7. Pour the filling into the prebaked pie crust. Place in the refrigerator for 2 to 3 hours until completely cool. Any leftover filling makes a delicious pudding.

8. Using a 16-inch piping bag fitted with a No. 824 star tip, pipe the whipped cream in 2 concentric circles of star swirl border (see Piping Styles on page 242), or spoon the cream around the outer edge of the pie. Place 12 of the reserved chocolate chunk cookies in the whipped cream border, evenly spaced. Crush the remaining 2 cookies with your hand and sprinkle the crumbs over the whipped cream border. Sprinkle the dark chocolate curls over the cookies and whipped cream. Store, covered, at room temperature for 1 day or in the refrigerator for up to 6 days.

Cinnamon Toffee Pie

Makes one 9-inch pie,
serves 6 to 8

One of our favourite days of the year is Pie Pop-up Day! We have been hosting an annual celebration of pie on the Sunday of Thanksgiving weekend for several years. We make all the pies on our Thanksgiving menu, plus four to six secret pie flavours that we do not announce until that week. We also make the cutest mini versions of all the pies so that folks can mix and match and have pie parties with their friends and family. It is an exciting day for the bakery because we get to flex our creativity and it concludes a long week of overnight baking and hundreds of handmade pies before some well-deserved rest and relaxation. We are all exhausted, but we are also incredibly excited to share our pie love with our customers. This silky and perfectly sweet pie was first served as a surprise pie at a pop-up. It is much like a giant crème brûlée but with a maple syrup sweetness and just the right amount of spicy cinnamon to cut through the sweet. The cinnamon sugar is sprinkled over the pie as soon as it comes out of the oven so that it melts to create a crust. If your timing is not quite right and the sugar does not melt, you can always hit it with a small kitchen torch to caramelize the loose sugar.

1. Preheat the oven to 400°F.

2. Prepare the crust: On a lightly floured work surface, roll out the butter pastry dough into an 11- to 12-inch circle about ⅛ inch thick (depending on the depth of the pie plate). Fold the dough in half to lift it without stretching and gently unfold it in a 9-inch pie plate. Gently press the dough into the sides and bottom of the plate, making sure not to stretch the dough. Trim the dough as needed and crimp the edges of the pastry. Place the pie plate in the refrigerator to relax and firm up a bit, at least 15 minutes.

3. Make the cinnamon toffee filling: In a large bowl, whisk together the sugar, butter, vanilla bean paste, cinnamon, and salt until smooth. Add the corn syrup and maple syrup and whisk until smooth. Add the eggs and cream and continue whisking until smooth. Stir in the vinegar and whisk again until smooth.

4. Pour the mixture through a fine-mesh sieve into the pie shell and bake for 45 to 50 minutes, or until the top has bubbled and puffed up and the crust is golden brown. The filling will settle back down as it cools.

5. Make the cinnamon sugar: In a small bowl, combine the sugar and cinnamon.

6. As soon as the pie is removed from the oven, sprinkle the cinnamon sugar overtop. Allow the pie to cool completely before serving, 2 to 3 hours. Store, covered, at room temperature for 1 day or in the refrigerator for up to 6 days.

Butter Pastry
1 batch Butter Pastry (page 262)

Cinnamon Toffee Filling
¾ cup granulated sugar
½ cup unsalted butter, melted and cooled
1 teaspoon vanilla bean paste (or 2 teaspoons pure vanilla extract)
¾ teaspoon cinnamon
½ teaspoon salt
⅔ cup white corn syrup
⅓ cup pure maple syrup
4 large eggs, room temperature
½ cup whipping (35%) cream
2 teaspoons white vinegar

Cinnamon Sugar
2 tablespoons granulated sugar
½ teaspoon cinnamon

Banana Chocolate Cream Pie

Makes one 9-inch pie,
serves 6 to 8

This was one of the first pies developed at the bakery. It will forever remind us of one of our first bakers, Trish, the Queen of Pies. Trish introduced us to Pi Day, now celebrated annually at the bakery on March 14. Not content to stick with a simple banana cream pie, she added a luscious dark chocolate layer—we think it makes all the difference and helps keep your pastry from getting soggy. Ideally, you want nice firm bananas to cut up for the base but very ripe bananas for the pudding. Since that can be hard to arrange, frozen bananas work just fine for the pudding! If the idea of banana pudding has you turning up your nose, think again. Josie had to be convinced too, but now this is one of her favourite pies.

1. Preheat the oven to 400°F.

2. Prepare the crust: On a lightly floured work surface, roll out the butter pastry dough into an 11- to 12-inch circle about ⅛ inch thick (depending on the depth of the pie plate). Fold the dough in half to lift it without stretching and gently unfold it in a 9-inch pie plate. Gently press the dough into the sides and bottom of the plate, making sure not to stretch the dough. Trim the dough as needed and crimp the edges of the pastry. Place the pie plate in the refrigerator to relax and firm up a bit, at least 15 minutes.

3. Blind-bake the crust. Line the shell with parchment paper and fill it with about 3 cups of dried beans or fill it with pie weights. Bake for 20 to 25 minutes, or until the crust is a deep golden brown. Remove the parchment paper beans or pie weights. Allow the pie shell to cool completely on a wire rack.

4. Make the chocolate ganache: In a medium heat-resistant bowl, heat the chocolate and cream in the microwave in 30-second intervals, stirring vigorously after each interval, until the ganache is smooth and the chocolate is melted. Stir the ganache until silky smooth. Pour it into the base of the baked pie shell. Slice the 2 just-ripe firm bananas into ½-inch slices and line the bottom of the entire pie, pushing the slices into the ganache. Place the pie in the fridge, uncovered, for 15 to 20 minutes so that the ganache can firm up a little before the hot pudding goes on top.

5. Make the banana pudding: Place the 2 very ripe bananas, milk, and sugar in a 4-cup liquid measuring cup. Pureé with an immersion blender. (Alternatively, you can use a blender.) Transfer the mixture to a large pot and bring to a simmer over high heat, stirring frequently. Simmer for 1 full minute, then remove from the heat.

6. In a large bowl, mix the egg yolks, cornstarch, vanilla, and salt until the cornstarch is fully dissolved. Add the hot banana mixture, ¼ cup at a time, stirring constantly. Pour the filling back into the pot and bring to a boil over medium-high heat, stirring constantly. Reduce the heat to medium and boil, stirring frequently, for 4 to 5 minutes, or until the mixture has thickened.

Butter Pastry

1 batch Butter Pastry (page 262)

Chocolate Ganache

6 ounces (170 g/¾ cups)
    semi-sweet chocolate callets or
    chopped chocolate
⅓ cup whipping (35%) cream

Banana Pudding

2 just-ripe firm bananas + 2 very
    ripe bananas, divided
1½ cups whole milk
½ cup granulated sugar
4 large egg yolks, room
    temperature
¼ cup cornstarch
1 teaspoon pure vanilla extract
¼ teaspoon salt
¼ cup unsalted butter, room
    temperature

Whipped Cream

2 batches Whipped Cream
    (page 275)

For assembly

2 tablespoons dark chocolate
    curls
1 Skor chocolate bar, crushed

Continued on next page

*Banana Chocolate Cream Pie
continued*

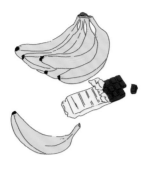

7. Remove the banana pudding from the heat. Stir in the butter until the mixture is smooth. Pour the pudding into the prebaked pie crust on top of the bananas and ganache. Place the pie in the fridge, uncovered, for 1 to 2 hours until completely cool. Any leftover filling makes a delicious pudding.

8. Spread the whipped cream over the pie. Alternatively, fill a 16-inch piping bag fitted with a No. 824 star tip with the whipped cream and pipe it in lines of star swirl border on top of the pie (see Piping Styles on page 242). Sprinkle with the chocolate curls and the crushed Skor chocolate bar. Store, covered, at room temperature for 1 day or in the refrigerator for up to 6 days.

Boston Cream Pie

Makes one 9-inch pie,
serves 6 to 8

Our Thanksgiving pie season highlights our pastry crew, celebrating all of their well-honed skills and tireless work to produce an insane amount of pies every season. With our annual Sunday Pie Pop-up Day, we bake our signature Thanksgiving lineup but also include some "top-secret, not-so-secret surprise" pies. These are creations we encourage our staff to develop, chasing their cravings and allowing their creativity to flow. This cake masquerading as a pie was so well received when it made its first appearance at our second Pie Pop-up Day, we actually featured it for a few years. It has a vanilla cake base, vanilla custard centre sandwiched with more cake, and a healthy amount of dark chocolate ganache decorated with whipped cream. We are sure that this recipe will give those cake, and Boston cream doughnut, lovers a great option at pie time.

1. Prepare the pastry cream and simple syrup in advance and store, covered, in the refrigerator until needed.

2. Preheat the oven to 350°F. Grease a 9-inch deep-dish pie plate with canola oil cooking spray.

3. Make the vanilla cake: Sift the flour, baking powder, and salt into a medium bowl and stir together.

4. In the bowl of a stand mixer fitted with the whisk attachment, combine the sugar, eggs, canola oil, vanilla extract, and vanilla bean paste. Whip on high speed until the mixture is pale in colour and has reached the ribbon stage, 10 to 15 minutes. Once you have reached the right consistency, you will see the batter lighten to a pale tone and thicken noticeably. Test it by stopping the mixer and lifting the whisk attachment; the batter should fall in long ribbons into the bowl.

5. Add half the dry ingredients to the wet ingredients and whisk on medium speed until almost fully incorporated. Scrape down the sides and bottom of the bowl. Add the buttermilk and whisk on medium-high speed just until combined. Scrape down the sides and bottom of the bowl. Add the remaining dry ingredients and whisk on medium speed just until combined. Scrape down the sides and bottom of the bowl and mix one final time to ensure the batter is smooth and no lumps remain, about 1 minute. Do not overmix, as doing so may deflate the air bubbles.

6. Pour the batter into the pie plate, filling it three-quarters full. (Any leftover batter will make a couple of cupcakes.) Bake for 20 to 35 minutes, or until a toothpick inserted into the centre of the cake comes out clean. Allow the cake to cool in the pan on a wire rack for at least 2 hours before assembling this classic pie.

7. Make the chocolate ganache while the cake is cooling.

8. Make the filling: When the cake is cool, in the bowl of a stand mixer fitted with the paddle attachment, beat the pastry cream on medium speed to return it to a smooth consistency, about 2 minutes.

Pastry Cream
½ batch Pastry Cream (page 274)

Simple Syrup
1 batch Simple Syrup (page 267)

Vanilla Cake
1¼ cups all-purpose flour
1⅛ teaspoons baking powder
½ teaspoon salt
1 cup granulated sugar
2 large eggs, room temperature
6 tablespoons canola oil
1½ teaspoons pure vanilla extract
1½ teaspoons vanilla bean paste
½ cup buttermilk,
   room temperature

Chocolate Ganache
1½ batches Dark Chocolate
   Ganache (page 254)

Vanilla Bean Whipped Cream
1 cup cold whipping (35%) cream
1 tablespoon icing sugar
1 teaspoon pure vanilla extract
1 tablespoon vanilla bean paste

Continued on next page

9. Carefully remove the cake from the pie plate by running a butter knife along the sides. Turn the cake upside down and place it on a flat surface. Using a serrated knife, cut the cake in half horizontally. Place the bottom layer, cut side up, back in the pie plate.

10. Using a pastry brush, moisten the bottom layer with 2 to 3 tablespoons of the simple syrup. Spread the pastry cream over the bottom layer, leaving a ¼-inch border around the outer edge of the cake.

11. Moisten the underside of the top layer with 2 to 3 tablespoons of the simple syrup. Place the top layer, cut side down, on top of the pastry cream. Gently push down on the top layer to form a bond but be sure not to squish all the pastry cream out along the sides.

12. If needed, reheat the chocolate ganache in the microwave in 30-second intervals. You want it to be fluid but not thick. Pour the ganache over the cake and smooth it with a small offset palette knife. (Do not worry if the ganache is a bit too liquid and it pours into the sides of the cake. Put a little more whipped cream on top and nobody will know!) Chill the pie in the refrigerator until the ganache is firm to the touch, about 10 minutes.

13. Make the vanilla bean whipped cream: In the bowl of a stand mixer fitted with the whisk attachment, combine the cold cream, icing sugar, vanilla extract, and vanilla bean paste and whip on medium speed. The cream will start to get frothy and begin to thicken after 2 to 3 minutes. Increase the speed to high and whip for another 30 seconds to 1 minute, or until the mixture looks fluffy and the whisk leaves deep markings in the whipped cream. Fill a piping bag fitted with a No. 824 star tip with the whipped cream and pipe a rosette border around the outer edge of the pie. (See Piping Styles on page 242 for different styles to use.) Store, covered, at room temperature for 1 day or in the refrigerator for up to 4 days.

Icings, Buttercreams, and Fillings

Piping Styles

You will find a variety of piping styles adorning some of our favourite baked goods throughout this book. Below, you will see examples of all the ones we love! Feel free to experiment and change it up. No matter if it's buttercream or whipped cream, we tend to use a large No. 804 round tip or a slightly fatter No. 806 round tip for round piping. We use a No. 824 star tip or a slightly more open No. 825 start tip for piping star shapes and designs. For small details like writing on cakes or for finer decorative pieces, we use smaller tips ranging from No. 1 to No. 10 round tips and various star, leaf, and basket weave tips. However, do not limit yourself to these tips—let your imagination play! Build a collection of different tips. We highly recommend adding at least three large and six small couplers to your collection so that you can easily swap out tips without emptying your piping bags.

1. **Round Swirl Border** (No. 804 round tip): used for cakes or pies
2. **Big/Small Pearl Border** (No. 804 round tip): used for wedding cakes or celebration cakes
3. **Classic Rosette and Star Drop** (No. 825 star tip): used for cakes, doughnuts, or bars
4. **Star Swirl Border** (No. 825 star tip): used for cakes or pies
5. **Round Shell Border** (No. 825 star tip): used for cakes or pies
6. **Classic Star Shell Border** (No. 825 star tip): used for cakes
7. **Round Reverse Shell Border** (No. 804 round tip): used for cakes
8. **Star Reverse Shell Border** (No. 825 star tip): used for cakes

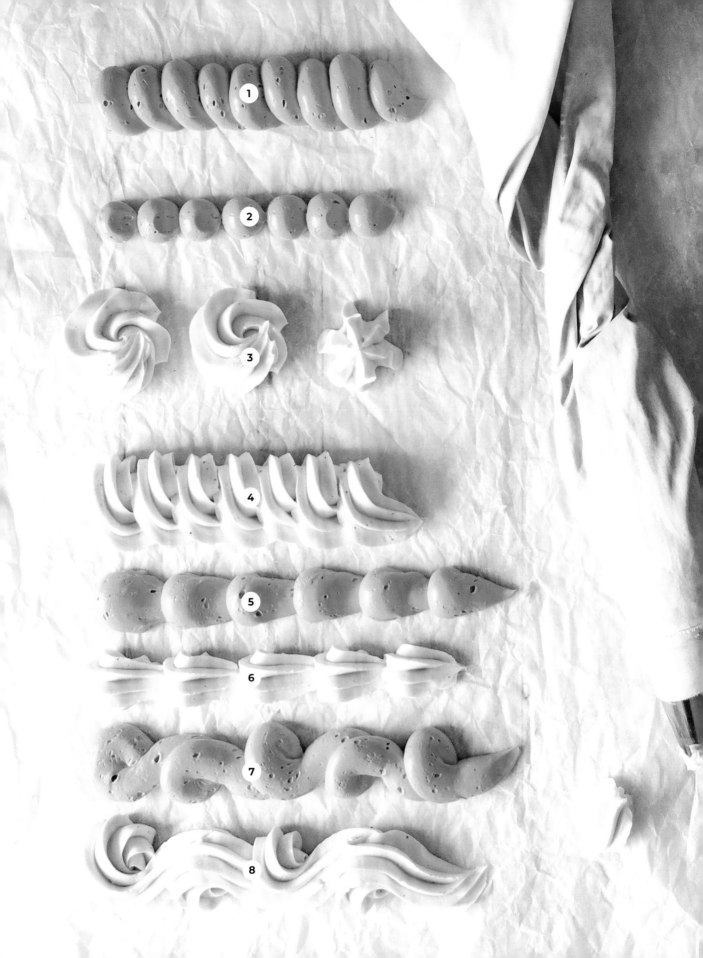

Icings and Buttercreams

3½ cups icing sugar
1 cup unsalted butter, room
    temperature
1¾ pounds (790 g) cream cheese,
    cut into 1-inch cubes,
    room temperature

DREAMY CREAM CHEESE ICING

It is imperative to use soft, room-temperature cream cheese to avoid lumps and achieve a satin-like smoothness in this icing. If your kitchen is cool, you may even want to microwave the cream cheese for 30 seconds to remove the chill. This sweet but slightly tart, versatile icing is great to have on hand to spread on banana bread, swap out for buttercream in cake fillings, and if you are feeling super indulgent, even use as a dip for cookies.

1. In the bowl of a stand mixer fitted with the paddle attachment, combine the icing sugar and butter. Starting with the mixer on low speed and slowly increasing to high speed to avoid creating a white icing powder storm, mix until combined. Then beat on high speed until light and fluffy, about 10 minutes. Scrape down the sides and bottom of the bowl.

2. With the mixer on medium-high speed, add the cream cheese in 3 additions, scraping down the sides and bottom of the bowl after each addition.

3. When the cream cheese has been incorporated, scrape down the sides and bottom of the bowl, then beat the icing for just 1 minute. Use immediately or store in the refrigerator for up to 1 month or in the freezer for up to 2 months. If refrigerated, let soften at room temperature. If frozen, thaw in the refrigerator overnight. When ready to use, in the bowl of a stand mixer fitted with the paddle attachment, beat on high speed for 5 to 10 minutes.

VANILLA BEAN AMERICAN BUTTERCREAM

Makes about 3 cups

Sweet and fluffy, this buttercream is the most basic combination of butter and icing sugar with just a touch of cream to lighten it up and vanilla for flavour. It stands up well for extended periods at room temperature and can be used to ice cakes if you prefer a sweeter icing, although it will never have the beautiful smooth finish of Swiss meringue buttercream.

1 cup unsalted butter, cut into
    1-inch cubes, room temperature
3½ cups icing sugar
1 tablespoon vanilla bean paste
1 to 3 tablespoons whipping (35%)
    cream, divided

1. In the bowl of a stand mixer fitted with the paddle attachment, beat the butter, icing sugar, vanilla bean paste, and 1 tablespoon of the cream, starting on low speed and increasing to high speed as the icing sugar incorporates. Mix on high speed for 6 to 8 minutes, stopping to scrape down the sides and bottom of the bowl once or twice, until the icing is light and fluffy. This can take up to 10 minutes, depending on the temperature of the butter.

2. Add up to 2 tablespoons of the remaining cream, mixing well after each addition, to adjust the consistency, if needed.

3. Use immediately or store in the refrigerator for up to 1 month or in the freezer for up to 6 months. If refrigerated, let soften at room temperature. If frozen, thaw in the refrigerator overnight. When ready to use, in the bowl of a stand mixer fitted with the paddle attachment, beat on high speed for 5 to 10 minutes.

CHOCOLATE AMERICAN BUTTERCREAM

Makes about 3½ cups

The combination of cocoa powder and semi-sweet chocolate gives this sweet icing a deep chocolate flavour. Fluffy, melt in your mouth, and very sweet, this icing is the closest we get to canned icing at the bakery.

3½ cups icing sugar
1 cup unsalted butter, cut into
    1-inch cubes, room temperature
1 tablespoon vanilla bean paste
1 to 3 tablespoons whipping (35%)
    cream, divided
3½ ounces (100 g) semi-sweet
    chocolate, melted and cooled
    but still liquid
2 tablespoons cocoa powder

1. In the bowl of a stand mixer fitted with the paddle attachment, beat the icing sugar, butter, vanilla bean paste, and 1 tablespoon of the cream, starting on low speed and increasing to high speed as the icing sugar incorporates. Mix on high speed for 6 to 8 minutes, stopping to scrape down the sides and bottom of the bowl once or twice, until the icing is light and fluffy. This can take up to 10 minutes, depending on the temperature of the butter. Scrape down the sides and bottom of the bowl.

2. Add the chocolate and beat the icing on high speed for 30 seconds just until the chocolate is incorporated. Sift the cocoa powder over the bowl and beat, starting at slow speed and slowly increasing to high speed. Beat on high speed for 2 full minutes.

3. Add up to 2 tablespoons of the remaining cream, mixing well after each addition, to adjust the consistency, if needed.

4. Use immediately or store in the refrigerator for up to 1 month or in the freezer for up to 6 months. If refrigerated, let soften at room temperature. If frozen, thaw in the refrigerator overnight. When ready to use, in the bowl of a stand mixer fitted with the paddle attachment, beat on high speed for 5 to 10 minutes.

PEANUT BUTTER AMERICAN BUTTERCREAM

Makes about 3½ cups

3 cups icing sugar

1½ cups smooth peanut butter (sweetened, not natural)

¾ cup unsalted butter, cut into 1-inch cubes, room temperature

1 to 3 tablespoons whipping (35%) cream

We really tried to jam as much peanut butter flavour in this recipe as possible, and we think you will be pleased with the results. Just like its base recipe, this icing is sweet and fluffy, but it also has a stick-to-the-roof-of-your-mouth finish that pairs beautifully with chocolate or fruit jams.

1. In the bowl of a stand mixer fitted with the paddle attachment, beat the icing sugar, peanut butter, butter, and 1 tablespoon of the cream, starting on low speed and increasing to high speed as the icing sugar incorporates. Mix on high speed for 6 to 8 minutes, stopping to scrape down the sides and bottom of the bowl once or twice, until the icing is light and fluffy. This can take up to 10 minutes, depending on the temperature of the butter.

2. Add up to 2 tablespoons of the remaining cream, mixing well after each addition, to adjust the consistency, if needed.

3. Use immediately or store in the refrigerator for up to 1 month or in the freezer for up to 6 months. If refrigerated, let soften at room temperature. If frozen, thaw in the refrigerator overnight. When ready to use, in the bowl of a stand mixer fitted with the paddle attachment, beat on high speed for 5 to 10 minutes.

BIRD'S CUSTARD AMERICAN BUTTERCREAM

Makes about 3 cups

3½ cups icing sugar

¼ cup Bird's Custard Powder

1 cup unsalted butter, cut into 1-inch cubes, room temperature

1 to 3 tablespoons whipping (35%) cream, divided

Josie's parents immigrated from England and Scotland before meeting in Canada, so she has brought a lot of British influence to the bakery. Bird's custard was a dessert staple at her grandparents' table for years. If you find yourself with extra custard powder to use up, try making the custard and serving it over our Fruit Crumble Pie (page 221). The custard powder adds a vibrant yellow colour and delicate custard flavour to this icing that pairs very well with chocolate.

1. In the bowl of a stand mixer, using a hand whisk, whisk together the icing sugar and custard powder until well blended. Place the bowl on a stand mixer fitted with the paddle attachment. Add the butter and 1 tablespoon of the cream and mix, starting on low speed and increasing to high speed as the icing sugar incorporates, for 6 to 8 minutes, stopping to scrape down the sides and bottom of the bowl once or twice, until the icing is light and fluffy. This can take up to 10 minutes, depending on the temperature of the butter.

2. Add up to 2 tablespoons of the remaining cream, mixing well after each addition, to adjust the consistency, if needed.

3. Use immediately or store in the refrigerator for up to 1 month or in the freezer for up to 6 months. If refrigerated, let soften at room temperature. If frozen, thaw in the refrigerator overnight. When ready to use, in the bowl of a stand mixer fitted with the paddle attachment, beat on high speed for 5 to 10 minutes.

VEGAN VANILLA BEAN BUTTERCREAM

Makes about 5½ cups

We always strive to create vegan counterparts that are as delicious as the original recipes. We have worked hard to create a vegan icing that is stable enough to build cakes but also sweet and fluffy. Use our recommended brands, as margarines and vegan butters can vary greatly in flavour and moisture content. If you cannot find these brands, look for a margarine that is soft and spreadable even when refrigerated and a vegan butter that's firm and salted and has a subtle butter flavour. If making the buttercream to fill sandwich cookies, omit the soy milk.

6 cups icing sugar, sifted

¾ cup soft vegan margarine (we use Crystal), room temperature

¾ cup vegan butter (we use Earth Balance Buttery Sticks), room temperature

1½ tablespoons vanilla bean paste

1 to 3 tablespoons soy milk (optional; omit if icing sandwich cookies)

1. In the bowl of a stand mixer fitted with the paddle attachment, combine the icing sugar, vegan margarine and butter, and vanilla bean paste and beat on low speed until combined. Scrape down the sides and bottom of the bowl. With the mixer on high speed, beat until light and fluffy, about 10 minutes.

2. If the buttercream is too thick, add 1 tablespoon of the soy milk at a time, beating after each addition and testing the buttercream's spreadability. You are looking for soft and fluffy, not thick like peanut butter.

3. Use immediately or store in the refrigerator for up to 1 month or in the freezer for up to 6 months. If refrigerated, let soften at room temperature. If frozen, thaw in the refrigerator overnight. When ready to use, in the bowl of a stand mixer fitted with the paddle attachment, beat on high speed for 5 to 10 minutes.

VEGAN CHOCOLATE BUTTERCREAM

Makes about 6 cups

6 cups icing sugar, sifted

¾ cup vegan margarine (we use Crystal), room temperature

¾ cup vegan butter (we use Earth Balance Buttery Sticks), room temperature

1 tablespoon vanilla bean paste

4 ounces (115 g) bittersweet couverture chocolate, melted and room temperature but still liquid, more if needed

2 tablespoons cocoa powder

1 to 3 tablespoons soy milk (optional; omit if icing sandwich cookies)

Just like its vanilla sister, this icing will please any palette, vegan or not. Using both cocoa powder and semi-sweet chocolate gives it a deep chocolate flavour, and the salt in the vegan margarine and butter really amp up the richness. Use our recommended brands, as margarines and vegan butters can vary greatly in flavour and moisture content. If you cannot find these brands, look for a margarine that is soft and spreadable even when refrigerated and a vegan butter that's firm and salted and has a subtle butter flavour. If making the buttercream to fill sandwich cookies, omit the soy milk.

1. In the bowl of a stand mixer fitted with the paddle attachment, combine the icing sugar, vegan margarine and butter, and vanilla bean paste and beat on low speed just until combined. Scrape down the sides and bottom of the bowl. With the mixer on high speed, whip until light and fluffy, about 10 minutes. Scrape down the sides and bottom of the bowl.

2. Add the melted chocolate and sift the cocoa powder on top. Whip on low speed and then increase the speed to high and whip for 30 seconds. Scrape down the sides and bottom of the bowl. With the mixer on high speed, whip until light and fluffy.

3. Taste the buttercream to ensure it is chocolatey enough for you. If not, add up to another 2 ounces (55 g) of melted room-temperature chocolate.

4. If the buttercream is too thick, add 1 tablespoon of the soy milk at a time, beating after each addition and testing the buttercream's spreadability. You are looking for soft and fluffy, not thick like peanut butter.

5. Use immediately or store in the refrigerator for up to 1 month or in the freezer for up to 6 months. If refrigerated, let soften at room temperature. If frozen, thaw in the refrigerator overnight. When ready to use, in the bowl of a stand mixer fitted with the paddle attachment, beat on high speed for 5 to 10 minutes.

VANILLA BEAN BUTTERCREAM

Makes about 6 cups

6 large egg whites (about 1 cup)

1¼ cups granulated sugar

⅛ teaspoon salt

2 cups unsalted butter, cut into 1-inch pieces, room temperature

1 tablespoon pure vanilla extract

1 tablespoon vanilla bean paste

There are two main egg white-based buttercream styles, Italian and Swiss. Both have their advantages, but we love the stability of Swiss meringue, especially for cakes. This recipe can be finicky, but by keeping a few key points in mind you will be whipping it up confidently in no time! Always, always, always start with an immaculately clean and dry mixing bowl and whisk attachment, free of any grease or soap residue. Fats and foreign substances are not friends of meringue. Separate your egg whites very carefully by cracking an egg over a small bowl. Allow the white to fall into the bowl and place the yolk in a storage container; refrigerate the yolks when done to use in another recipe. If the white is completely yolk-free, add it to the medium bowl you are using for your double boiler. Continue with this process until you are done separating your eggs. If you tear a yolk and it ends up in the whites, save the mixture for another dish and start separating a new egg! There cannot be any yolks in the whites. This buttercream is very butter forward and not too sweet—the complete opposite of the American buttercream.

Avoid refrigerating iced baked goods or allow them to warm up to room temperature before consuming them, or the icing will be a little like biting into a stick of butter. If you have stored your buttercream in the fridge or it was previously frozen, place it in a heat-resistant bowl and heat in the microwave for 30 to 40 seconds before rebeating it. It should not be melted to a liquid, just soft. Place the buttercream in the bowl of a stand mixer fitted with the paddle attachment and beat on medium-high speed for 7 to 10 minutes. If the buttercream turns into a soupy, wet mess, it has separated. This is most likely to happen when rebeating buttercream that is not at room temperature, and it is fixable! Simply return the buttercream to the heat-resistant bowl and heat in the microwave for another 30 seconds. Pop it back on the mixer and beat on medium-high speed for 7 to 10 more minutes. If you freeze the buttercream, ensure you thaw it out completely in the fridge and then bring it to room temperature before rebeating.

1. Fill a medium saucepan with 2 to 3 inches of hot water as part of a double boiler and bring to a boil over high heat. Once boiling, reduce the heat to low to maintain a simmer.

2. In a medium glass or stainless steel bowl that will fit nicely over the pan of hot water but not touch the simmering water below, whisk together the egg whites, sugar, and salt. Place the bowl over the simmering water bath. Whisk constantly until the sugar has dissolved and the mixture has a sticky, tacky-looking texture. As it is heating, you will notice the mixture becoming more fluid; keep whisking until it reaches 140°F on a candy thermometer or the mixture is body temperature to the touch and the sugar is dissolved.

3. Transfer the meringue mixture to the bowl of a stand mixer fitted with the whisk attachment. Whisk on high speed for 10 to 15 minutes or until stiff peaks have formed and you can no longer feel any heat coming from the bottom of the mixing bowl.

4. Reduce the speed to medium-high and start adding the butter pieces, waiting until each addition is fully incorporated before adding the next. Scrape down the sides of the bowl at least twice while making your additions.

5. Once all the butter is incorporated and the buttercream is smooth, beat for 5 minutes on high speed. Give the bowl one final scrape and then add the vanilla extract and vanilla bean paste and continue to beat on high speed for 2 more minutes.

6. Use immediately or keep covered at room temperature for up to 1 day until ready to use. When ready to use, in the bowl of a stand mixer fitted with the paddle attachment, beat on high speed for 5 to 10 minutes. Store in an airtight container in the refrigerator for up to 2 months or in the freezer for up to 6 months. If refrigerated, let soften at room temperature. If frozen, thaw in the refrigerator overnight. When ready to use, in the bowl of a stand mixer fitted with the paddle attachment, beat on high speed for 5 to 10 minutes.

Makes about 6 cups

1 batch Vanilla Bean Buttercream
   (page 248)
7 ounces (200 g) bittersweet
   chocolate, melted and room
   temperature but still liquid,
   more if needed
2 tablespoons cocoa powder

CHOCOLATE BUTTERCREAM

This deep chocolate–flavoured buttercream complements our rich chocolate cake perfectly for dark chocolate lovers. If you prefer a sweeter, more malty chocolate buttercream that is reminiscent of hot chocolate, swap milk chocolate for the bittersweet chocolate and Ovaltine for the cocoa powder. Make sure your chocolate is at room temperature but still liquid when you are ready to add it and then get the mixer up to high speed as quickly as possible. If you are too timid while mixing, the chocolate may harden before incorporating fully into the buttercream and you can end up with little bits of hard chocolate in your buttercream. Have your silicone spatula handy to scrape down the sides and bottom of the bowl.

1. Prepare the vanilla bean buttercream. At the end of step 5 (see page 249), add the melted chocolate and sift the cocoa powder on top, then mix on low speed for 1 minute. Increase the speed to high and beat for 30 seconds. Scrape down the sides and bottom of the bowl and beat on high speed until light and fluffy, about 5 minutes.

2. Taste the buttercream to ensure it is chocolatey enough for you. If not, add another ¼ to ½ cup of melted room-temperature chocolate. Scrape down the sides and bottom of the bowl. Beat on high speed until light and fluffy, about 5 minutes.

3. Use immediately or keep covered at room temperature for up to 1 day. When ready to use, in the bowl of a stand mixer fitted with the paddle attachment, beat on high speed for 5 to 10 minutes. Store in an airtight container in the refrigerator for up to 2 months or in the freezer for up to 6 months. If refrigerated, let soften at room temperature. If frozen, thaw in the refrigerator overnight. When ready to use, in the bowl of a stand mixer fitted with the paddle attachment, beat on high speed for 5 to 10 minutes.

HAZELNUT CHOCOLATE BUTTERCREAM

Makes about 8 cups

1 batch Vanilla Bean Buttercream
  (page 248)
3 to 3½ cups hazelnut chocolate
  spread, divided
½ teaspoon salt (optional)

It seems that hazelnut chocolate spread falls into two camps: either you grew up with it on the breakfast table and have been appreciating its nutty sweetness your whole life, or it was an elusive treat. In Nickey's Italian household, hazelnut chocolate spread was a pantry staple that made its way onto crusty Calabrese bread slices regularly. Josie falls into the second camp, so it was one of the foods she bought on her first independent grocery store trip, and she has never looked back. Now it goes into any baked good we can imagine at the bakery, and this luxurious buttercream is no exception. This icing has a very prominent chocolate hazelnut flavour and a touch of that stick-to-the-roof-of-your-mouth nuttiness. If you want to elevate the chocolate and hazelnut even more, or just enjoy a salty edge to your sweet, try the addition of optional salt.

1. Prepare the vanilla bean buttercream. At the end of step 5 (see page 249), add 3 cups of the hazelnut chocolate spread and the salt (if using), then beat on high speed until light and fluffy, about 7 minutes. Stop the mixer to scrape down the sides and bottom of the bowl at least twice during the process.

2. Taste the buttercream to ensure it has enough hazelnut chocolate flavour for you. If not, add another ½ cup hazelnut chocolate spread. Scrape down the sides and bottom of the bowl. Beat on high speed until light and fluffy, about 5 minutes.

3. Use immediately or keep covered at room temperature for up to 1 day. When ready to use, in the bowl of a stand mixer fitted with the paddle attachment, beat on high speed for 5 to 10 minutes. Store in an airtight container in the refrigerator for up to 2 months or in the freezer for up to 6 months. If refrigerated, let soften at room temperature. If frozen, thaw in the refrigerator overnight. When ready to use, in the bowl of a stand mixer fitted with the paddle attachment, beat on high speed for 5 to 10 minutes.

MAPLE BUTTERCREAM

Makes about 6 cups

1 batch Vanilla Bean Buttercream
(page 248)
¾ to 1 cup grade A dark maple
syrup, divided
1 tablespoon good-quality maple
extract (optional)

We are wary of extracts, mostly because the natural source is always so much better than the extract. However, intense maple flavour can be hard to nail down, especially if you cannot find dark maple syrup and have to use a lighter variety. While mixing the buttercream, taste it to ensure it is maple-y enough for you. If not, add the optional extract. Regardless, this buttercream has a wonderful butterscotch maple flavour to it that you are sure to love.

1. Prepare the vanilla bean buttercream. At the end of step 5 (see page 249), add ¾ cup of the maple syrup, then mix on low speed for 1 minute. Increase the speed to high and beat for 30 seconds. Scrape down the sides and bottom of the bowl. Beat on high speed until light and fluffy, about 5 minutes.

2. Taste the buttercream to ensure it has enough maple flavour for you. If not, add the remaining ¼ cup maple syrup and/or the optional maple extract. Scrape down the sides and bottom of the bowl. Beat on high speed until light and fluffy, about 5 minutes.

3. Use immediately or keep covered at room temperature for up to 1 day. When ready to use, in the bowl of a stand mixer fitted with the paddle attachment, beat on high speed for 5 to 10 minutes. Store in an airtight container in the refrigerator for up to 2 months or in the freezer for up to 6 months. If refrigerated, let soften at room temperature. If frozen, thaw in the refrigerator overnight. When ready to use, in the bowl of a stand mixer fitted with the paddle attachment, beat on high speed for 5 to 10 minutes.

CARAMEL BUTTERCREAM

Makes about 6 cups

1 batch Vanilla Bean Buttercream
(page 248)
1 batch Caramel (page 275)
½ teaspoon salt (optional)

This buttercream has a gorgeous warm caramel colour to it that looks beautiful against chocolate on cakes. Caramel pairs naturally with salt, as the salt cuts through the sweetness of the caramel to highlight the buttery complexity of the cooked sugar. So, feel free to add the optional salt if you like a salty edge to your sweet caramel.

1. Prepare the vanilla bean buttercream. At the end of step 5 (see page 249), add 1 cup of the caramel and the salt (if using), then mix on low speed for 1 minute. Increase the speed to high and beat for 30 seconds. Scrape down the sides and bottom of the bowl and beat on high until light and fluffy, about 5 minutes.

2. Taste the buttercream to ensure it has enough caramel flavour for you. If not, add another ¼ cup of the caramel. Scrape down the sides and bottom of the bowl. Beat on high speed until light and fluffy, about 5 minutes.

3. Use immediately or keep covered at room temperature for up to 1 day. When ready to use, in the bowl of a stand mixer fitted with the paddle attachment, beat on high speed for 5 to 10 minutes. Store in an airtight container in the refrigerator for up to 2 months or in the freezer for up to 6 months. If refrigerated, let soften at room temperature. If frozen, thaw in the refrigerator overnight. When ready to use, in the bowl of a stand mixer fitted with the paddle attachment, beat on high speed for 5 to 10 minutes.

LEMON BUTTERCREAM

Makes about 6 cups

This lemon buttercream has the flavour of a lemon drop candy and will have you dreaming of warm sunshine. It is not tart, just sweet and smooth. It would make a lovely icing for our Lemon Poppy Seed Loaf (page 39). If you do not like the flavour of lemon oil or have a hard time sourcing it, you can swap it out for the zest of a second lemon instead.

1 batch Vanilla Bean Buttercream (page 248)

Zest of 1 lemon

2 to 3 drops lemon oil, depending on potency and desired flavour

1. Prepare the vanilla bean buttercream, adding the lemon zest and 2 drops of the lemon oil to the bowl with the vanilla in step 5 (see page 249).

2. Beat on high speed for 3 minutes until light and fluffy. Scrape down the sides and bottom of the bowl to ensure the ingredients are fully incorporated. Taste and add more lemon oil if you want a stronger lemon flavour. Beat the buttercream for 1 to 2 more minutes after adding any additional oil.

3. Use immediately or keep covered at room temperature for up to 1 day. When ready to use, in the bowl of a stand mixer fitted with the paddle attachment, beat on high speed for 5 to 10 minutes. Store in an airtight container in the refrigerator for up to 2 months or in the freezer for up to 6 months. If refrigerated, let soften at room temperature. If frozen, thaw in the refrigerator overnight. When ready to use, in the bowl of a stand mixer fitted with the paddle attachment, beat on high speed for 5 to 10 minutes.

RASPBERRY BUTTERCREAM

Makes about 6 cups

Really, any jam would work here, so if you prefer strawberry jam or grape jelly, go for it! The jam adds both fruit flavour and a little colour to the buttercream. We like to leave the seeds in the raspberry jam for extra texture and visual effect, but seedless jams will also be delicious. You can also add a drop or two of gel food colouring along with the jam to amp up the berry colour, if desired.

1 batch Vanilla Bean Buttercream (page 248)

½ to ¾ cup seedless raspberry jam, divided

1. Prepare the vanilla bean buttercream. At the end of step 5 (see page 249), add ½ cup of the raspberry jam, then mix on low speed for 1 minute. Increase the speed to high and beat for 30 seconds. Scrape down the sides and bottom of the bowl. Beat on high speed until light and fluffy, about 5 minutes.

2. Taste the buttercream to ensure it has enough raspberry flavour for you. If not, add the remaining ¼ cup raspberry jam. Scrape down the sides and bottom of the bowl. Beat on high speed until light and fluffy, about 5 minutes.

3. Use immediately or keep covered at room temperature for up to 1 day. When ready to use, in the bowl of a stand mixer fitted with the paddle attachment, beat on high speed for 5 to 10 minutes. Store in an airtight container in the refrigerator for up to 2 months or in the freezer for up to 6 months. If refrigerated, let soften at room temperature. If frozen, thaw in the refrigerator overnight. When ready to use, in the bowl of a stand mixer fitted with the paddle attachment, beat on high speed for 5 to 10 minutes.

Chocolate Ganaches

Makes about ½ cup

3½ ounces (100 g) semi-sweet
    chocolate callets or semi-sweet
    chocolate, chopped
¼ cup whipping (35%) cream
3 tablespoons white corn syrup

DARK CHOCOLATE GANACHE

Ganache is a flexible addition to many recipes and very common around the bakery. We sometimes have four or five different ganache recipes being used at a time for slightly different needs. For simplicity, we have provided you with our easiest, most failproof version and its variations. This is a very straightforward recipe that requires only that you start with good-quality chocolate and cream for great results. After that, you just need to avoid overheating and scorching the chocolate. Thirty seconds might seem like nothing, but in most microwaves it is usually enough time to get the mixture warm enough that it will continue to melt as you stir.

1. Combine all the ingredients in a small heat-resistant bowl and heat in the microwave for 30 seconds. Vigorously stir until the ingredients are incorporated and the mixture is glossy and smooth. If you see any lumps, heat in the microwave in 15-second intervals, stirring after each interval, until smooth.

2. Store in an airtight container in the refrigerator for up to 2 weeks or in the freezer for up to 6 months. When ready to use, in a small heat-resistant bowl, reheat in the microwave in 15-second intervals, stirring after each interval, until a pourable consistency is achieved. If frozen, thaw in the refrigerator overnight before reheating.

MILK CHOCOLATE GANACHE

Makes about ½ cup

When we make this ganache at the bakery, it always smells like butterscotch and fresh cream. There is just something so comforting about the creamy aroma of milk chocolate; it has none of the bitter notes of dark chocolate, just smooth sweetness. If you have a favourite chocolate, feel free to swap the ganaches used in our recipes and personalize those recipes to your own tastes.

3½ ounces (100 g) milk chocolate callets or milk chocolate, chopped
3 tablespoons whipping (35%) cream
3 tablespoons white corn syrup

1. Combine all the ingredients in a small heat-resistant bowl and heat in the microwave for 30 seconds. Vigorously stir until the ingredients are incorporated and the mixture is glossy and smooth. If you see any lumps, heat in the microwave in 15-second intervals, stirring after each interval, until smooth.

2. Store in an airtight container in the refrigerator for up to 2 weeks or in the freezer for up to 6 months. When ready to use, in a small heat-resistant bowl, reheat in the microwave in 15-second intervals, stirring after each interval, until a pourable consistency is achieved. If frozen, thaw in the refrigerator overnight before reheating.

WHITE CHOCOLATE GANACHE

Makes about ½ cup

This ganache is used mostly to add a punch of colour to our baked goods. Honestly, there are not too many white chocolate lovers in our ranks. However, just like in our other ganaches, good-quality chocolate is the key here. Pick a chocolate you enjoy eating, but it is not necessary that you buy the most expensive one.

3 ounces (85 g) white chocolate callets or white chocolate, chopped
2 tablespoons whipping (35%) cream
3 tablespoons white corn syrup

1. Combine all the ingredients in a small heat-resistant bowl and heat in the microwave for 30 seconds. Vigorously stir until the ingredients are incorporated and the mixture is glossy and smooth. If you see any lumps, heat in the microwave in 30-second intervals, stirring after each interval, until smooth.

2. Store in an airtight container in the refrigerator for up to 2 weeks or in the freezer for up to 6 months. When ready to use, in a small heat-resistant bowl, reheat in the microwave in 15-second intervals, stirring after each interval, until a pourable consistency is achieved. If frozen, thaw in the refrigerator overnight before reheating.

Makes about ½ cup

1 batch White Chocolate Ganache
(page 255)
1 to 2 drops white gel food
colouring
1 to 2 drops gel food colouring of
your choice

COLOURED WHITE CHOCOLATE GANACHE

We love jewel tones, but we also want them to taste amazing. White chocolate is the perfect delicious carrier for all the rainbow tones you need to finish off your cakes in unique style. It is easy to cut and melts in your mouth, even when refrigerated—a trick that other finishes that are easy to colour, like royal icing, just cannot pull off.

1. Prepare the white chocolate ganache and mix in the white food colouring first until fully combined. The white food colouring cuts out the yellow undertone and provides a more opaque base to give the ganache a bright, vibrant final colour.

2. Add the food colouring of your choice, one drop at a time, and stir until completely combined and you have reached your preferred colour.

3. Store in an airtight container in the refrigerator for up to 2 weeks or in the freezer for up to 6 months. When ready to use, in a small heat-resistant bowl, reheat in the microwave in 15-second intervals, stirring after each interval, until a pourable consistency is achieved. If frozen, thaw in the refrigerator overnight before reheating.

Makes about ½ cup

1 batch White Chocolate Ganache
(page 255)
1 drop white gel food colouring
1 drop sky blue gel food colouring
½ drop teal gel food colouring

BLUE GANACHE

We use this lovely, tinted ganache in our Birthday Party Cake (page 183) and anywhere else we want a hit of our iconic blue. It has a beautiful blue-teal colour that we have developed over the years that just makes us smile. We wear it as our uniforms, it graces our coffee cups, and we even painted some of the walls in the bakery this colour.

1. Prepare the white chocolate ganache and mix in the white food colouring first until fully combined. Add the sky blue and teal food colourings and stir until you have achieved a solid colour throughout.

2. Store in an airtight container in the refrigerator for up to 2 weeks or in the freezer for up to 6 months. When ready to use, in a small heat-resistant bowl, reheat in the microwave in 15-second intervals, stirring after each interval, until a pourable consistency is achieved. If frozen, thaw in the refrigerator overnight before reheating.

RASPBERRY WHITE CHOCOLATE GANACHE

Makes about ½ cup

Just like in our Raspberry Buttercream (page 253), any jam will work here. If your jam is chunky or you prefer it without seeds, strain the jam to remove the chunks or seeds before measuring out two tablespoons and stirring it into the ganache.

1 batch White Chocolate Ganache (page 255)
2 tablespoons seedless raspberry jam

1. Prepare the white chocolate ganache and, while still warm, add the raspberry jam and stir until completely combined.

2. Store in an airtight container in the refrigerator for up to 2 weeks or in the freezer for up to 6 months. When ready to use, in a small heat-resistant bowl, reheat in the microwave in 15-second intervals, stirring after each interval, until a pourable consistency is achieved. If frozen, thaw in the refrigerator overnight before reheating.

VEGAN DARK CHOCOLATE GANACHE

Makes about 1¼ cups

Be careful when purchasing semi-sweet chocolate for vegan recipes. Most are vegan, but some manufacturers sneak in non-vegan ingredients, so check the ingredient lists carefully. If you do not have soy milk on hand, most non-dairy milks will work, even if they are slightly sweetened.

9 ounces (255 g) semi-sweet chocolate callets or semi-sweet chocolate, chopped
½ cup unsweetened soy milk
¼ cup white corn syrup

1. Combine all the ingredients in a small heat-resistant bowl and heat in the microwave for 1 minute. Vigorously stir until the ingredients are incorporated and the mixture is glossy and smooth. If you see any lumps, heat in the microwave in 30-second intervals, stirring after each interval, until smooth.

2. Store in an airtight container in the refrigerator for up to 2 weeks or in the freezer for up to 6 months. When ready to use, in a small heat-resistant bowl, reheat in the microwave in 15-second intervals, stirring after each interval, until a pourable consistency is achieved. If frozen, thaw in the refrigerator overnight before reheating.

Compotes

3 cups fresh or frozen
    strawberries, hulled
¼ cup granulated sugar
1 tablespoon lemon juice

STRAWBERRY COMPOTE

Like jam but with much less sugar, fruit compotes are the perfect way to capture the flavour of fresh fruits and keep them preserved for later use. They are also a great way to use up any fruit that is about to be past its prime, because it is no problem if the fruit is blemished or a little overripe. Depending on the size of your strawberries, you may want to quarter the fruit, but we love a chunky compote with big pieces of fruit that burst in your mouth.

1. Place the ingredients in a heavy medium pot over medium-high heat. Using a wooden spoon, stir together to coat the strawberries evenly in the sugar and lemon juice. Stir occasionally, breaking up any larger berries with the spoon, until the mixture comes to a boil, and then reduce the heat to low. Keep the mixture at a low rolling boil, stirring occasionally, for 15 to 20 minutes until the strawberries start to soften and lose shape. You will notice that the juices evaporate and thicken. Depending on your desired final thickness, you can simmer for up to 30 minutes. The compote will thicken more as it cools. Remove from the heat and allow to cool completely.

2. Store in an airtight container in the refrigerator for up to 2 weeks or in the freezer for up to 4 months. If frozen, thaw in the refrigerator overnight before using.

2 cups fresh or frozen wild
    blueberries
¼ cup water
¼ cup granulated sugar
2 tablespoons lemon juice

BLUEBERRY COMPOTE

Wild blueberries are best for this compote. They contain much more flavour than their juicier but blander cultivated counterpart. In addition, they contain a higher concentration of antioxidants and more fibre, so it is a win-win. If you cannot find wild blueberries, regular blueberries will work.

1. Place the ingredients in a heavy medium pot over medium-high heat and stir together to coat the blueberries evenly in the sugar and liquids. Stir occasionally until the mixture comes to a boil and then reduce the heat to low. Keep the mixture at a low rolling boil, stirring occasionally, for 15 to 20 minutes until the blueberries have burst and started to soften. You will notice that the juices evaporate and thicken. The compote will thicken more as it cools. Remove from the heat and allow to cool completely. Refrigerate the compote in an airtight container for 4 to 6 hours to thicken before using.

2. Store in an airtight container in the refrigerator for up to 2 weeks or in the freezer for up to 4 months. If frozen, thaw in the refrigerator overnight before using.

RASPBERRY COMPOTE

Makes 1½ cups

You may already know that raspberries are not actually individual berries like blueberries or strawberries but that each raspberry contains about a hundred tiny fruits called drupelets. Each drupelet has a seed at its centre, and the drupelets grow as a cluster around each stem. As you cook the raspberries in this compote, you will see the drupelets separate from each other. If you do not like seeds in your compote, you can push the mixture through a strainer before you cool it, but you will end up with just under a cup of compote and still a few seeds.

3 cups fresh or frozen raspberries
¼ cup granulated sugar
1 tablespoon lemon juice

1. Place the ingredients in a heavy medium pot over medium-high heat and stir together to coat the raspberries evenly in the sugar and lemon juice. Stir occasionally until the mixture comes to a boil and then reduce the heat to low. Keep the mixture at a rolling simmer, stirring occasionally, for 10 to 15 minutes until the raspberries soften and lose their shape. You will notice that the juices evaporate and thicken. The compote will thicken more as it cools. Remove from the heat and allow to cool completely. Refrigerate the compote in an airtight container for 4 to 6 hours to thicken before using.

2. Store in an airtight container in the refrigerator for up to 2 weeks or in the freezer for up to 4 months. If frozen, thaw in the refrigerator overnight before using.

PEACH COMPOTE

Makes 2¾ cups

Almond extract may seem like a weird addition to this compote. However, peach and almond trees are closely related, and these ingredients complement each other's flavour well. Imitation almond extract is often made from apricot and peach pits because they contain the organic compound benzaldehyde, which is used to flavour the extract. So, give it a try—we think the almond flavour brings out a buttery richness in the peaches.

3 cups fresh or frozen pitted and sliced peaches (5 medium peaches)
¼ cup packed brown sugar
2 tablespoons cold water
1 teaspoon cinnamon
1 teaspoon vanilla bean paste
⅛ teaspoon almond extract (optional)

1. Place the ingredients in a heavy medium pot over medium-high heat and stir together to coat the peaches evenly. Stir occasionally until the mixture comes to a boil and then reduce the heat to low. Keep the mixture at a rolling simmer, stirring occasionally, for 15 to 20 minutes until the peaches are soft and the juices start to thicken. The compote will thicken more as it cools. Remove from the heat and allow to cool completely. Refrigerate the compote in an airtight container for 4 to 6 hours to thicken before using. Store in an airtight container in the refrigerator for up to 2 weeks or in the freezer for up to 4 months. If frozen, thaw in the refrigerator overnight before using.

2. Store in an airtight container in the refrigerator for up to 2 weeks or in the freezer for up to 4 months. If frozen, thaw in the refrigerator overnight before using.

Makes 4 cups

6 cups peeled and cubed apples
 (Mutsu or Jonagold)
2 tablespoons lemon juice
½ cup granulated sugar
½ cup packed brown sugar
1 teaspoon cinnamon
¼ teaspoon freshly grated or
 ground nutmeg
¼ cup cornstarch
¼ teaspoon salt
2 cups water

CINNAMON APPLE COMPOTE

The size of the apple cubes in this compote is up to you. We love larger chunks, 1½ inches or bigger, because it is more visually appealing and gives you a satisfying tart burst in the centre of the apple chunks. Smaller apple pieces, less than 1-inch cubed, will break down faster and give you more of a chunky caramel applesauce. Either way, we suggest you make a double batch because you know you are going to want this on standby for ice cream topping, yogurt parfait, and whatever other craving you may have.

1. In a medium bowl, drizzle the lemon juice over the apples and toss to coat. This will help prevent the apples from browning. Set aside.

2. In a large saucepan, stir together the granulated sugar, brown sugar, cinnamon, nutmeg, cornstarch, and salt. Using a whisk, stir in the water until everything has dissolved.

3. Bring the mixture to a boil over medium-high heat. Reduce the heat to low and simmer for 2 minutes to cook out the starch and thicken the mixture, stirring occasionally with a wooden spoon or silicone spatula. Stir in the apples, increase the heat to medium-high, and bring the mixture to a full boil again. Reduce the heat to low and simmer, stirring occasionally, for 10 to 12 minutes until the apples have softened but still maintain their shape. Remove from the heat and let the mixture cool completely. You can pour it into a shallow casserole dish to speed up the cooling process. Place the compote in an airtight container for 4 to 6 hours to thicken before using.

4. Store in an airtight container in the refrigerator for up to 2 weeks or in the freezer for up to 4 months. If frozen, thaw in the refrigerator overnight before using.

Crumbles

Makes 2½ cups,
enough for one 9-inch pie

1 cup lightly packed dark
 brown sugar
¾ cup all-purpose flour
¾ cup large oat flakes
½ cup unsalted butter, room
 temperature and cut into
 1-inch cubes
½ teaspoon cinnamon
½ teaspoon salt

BROWN SUGAR OAT CRUMBLE

The chunkier the oats, the better in this crumble. Once baked, the brown sugar and flour form a beautiful crunchy coating for the creamy oats, who are really the star here. If you like a little more spice, you can always increase the cinnamon or replace it with our Pumpkin Spice (page 267) for a different twist. As you rub the ingredients together, keep in mind that you want the oats to stay as whole as possible, the sugar and flour should form a sandy base to the crumble, and small butter chunks should be visible throughout the crumble and coated in the flour and sugar. You are not trying to create a homogenous paste.

1. Place the ingredients in a large bowl. Rub the mixture together with your fingers until it has formed coarse crumbs, pea-size butter chunks, and the oats are still intact.

2. Store in an airtight container in the refrigerator for up to 1 month or in the freezer for up to 6 months. If frozen, thaw in the refrigerator overnight before using.

MUM'S SHORTBREAD CRUMBLE

This is one of Josie's family recipes and the crumble she grew up with on her grandmother's pies. Josie's grandma, Mary, received the recipe from her mother-in-law, and it emigrated with the family from England in the 1960s. It is rare that a meal does not end in pie at her grandparents' house, and we are still attempting to duplicate the perfect flaky, light crusts Josie grew up with. Peach is our favourite fruit pairing with this crumble, although it's magic with the tartness of rhubarb too.

1. Place all the ingredients in a large bowl. Rub the mixture together with your fingers until it has formed coarse crumbs.

2. Store in an airtight container in the refrigerator for up to 1 month or in the freezer for up to 6 months. If frozen, thaw in the refrigerator overnight before using.

Makes 2½ cups, enough for one 9-inch pie or crumble

¾ cup salted butter or margarine, cold and cut into ½-inch slices
¾ cup granulated sugar
1½ cups all-purpose flour

VEGAN SHORTBREAD CRUMBLE

A little less sweet than Mum's Shortbread Crumble (recipe above) and with a subtle brown sugar flavour, this vegan crumble is perfect for topping pies, muffins, and even cookies. Try our vegan chocolate cookies (found in the Cookies and Cream Sandwich Cookies, page 139) baked with crumble on top for a coffee cake cookie experience.

1. Place the ingredients in a large bowl. Rub the mixture together with your fingers until it has formed coarse crumbs.

2. Store in an airtight container in the refrigerator for up to 1 month or in the freezer for up to 6 months. If frozen, thaw in the refrigerator overnight before using.

Makes 2½ cups, enough for one 9-inch pie or crumble

1½ cups all-purpose flour
¾ cup soft vegan margarine, room temperature
½ cup packed dark brown sugar
½ teaspoon salt

Crusts and Pastries

Makes enough for 9 large tarts or
one 9-inch pie base

1 cup unsalted butter, frozen
½ cup cold water, more if needed
1½ teaspoons granulated sugar
1 teaspoon salt
2½ cups all-purpose flour

BUTTER PASTRY

There are many variations on basic pie dough and much debate about the "right" fat to use. Some of the best pies we have ever tried have used a lard-based pastry. If you have a source for fresh farm lard, we highly suggest you try it out. If you tasted a Cake & Loaf pie in our first couple of years, they were fifty percent fresh lard from our pork farmer and fifty percent butter. Our farmer retired and it became too hard to source consistently high-quality lard, so we switched to a vegetarian-friendly pie crust. Vegetable shortening is a cheap and cheerful option and the favourite of many grandmothers; we cannot deny it makes a tender pie crust! However, for us, butter is the key to a flavourful, flaky, substantial crust.

1. Using a box grater, grate the frozen butter into a large bowl. Place in the freezer for 10 to 15 minutes to make sure the butter is still frozen.

2. In a liquid measuring cup, mix together the cold water, sugar, and salt until the solids are fully dissolved. Place in the refrigerator until ready to use.

3. Remove the bowl from the freezer and toss the flour with the grated butter to distribute the butter evenly throughout the flour.

4. Using a fork, mix the cold water mixture into the flour mixture, causing as little friction as possible, until you have a shaggy dough. You want to try to maintain those butter pieces. Resist the urge to add more water unless absolutely necessary to bring the pastry together into a shaggy dough with just a little dry flour. If needed, add 2 to 3 more tablespoons of cold water to the dough, 1 tablespoon at a time.

5. Bring the pastry together by gently folding it into a rough disc, then wrap it tightly in plastic wrap and refrigerate for at least 1 hour before rolling it out. The pastry can be made in advance, wrapped tightly in plastic wrap, and stored in the refrigerator for up to 1 week or in the freezer for up to 6 months. If frozen, thaw in the refrigerator overnight before using.

VEGAN PASTRY

Makes enough for 9 large tarts or one 9-inch pie base

It is possible to simply swap vegan shortening, like Crisco, for the butter in our Butter Pastry (page 262), and doing so would make a very respectable vegan pastry. However, we have found that if you want to use a higher quality vegan butter, then apple cider vinegar and an increase in moisture really helps to round out the flavour and increase the strength of this pastry. This pastry can be used interchangeably with the butter pastry in any recipe found in this book.

1. Using a box grater, grate the frozen vegan butter into a large bowl. Place the bowl in the freezer for 10 to 15 minutes to make sure the butter is still frozen.

2. In a liquid measuring cup, mix together the apple cider vinegar, cold water, salt, and sugar until the solids are fully dissolved. Place in the refrigerator until ready to use.

3. Remove the bowl from the freezer and toss the flour with the grated vegan butter to distribute the butter evenly throughout the flour.

4. Using a fork, mix the cold water mixture into the flour mixture, causing as little friction as possible, until you have a shaggy dough. You want to try to maintain those butter pieces. Resist the urge to add more water unless absolutely necessary to bring the pastry together into a shaggy dough with just a little dry flour. If needed, add 2 to 3 more tablespoons of cold water to the dough, 1 tablespoon at a time.

5. Bring the pastry together by gently folding it into a rough disc, then wrap it tightly with plastic wrap and refrigerate for at least 1 hour before rolling it out. The pastry can be made in advance, wrapped tightly in plastic wrap, and stored in the refrigerator for up to 1 week or in the freezer for up to 6 months. If frozen, thaw in the refrigerator overnight before using.

1 cup vegan butter, frozen (we use Earth Balance Buttery Sticks)
2 tablespoons apple cider vinegar
⅓ cup cold water, more if needed
1 teaspoon salt
1½ teaspoons granulated sugar
2½ cups all-purpose flour

GRAHAM CRUMB BASE

Makes enough for two 6-inch cheesecake bases or one 9-inch pie base

2 cups graham cracker crumbs

6 tablespoons unsalted butter, melted and warm

½ cup lightly packed dark brown sugar

This simple crust is the base for our cheesecakes and some pies. Depending on the humidity of your kitchen and the graham cracker crumbs you use, you might need to adjust this recipe slightly. To test that your crumb base is the right texture, squeeze some in the palm of your hand. It should stay in large clumps once you open your palm. If it crumbles, add another tablespoon of melted butter.

1. In a medium bowl, mix together the graham cracker crumbs, melted butter, and brown sugar until well combined.

2. Use immediately and bake according to recipe requirements or store in an airtight container in the refrigerator for up to 1 month or in the freezer for up to 6 months. If frozen, thaw in the refrigerator overnight before using.

CHOCOLATE GRAHAM CRACKER BASE

Makes enough for two 6-inch cheesecake bases or one 9-inch pie base

2 cups graham cracker crumbs

½ cup unsalted butter, melted and warm

¼ cup cocoa powder

2 tablespoons granulated sugar

½ teaspoon salt

If you would like to add a little chocolate kick to any of our graham crust recipes, swap out this rich chocolate base for the regular graham base; they can be used interchangeably. After a few rounds of testing, we found that the salt makes all the difference in this graham base, so do not leave it out.

1. In a medium bowl, mix together the graham cracker crumbs, melted butter, cocoa powder, sugar, and salt until well combined.

2. Use immediately and bake according to recipe requirements or store in an airtight container in the refrigerator for up to 1 month or in the freezer for up to 6 months. If frozen, thaw in the refrigerator overnight before using.

Bakery Essentials

MERINGUE

With so many talented bakers at Cake & Loaf and with so many different products, we often have two different versions of recipes in use. Meringue is a controversial item at the bakery, and we have never really been able to decide which style of meringue we prefer. Swiss meringue is definitely the easier technique if you have not made meringue before. The Italian meringue is more stable and forgiving if you want your pie to stand up for a few days. Either way, these meringues taste delicious and you can use either of them in the recipes in this book.

ITALIAN MERINGUE

Makes about 2½ cups

¾ cup granulated sugar
¼ cup water
¼ cup egg whites, room temperature (from about 2 large eggs)

1. In a medium saucepan, combine the sugar and water and cook over low- heat, stirring until the sugar has dissolved. When the sugar has dissolved, increase the heat to high and allow the syrup to come to a boil. Boil until the syrup reaches 240°F on a candy thermometer. Carefully remove from the heat.

2. While the syrup is boiling, in the bowl of a stand mixer fitted with the whisk attachment, whip the egg whites on medium-high speed until foamy white and you can start to see soft peaks forming, 2 to 3 minutes.

3. Reduce the speed to low (this will help avoid splashing) and slowly drizzle the hot syrup into the mixing bowl. It is important not to pour the syrup onto the whisk or the syrup may splatter against the sides of the bowl or into your face.

4. When all the syrup has been added, increase the speed to medium-high and whip until opaque, glossy white, stiff peaks form and the bottom of the bowl feels room temperature to the touch, 4 to 5 minutes. Use immediately. Prepared meringue cannot be stored.

SWISS MERINGUE

Makes about 2 cups

½ cup + 1 tablespoon granulated sugar
¼ cup egg whites, room temperature (from about 2 large eggs)

1. Select a medium saucepan that fits the bottom of your stand mixer bowl. You will be using the bowl and pan to create a double boiler. Fill the pan with 2 inches of water and bring to a boil over high heat. Once the water has come to a boil, reduce the heat to a simmer.

2. In the bowl of the stand mixer, add the sugar and egg whites and gently whisk by hand just to wet all the sugar. Place the mixer bowl over the simmering water and continue whisking constantly until the mixture reaches 140°F on a candy thermometer. If testing by hand, rub a bit of the mixture between 2 fingertips. It should feel smooth, not gritty, and warm to the touch. (Whisking keeps the egg whites moving so that you do not end up cooking them by accident.)

3. Place the bowl onto the stand mixer fitted with the whisk attachment. Whip on high speed until opaque, glossy white, stiff peaks form and you can no longer feel heat coming from the bottom of the bowl, 7 to 10 minutes. Use immediately. Prepared meringue cannot be stored.

1 cup granulated sugar
½ cup water
½ teaspoon salt
2 cups unsalted peanuts

CANDIED PEANUTS

During our annual holiday light festival, we set up a peanut station and cook and serve warm fresh candied peanuts to our guests. The aroma of caramelizing peanuts carries across the neighbourhood, and kids often gather around the station to stay warm and watch the magical transformation from sugar granules to caramel. You might want to double this recipe to have it on hand for an added decorative touch to all your desserts or for pure snacking.

1. Line a baking sheet with parchment paper or a silicone baking mat.

2. In a medium saucepan, combine the sugar, water, and salt over medium heat and stir for 1 to 2 minutes until the sugar dissolves.

3. Add the peanuts and cook, stirring constantly, until completely coated in caramelized sugar and all the liquid has evaporated, 15 to 25 minutes. Watch the mixture carefully and adjust your heat to avoid any burning. You want the heat high enough to caramelize the sugar but low enough to do it slowly to avoid the sugar cooking unevenly and burning.

4. Carefully pour the peanut mixture onto the prepared baking sheet and spread it out in a single layer to cool. Allow the nuts to cool completely. Store in an airtight container at room temperature for up to 2 months.

Makes 1½ cups

1½ cups pecan halves
¼ cup pure maple syrup
¼ teaspoon salt

Variation
Maple Candied Walnuts: Replace the pecan halves with the same amount of walnut halves.

MAPLE CANDIED PECANS

The easiest way to make candied nuts is to use maple syrup. It is not quite as stable as the method used in the Candied Peanuts (recipe above) and depending on how humid your kitchen is and the time of year, your nuts might get a little sticky after a few days, but they will remain delicious. However, this is a fast and effective way to make candied nuts! We always have some of these maple pecans on hand at the bakery for topping cheesecakes or adding to scones. This technique works well for walnuts, too.

1. Preheat the oven to 375°F. Line a baking sheet with parchment paper or a silicone baking mat.

2. In a small bowl, gently mix together the pecans, maple syrup, and salt until the maple syrup has fully coated the pecans and flooded all the little crevices of the nuts. Spread the pecan mixture onto the prepared baking sheet, pouring any extra syrup in the bottom of the bowl over the nuts. Bake for 8 to 10 minutes until the maple syrup starts bubbling up. Stir the pecans, recoating them in the bubbly syrup, then continue baking for 3 to 5 more minutes or until you can smell the pecans toasting and the maple syrup has darkened just slightly. The maple coating will harden as the nuts cool. Allow the nuts to cool completely on the baking sheet. Store in an airtight container at room temperature for up to 2 months.

SIMPLE SYRUP

Makes 1 cup

Simple syrup is the baker's secret weapon that will transform your cakes from amateur to professional. When you are building multiple layers and sometimes decorating a cake over several days, simple syrup keeps your cakes moist and enhances all the flavour elements. It also helps keep leftover cake delicious, even when refrigerated. Simple syrup is also a common cocktail ingredient, so maybe double the recipe and whip up some mojitos to go with your baking.

1 cup water
1 cup granulated sugar
1 teaspoon lemon juice

Variations

Raspberry Flavour: Add 2 tablespoons raspberry jam after the simple syrup has cooled. Strain out any seeds using a fine-mesh sieve.

1. Place the ingredients in a heavy medium saucepan over high heat and stir to dissolve the sugar completely. Bring the mixture to a boil without stirring and let boil for 3 minutes. Allow to cool completely and store in an airtight container in the refrigerator for up to 3 weeks.

Lemon Flavour: Add the juice of 2 lemons.

Maple Flavour: Add 3 tablespoons of pure maple syrup after the simple syrup has cooled.

PUMPKIN SPICE

Makes about ¾ cup

We make our own special pumpkin spice blend at the bakery that evolved from a whole spice, chai tea mix that Josie has been making for more than two decades. It was influenced by her time in high school as a waitress at an Indian restaurant, where she fell in love with gulab jamun, fluffy fried milk dough balls in cardamom syrup. After that, she was always looking for ways to include cardamom, with its delicate citrus notes and herbal qualities, in her baking. We think it really rounds out our pumpkin spice and gives it a distinctive flavour. In simple pumpkin recipes, it really shines. Josie served her chai tea mix to Nickey the first time they hung out in an attempt to impress. It worked and was what solidified Nickey's impression of Josie—as a foodie she wanted to know!

¼ cup cinnamon
¼ cup ground ginger
1 tablespoon ground allspice
1 tablespoon ground cardamom
1 tablespoon freshly grated or
   ground nutmeg
1½ teaspoons ground cloves

1. In a medium bowl, whisk together the ingredients until fully combined. Store in an airtight container at room temperature for up to 6 months.

Makes about 2 cups

Domes of 2 cake layers (same
   flavour) (or ½ batch batter of
   Vanilla Cake, page 180,
   Chocolate Cake, page 181, or
   Red Velvet Beet Cake, page 193)

CAKE CRUMBS

When you cut off the domes of your baked cakes to make them level for layering, save the domes and make cake crumbs. Alternately, you can use a freshly baked cake, torn into pieces and toasted. Do not forget that vegan cakes need vegan crumbs.

MAKE FROM FRESH CAKE

1. Preheat the oven to 350°F. Grease an 8-inch square baking pan with canola oil cooking spray and line with parchment paper.

2. Prepare the ½ batch cake batter of your choice following the directions in the recipe. Pour the batter into the prepared pan.

3. Bake for 15 to 25 minutes, or until a toothpick inserted into the centre of the cake comes out clean. Transfer the pan to a wire rack and allow the cake to cool completely before removing it from the pan.

4. When cooled, remove the cake from the pan, then follow the instructions in Make from Cake Domes (see below).

MAKE FROM CAKE DOMES

1. Preheat the oven to 200°F. Line a baking sheet with parchment paper or a silicone baking mat. Tear the cake domes into ½-inch pieces and spread out in a single layer on the prepared baking sheet. Bake for 30 to 45 minutes, or until completely dried. A slow drying process is used so that the cake pieces do not brown.

2. Allow the cake pieces to cool completely on the baking sheet, at least 2 hours.

3. In small batches, blitz the toasted cake pieces in a food processor or blender until they resemble medium-fine crumbs. Store in an airtight container at room temperature for up to 1 month.

HOMEMADE MASCARPONE

Makes 2½ cups

This versatile mascarpone takes a few days to complete but requires very little active effort. You will impress yourself and everyone around you with your amazing cheese-making skills, and no one needs to know how simple it is. If you double the batch, it is also delicious as creamy herb cheese spread, similar to Boursin. Chop up your favourite fresh herbs (we like thyme, parsley, basil, and chives), crush some garlic, and add salt and freshly ground pepper to taste and mix them into your fresh cheese. Alternatively, try a sweet version by whipping it with some honey and folding in fresh berries for a light dessert. You can even serve it as part of an antipasto spread topped with a spicy red pepper jelly.

4 cups whipping (35%) cream
¼ cup freshly squeezed lemon
   juice (2 to 3 lemons)

1. In a heavy medium saucepan, heat the cream over medium-high heat for 3 to 5 minutes, stirring constantly all the way to the bottom of the pot with a silicone spatula, until it reaches 190°F on a candy thermometer. Do not let the cream boil.

2. Remove from the heat and stir in the lemon juice until fully distributed in the cream. Return the pot to low heat and bring the temperature back up to 190°F, then continue stirring constantly over low heat for 5 minutes while maintaining the 190°F temperature. Do not let the cream boil. Remove from the heat and let rest at room temperature for 30 minutes.

3. Set a plastic colander or sieve over a large bowl, then line it with wet coffee filters generously overlapped to fully cover the straining surface. Strain the cream mixture through the coffee filters. Discard the liquid or use it in place of buttermilk for baking. Place the strainer over a bowl that will fit well into your fridge and wrap the entire bowl with plastic wrap. The liquid from the cheese will continue to drip slowly through the strainer, and the cheese will continue to firm up. Transfer the wrapped bowl to the refrigerator for 3 to 4 days until the mascarpone reaches desired thickness. It can be left in the strainer, wrapped, in the refrigerator for up to 1 week.

4. Lift the coffee filters from the strainer and flip the mascarpone into a medium bowl. Carefully remove and discard any remaining pieces of coffee filter that might have ripped. Store the mascarpone in an airtight container in the refrigerator for up to 2 weeks.

Makes 2½ cups

1 batch Homemade Mascarpone
    (page 269) or 1 pound (450 g)
    store-bought, room
    temperature
½ cup icing sugar
½ cup whipping (35%) cream

MASCARPONE FILLING

As delicious as this filling is in cakes, it might be even better as a dip for fresh fruit or cookies. It is creamy and sweet and, especially if made with Homemade Mascarpone (page 269), surprisingly light and fresh.

1. In the bowl of a stand mixer fitted with the paddle attachment, beat the mascarpone on high speed until silky smooth. Scrape down the sides and bottom of the bowl.

2. Sift the icing sugar into the bowl and beat on medium-high speed until smooth, about 1 minute. Do not overmix. Scrape down the sides and bottom of the bowl.

3. Add the cream and beat on high speed for 2 to 3 minutes until the filling is light and fluffy. Refrigerate in an airtight container for 4 to 6 hours to thicken before use. Store in an airtight container in the refrigerator for up to 1 week.

Makes about 4 cups

2½ cups granulated sugar
1¼ cups freshly squeezed lemon
    juice (about 7 lemons)
1 cup unsalted butter
Pinch of salt
4 eggs
8 egg yolks

LEMON CURD

Homemade lemon curd will take your baking from basic to remarkable. Our curd is more butter-heavy than other lemon curds, which gives it an extra-thick, creamy texture and helps it stand up well to freezing. If you are new to making curds or custards, watch the heat carefully to make sure you do not end up with scrambled eggs. You can reduce the heat and cook it slowly. It might take a little longer, but it will be worth it! Citrusy, silky smooth, and slightly sweet, this golden yellow beauty is perfect for filling cakes and sandwich cookies. It is also wonderful served over ice cream or with granola.

1. In a medium saucepan, heat the sugar, lemon juice, butter, and salt over medium heat, stirring occasionally with a wooden spoon until the butter has melted and the sugar has dissolved, about 3 minutes.

2. In a medium bowl, whisk together the eggs and egg yolks. While whisking, very slowly pour in the hot lemon mixture. It is important to keep whisking while you do this to avoid curdling the mixture.

3. Pour the egg and lemon mixture back into the saucepan and cook, stirring constantly, over medium-low heat until the mixture has thickened and coats the back of the wooden spoon, up to 10 minutes. Be careful not to overheat the mixture or you will end up with lemon-flavoured scrambled eggs.

4. When the mixture has thickened, remove from the heat and carefully strain the mixture through a fine-mesh sieve into a clean medium bowl to remove any eggy bits. Allow the mixture to cool completely. Store in an airtight container in the refrigerator for up to 1 month or in the freezer for up to 6 months. If frozen, thaw in the refrigerator overnight before using.

CANDIED LEMON PEEL

Makes 1 cup

To achieve the long zest strips needed for this recipe, remove the zest from the lemons with a vegetable peeler or paring knife, removing as little pith as possible. Then, using a sharp chef's knife, carefully julienne each piece of zest. You are creating long, delicate pieces. These sparkly beauties keep well for a few months, so they are nice to have around for a decorative touch to all your desserts, not just lemon desserts. You would be surprised how well they pair with dark chocolate.

6 to 8 lemons, peeled in long strips lengthwise, without the white pith (1 packed cup)
1½ cups granulated sugar
1 cup water

1. Place the lemon peel in a medium saucepan and cover with cold water. Bring to a boil over high heat. As soon as the mixture comes to a full rolling boil, strain the lemon peel, discarding the water. Return the lemon peel to the pot and cover with fresh cold water again. Bring to a full boil over high heat again. Strain the lemon peel, boil for a third time in fresh cold water, and strain again once boiled. This process removes the bitterness in the peel.

2. Add the strained lemon zest, sugar, and 1 cup of water to the medium saucepan and bring to a final boil over high heat. Boil the peel until translucent, 10 to 15 minutes. Remove from the heat and strain. Lay the zest in a single layer on a clean wire rack, using a heat-resistant spatula to separate the zest strands as best as you can. Allow to dry, uncovered, on the wire rack in a dry area.

3. The next day, toss the lemon zest on the wire rack to ensure it is completely dry on all sides. Dry, uncovered, on the wire rack or a baking sheet overnight.

4. Once completely dry and candied, store in an airtight container in a dry area for up to 2 months.

VEGAN HAZELNUT SPREAD

Makes 1½ cups

It is always better when you make it yourself. This spread may not have the silky-smooth quality of store-bought hazelnut chocolate spread, but it has a much more intense chocolate flavour and a rich nuttiness that elevates it from mundane to extraordinary. It's also vegan—a nice bonus if you avoid dairy and cannot enjoy most store-bought hazelnut chocolate spreads.

⅔ cup hazelnuts, roasted and peeled (or ½ cup store-bought hazelnut butter)
9 ounces (255 g) semi-sweet chocolate, melted and cooled
2 to 4 tablespoons canola oil, divided
3 tablespoons cocoa powder
¼ cup icing sugar
1 teaspoon pure vanilla extract
½ teaspoon salt

1. In a food processor, blend the hazelnuts until a smooth hazelnut butter forms. If using hazelnut butter, simply add it to the food processor with the ingredients in step 2.

2. Add the cooled melted chocolate and 2 tablespoons of the canola oil and blend until homogeneous. Scrape down the sides of the food processor bowl.

3. Sift the cocoa powder and icing sugar into the food processor. Add the vanilla and salt and blend until a smooth and spreadable consistency is reached. If the spread is too thick, add 1 tablespoon of the remaining canola oil at a time, to reach desired consistency. Store in an airtight container at room temperature for up to 1 month.

13 ounces (360 mL/1⅓ cups +
2 tablespoons) water, room
temperature, divided

1½ ounces (40 g/¼ cup) powdered
gelatin

1⅓ pounds (600 g/3 cups)
granulated sugar

15 ounces (425 g/1⅓ cups) liquid
glucose

1 tablespoon vanilla bean paste

¼ teaspoon salt

3⅓ cups icing sugar, divided

VANILLA BEAN MARSHMALLOWS

Once you have made these fluffy, melt-in-your-mouth, real vanilla cubes of sugary goodness, you will never eat a stale store-bought marshmallow again. They are a fun addition to recipes, as well as being desserts in their own right. Serve them topped with fruit compotes, ganaches, or lemon curd or toast some and have them atop ice cream with chocolate sauce. Glucose is not a common home baking ingredient, but it can be found at most bulk stores or online. It is not the same as white corn syrup, but is much thicker and acts as a stabilizer in this recipe. This is a sticky recipe! When working with the glucose, coat your tools with water or canola oil cooking spray to avoid sticking. We suggest you use a kitchen scale, as this is a recipe easier made by weight instead of cups, but we have included both measures here in case you do not have a scale.

1. Generously spray a 13- × 9-inch baking dish with canola oil cooking spray.

2. In the bowl of a 6-quart or larger stand mixer, combine half of the water and the gelatin powder and set aside to bloom. It will take 2 to 3 minutes for the gelatin to swell with the water and form a gel.

3. Pour the remaining water into a large pot. Pour the granulated sugar and glucose over the water. Do not stir. Bring the mixture to a boil over high heat and boil, without stirring, until a candy thermometer reaches 238°F.

4. Place the bowl with the bloomed gelatin on a stand mixer fitted with the whisk attachment. Carefully pour the hot sugar mixture into the bowl and immediately start mixing on low speed, gradually increasing to high speed. The mixture will foam and steam. Whip on high speed for 6 to 7 minutes. The whipped marshmallow will continue to increase in volume until it has almost filled the bowl. It is done when you can see the marshmallow forming stretchy bands like chewing gum as it whips and the mixture is opaque and glossy white. The marshmallow should still be warm when done. In the last minute of whipping, add the vanilla bean paste and salt.

5. Using a silicone spatula coated in canola oil cooking spray, heap the marshmallow into the prepared baking dish, scraping the bowl clean. Spread out the marshmallow evenly, then tap the bottom of the dish on the counter to settle the marshmallow. Sprinkle ⅓ cup of the icing sugar over the entire surface to prevent the marshmallow from forming a hard crust. Cover the dish with plastic wrap and let sit at room temperature overnight to firm up.

6. The next day, dust the countertop generously with 1 cup of the icing sugar and turn out the marshmallow onto the counter. Sprinkle 1 cup of the icing sugar over the bottom of the marshmallow slab (which is now facing up).

7. Place the remaining 1 cup icing sugar in a medium bowl to use for cutting and dusting the marshmallows. Using a 10-inch or longer chef's knife with the blade dusted with icing sugar, slice the marshmallow into forty-eight 1½-inch pieces by first cutting it into eight 9-inch-long strips. Cut each strip into 6 equal pieces. Dust the knife with icing sugar as you make each cut and dust all sides of the marshmallows as you cut them. This will prevent them sticking together. Store in an airtight container at room temperature for up to 2 months.

MARSHMALLOW FLUFF

Makes about 3 cups

Very similar in flavour to regular marshmallow, but with a more spreadable and pipeable consistency, this filling is excellent in cakes and sandwich cookies. It is best made just before you want to use it, especially if piping it, as it does firm up a bit as it cools and sets.

½ cup water, room temperature

1⅓ cups granulated sugar, divided

1 cup + 2 tablespoons white corn syrup

⅔ cup egg whites (about 4 eggs)

1 tablespoon vanilla bean paste

1. Pour the water into a small pot. Pour 1 cup of the sugar and the corn syrup on top of the water. Do not stir. Bring the mixture to a boil over high heat and boil, without stirring, until a candy thermometer reaches 250°F.

2. In the bowl of a stand mixer fitted with the whisk attachment, combine the egg whites and the remaining ⅓ cup sugar. Whip on high speed until the mixture reaches the soft peak stage, 2 to 3 minutes. You will see the egg whites go from foamy liquid to more opaque white, and if you stop the mixer and lift the whisk, you will see the egg whites briefly form soft peaks and then melt back into themselves after a second.

3. With the mixer on medium-low speed, carefully and slowly pour the hot sugar mixture into the egg whites in a steady stream. Do not add too much at a time or the egg whites will cook and curdle. After you have poured all the hot syrup into the bowl, increase the speed to high as quickly as possible. Whisk on high speed for 10 to 12 minutes until the outside of the bowl is room temperature to the touch and the fluff is thick and glossy with stiff peaks. Add the vanilla bean paste and mix on high speed just until combined, about 1 to 2 minutes.

4. Use the marshmallow fluff immediately for best results. It tastes best toasted immediately after piping. Leftover fluff can be stored in an airtight container in the refrigerator for up to 1 week.

Makes 2½ cups

2 cups whole milk

¼ cup + ⅓ cup granulated sugar, divided

¼ cup cornstarch

2 large egg yolks

1 egg, whole

2 tablespoons unsalted butter

1 tablespoon vanilla bean paste

1 teaspoon pure vanilla extract

½ teaspoon salt

PASTRY CREAM

Pastry cream, or thick vanilla custard, is one of those incredibly versatile and useful basic recipes that once you have made you will use all the time. Our version is very vanilla forward in flavour, just lightly sweet, and not too heavy since it uses just milk and no cream. Whenever Nickey makes pastry cream, she still uses the trick her pastry chef taught her at school. He always said to sprinkle the sugar on top of the milk before boiling and not touch it after that to avoid burning, and it has worked like a charm throughout her baking career.

1. In a heavy medium pot, combine the milk and ¼ cup of the sugar and bring to a simmer over medium heat, 2 to 3 minutes.

2. In a medium heat-resistant bowl, whisk together the remaining ⅓ cup sugar and the cornstarch to remove any lumps from the cornstarch. Add the egg yolks and whole egg to the mixture, whisking to a smooth consistency. Roll a clean kitchen towel into a tube and place it in a circle on the countertop. Place the bowl inside this nest to keep it in place.

3. When the milk comes to a simmer, carefully pour it into the bowl in a steady, slow stream while mixing vigorously with a whisk to prevent overheating the eggs. After you have tempered the mixture, pour it back into the pot and bring to a boil over medium-high heat, stirring constantly so that the eggs do not curdle or scorch on the bottom. When the mixture comes to a boil and thickens with fierce bubbles rising to the top, reduce the heat to medium-low and cook out the cornstarch, stirring constantly, for 1 minute. Remove from the heat and stir in the butter, vanilla bean paste, vanilla extract, and salt, mixing until the butter is completely melted and the pastry cream is smooth. Pour into a heat-resistant container and place a piece of plastic wrap directly on the surface to prevent a skin from forming. Refrigerate the pastry cream in an airtight container for 4 to 6 hours to thicken before use.

4. Store in an airtight container in the refrigerator for up to 2 weeks. When ready to use, place the chilled pastry cream in the bowl of a stand mixer fitted with the paddle attachment and beat on medium speed to return it to a smooth consistency, about 2 minutes.

WHIPPED CREAM

Makes 2 cups

Josie's kids always run to lick the whisk when she makes whipped cream at home, and we are not judging if that is your favourite part, too. Whipped cream is a staple at the bakery and an easy way to dress up dessert. Everyone loves those sweet, fluffy clouds of creamy goodness. This whipped cream is not very sweet, so if you prefer a sweeter flavour you can always double the icing sugar.

1 cup whipping (35%) cream, cold
1 tablespoon icing sugar
1 teaspoon pure vanilla extract

1. Pour the cream, icing sugar, and vanilla into the bowl of a stand mixer fitted with the whisk attachment and whip on medium speed. The cream will start to get frothy and begin to thicken after 2 to 3 minutes. Increase the speed to high and whip for another 30 seconds to 1 minute, or until the cream looks fluffy and the whisk leaves deep markings in the whipped cream.

2. Store in an airtight container in the fridge for up to 8 hours. After 8 hours the whipped cream will begin to liquify, but it can be rewhipped and used once more. Place the chilled whipped cream in the bowl of a stand mixer fitted with the whisk attachment and beat on medium-high speed to make it fluffy again, about 3 minutes.

CARAMEL

Makes 1½ cups

If you do not have a candy thermometer, you can still make this caramel; at the bakery we always make it by look, not by temperature. As the caramel starts to darken and go from clear to light brown to amber brown, be observant. When smaller, more condensed bubbles form on the surface of the sugar, the caramel is close to done. The bubbles themselves will be dark amber. To test, carefully dip a spoon into the mixture, drip a drop on a plate, and check the colour. If it's ready, move on to the next step; if it requires more time, let it bubble some more. However, do not walk away! Medium brown caramel can shift to burnt caramel faster than you think, and then you will be forced to start all over again.

1½ cups granulated sugar
⅓ cup water
1 teaspoon lemon juice
½ cup whipping (35%) cream, room temperature
1 teaspoon vanilla bean paste
½ teaspoon salt

1. In a heavy medium saucepan, stir together the sugar, water, and lemon juice until the sugar is dissolved. When the sugar is mostly dissolved, bring to a boil over high heat without stirring. The lemon juice is acidic and will help keep the sugar from crystallizing. Boil on high heat, without stirring, until the temperature reaches at least 345°F on a candy thermometer, about 10 minutes. Watch for a dark amber tone (not too dark, though; if it is black or the mixture smokes, you have gone too far).

2. When the caramel is a rich amber colour, carefully remove the pot from the heat and place it on a heat-resistant surface. Slowly pour the cream into the mixture in small additions, stirring carefully after each addition and backing away once it begins to climb the sides of the pot. Stir in the vanilla bean paste and salt. Leave the caramel in the pot and cool to room temperature. The cooling process may take 2 to 3 hours. When cooled, store in an airtight container at room temperature for up to 1 month.

Acknowledgments

THANK YOU, DAD, for lending us your woodworking and building talents, constructing and working with me at both locations. For rolling with the many last-minute requests, long days, and all the mini bakery builds against all odds. You have been such an important part of the bakery for both of us.

Mom, thank you for letting me take my first steps toward the sweeter side of cooking in your kitchen. By sharing your space in the later years, you allowed me to explore and create custom cakes, giving me the opportunity to expand my creativity and find my signature cake style.

Erin, sistor sistor, impromptu kitchen dance partner, and our kitchen manager extraordinaire. We know that with your positive attitude, creativity, care, and work ethic, we can rest assured that our kitchen is in good hands.

Close friends, confidants, personal cheerleaders, and consistent advice granters; you've kept me grounded, you've kept my goals in perspective and you've helped to nurture a stronger voice within throughout these many years. You know who you are and I am thankful for our friendships.

David and Amanda, without your willingness to share your camera gear and expertise, I wouldn't have had the confidence or tools to take all these pictures. Thank you for giving me the opportunity to expand my creativity in ways I never have before, an opportunity to push outside my comfort zone.

A big shout-out to everyone who came in droves for socially distanced porch pickups to grab all our baking after my many photo shoots. Thank you for enjoying the process with us and stopping by for some conversations during those strange times.

– Nickey

THANK YOU, LILY, for all your creative design input, honest feedback, and recipe ideas. Since the day you were born you have been making my life more meaningful and have challenged me to grow in ways I had not imagined were possible. Never stop shining your light; the world needs it.

To Finn, the best seven-year-old editor a mum could ask for, thank you for all your help testing recipes, early-morning candlelit editing sessions, and spelling assistance. Your compassion and kindness make my heart burst with pride and love.

To our first official hire and my fiercest supporter, Amanda, thank you for helping me live my dreams while being my dependable voice of reason. You ground me yet always seem to make me feel I can fly.

Thank you, Erica and Jeff, for letting us use your property for photographs, for your thoughts on recipe testing, and for your steadfast friendship. Erica, your creativity and generosity never cease to amaze me, and I feel so lucky to have our friendship.

To the best in-laws I could have asked for, the Rudderhams, thank you for your unwavering support. Thank you Debbie and Lyall for all the days of child care that allowed Cake & Loaf to grow and flourish, the occasional use of your freezer during holidays, and for making me feel so welcome from the first time we met. Lyall, thank you for keeping the bakery gardens beautiful and functional. Evan, I'm grateful for your loyal patronage, honest feedback, and all the lifting over the years.

Thank you, Mum, for being one of our best customers and for never clipping my wings but always providing a soft place to land. Thank you for teaching me to value what's really important in life and to stand up for what is right, even when the odds are stacked against me.

Thank you, Katie, for all your contributions to Cake & Loaf over the years and for being there to listen to my rants and provide intelligent, thoughtful advice. You continue to inspire me with your efforts to build a more compassionate world.

– Josie

THANK YOU TO ALL THE LOAFERS, past and present, who helped us build our business, believed in our vision, and contributed to these recipes. Especially to our COVID crew, who got us through the most challenging year of business yet with community and grace: Amanda, Erin, Helen, Huong, Kate, Kyle, Linda, Mary Ann, Melissa, Sarah, and Zoie.

To Andrea and everyone at Penguin Random House Canada, thank you for seeing potential in us and walking us through the foreign land of book writing. We never dreamed we would be doing this, and it has been such a gift.

Thank you to all the customers who have supported and believed in our team. We do this for you—for the light in your eyes when you bite into your favourite baked good, for the kindness and community you show us, for the daily connections that enliven us, and for the kinship we feel.

Thank you, Tamara, for all the gorgeous photographs and business chats over the years. You make us feel beautiful inside and out.

Thank you, Michael and Amy, for your many contributions to the bakery, recipes, and writing support. You've been a part of this journey in so many meaningful ways.

To everyone who tested recipes and read over drafts, thank you for helping us write this book: Dana, Caroline, Christine, Jane, Heather and Sharon, Jess, Gwen and John, and Ann Marie.

Thank you to the web of supportive small businesses in Hamilton, from our suppliers to our business buddies, that holds us up.

To our husbands, Alex and Luke, thank you for tolerating our erratic work hours and our consistent inconsistencies. We can only do what we do because of your unwavering support, so thanks for keeping the home fires burning.

– Nickey and Josie

Index